Value Chains in Development

Value Chains in Development
Emerging theory and practice

Edited by
Linda M. Jones

Practical Action Publishing
The Schumacher Centre
Bourton on Dunsmore, Rugby,
Warwickshire, CV23 9QZ, UK
www.practicalactionpublishing.org

© Practical Action Publishing, 2011

First published in 2011 by Practical Action Publishing
Reprinted 2013

ISBN 978 1 85339 678 6 Hardback
ISBN 978 1 85339 739 4 Paperback
ISBN 978 1 78044 678 3 Library Ebook
ISBN 978 1 78044 739 1 Ebook

http://dx.doi.org/10.3362/9781780446783

All rights reserved. No part of this publication may be reprinted or reproduced or utilized in any form or by any electronic, mechanical, or other means, now known or hereafter invented, including photocopying and recording, or in any information storage or retrieval system, without the written permission of the publishers.

A catalogue record for this book is available from the British Library.

The contributors have asserted their rights under the Copyright Designs and Patents Act 1988 to be identified as authors of their respective contributions.

Since 1974, Practical Action Publishing (formerly Intermediate Technology Publications and ITDG Publishing) has published and disseminated books and information in support of international development work throughout the world. Practical Action Publishing Ltd (Company Reg. No. 1159018) is the wholly owned publishing company of Practical Action Ltd. Practical Action Publishing trades only in support of its parent charity objectives and any profits are covenanted back to Practical Action (Charity Reg. No. 247257, Group VAT Registration No. 880 9924 76).

Typeset by SJI Services
Printed in the United Kingdom

Contents

Figures		vii
Tables		viii
Boxes		ix
1.	Introduction Linda M. Jones	1
2.	The Triple Trust – a threefold approach James Thomas	11
3.	The Judo Trick, or crowding in Paul Streeten	15
4.	Sub-sector Analysis – a macro-analytical tool for microenterprise support Matthew Gamser	29
5.	A sub-sectoral approach to small business and microenterprise development Biswajit Sen and Vijay Mahajan	33
6.	Business associations in countries in transition to market economies Jacob Levitsky	45
7.	Using franchises to promote small enterprise development Michael Henriques and Robert E. Nelson	59
8.	Towards success: impact and sustainability in the FIT programme Jim Tanburn	71
9.	Business development services – core principles and future challenges Alan Gibson	83
10.	Facilitating small producers' access to high-value markets: lessons from four development projects Jonathan Dawson	97
11.	Value chain programmes to integrate competitiveness, economic growth and poverty reduction Olaf Kula, Jeanne Downing and Michael Field	113

12. From behind the veil: industry-level methodologies for
    disadvantaged communities in Pakistan   129
    Linda M. Jones and Alexandra Snelgrove

13. Value chain financing in agriculture   141
    Calvin Miller and Carlos Da Silva

14. How to assess if markets work better for the poor: experiences
    from the Katalyst Project in Bangladesh   155
    Harald Bekkers, Alexandra Miehlbradt and Peter Roggekamp

15. Managing the process of change: useful frameworks for
    implementers of making markets work for the poor programmes   171
    Marshall Bear and Michael Field

16. Business environment reforms: Why it is necessary to rethink
    priorities and strategies   187
    Tilman Altenburg and Christian von Drachenfels

17. Integrated approaches to enabling the most vulnerable to
    participate in markets   199
    Alex Daniels and Andy Jeans

Index   217

Figures

1.1	The scope of value chain development	2
7.1	Flow of services and support	60
10.1	Creating linkages between small producers and 'distant' markets	104
10.2	Categorization of projects according to potential ripple benefits and difficulty of technical upgrading	108
11.1	Value chain map of Mozambique oilseeds industry	118
11.2	How market structure and co-operation affect competitiveness	123
11.3	Causal model for Kenya BDS and FINTRAC HDC project	126
13.1	A value chain at work	142
13.2	Financial flows within the rice chain	144
13.3	LAFISE group integrated service model	145
13.4	BASIX livelihood services model	152
14.1	Fish fingerling nursery training logic	158
14.2	Average growth in productivity for micro farmers	161
14.3	Average profits for micro farmers	161
14.4	Isolating project impact	165
15.1	An industry pathway	172
15.2	Knowledge management process	173
15.3	The beef market system	174
15.4	The vet services market	180
15.5	Advancing along the pathway	183
16.1	Effects of socially embedded institutional and normative market constraints on economic performance	190
17.1	LIFE Model	205
17.2	Promoting enterprise-based training	207
17.3	Approach to stimulating discriminated groups' participation as employers/employees	213

Tables

7.1	Potential franchise benefits	61
7.2	Potential disadvantages of franchising	62
10.1	Background information on four APT-supported projects	99
10.2	Marketing services provided by projects	100
11.1	Competitiveness assessment tools	112
13.1	Typology of value chain finance approaches	147
13.2	The opportunities and challenges in promoting value chain finance	150
15.1	Sales from herd health plan contracts	178
15.2	Vet services market changes	179
17.1	A brief summary of the population reached	203

Boxes

9.1	Extending the business-like principle to donor–counterpart relations	86
9.2	Developing services at the Chambers of Commerce and Industry in Brazil	88
11.1	Selecting industries in Zambia	117
11.2	Value chain analysis from Mozambique	118
11.3	Building an industry competitiveness strategy in Dominican Republic	122
11.4	Assessing the impact of USAID-Kenya's tree fruit projects	127
13.1	Contract poultry production	148
13.2	DrumNet: facilitating finance, marketing and information management	149
14.1	Mr Hossain's fish pond, Faridpur, Bangladesh	162
15.1	Market understanding of vet services	175
15.2	Multiple information sources trigger adjustments in intervention	179

CHAPTER 1
Introduction

Linda M. Jones

This volume traces the development of value chain theory and practice over the past two decades based on articles published in *Enterprise Development and Microfinance* journal (known until 2007 as *Small Enterprise Development* journal). Authored by leading thinkers and implementers, this collection of papers offers insights into fundamental challenges, significant findings, interesting models and new directions regarding the value chain approach. The majority of the papers are based on actual field experience, and so although the compilation is largely a retrospective, it enables us to examine 'history' in a way that can make a positive contribution to our present and future work.

Selection of the 16 articles included here resulted from an evaluation of their individual merit as well as an assessment of how each paper combines with the others to provide a representative overview of value chain development – taking into consideration thematic topic, geographic spread and theoretical versus practical perspectives. Due to the desire to create a balanced collection, as well as the inevitable space considerations of any such publication, many fine contributions to the journal have regretfully not been included. This introduction briefly defines value chain development and the related term market development (see box on the following page), reviews each article in the collection, and discusses their significance in the development of value chain theory and practice.

In the very first issue of the *EDM* journal in 1990, James Thomas, the then director of the Triple Trust Organization (TTO) in Cape Town, South Africa wrote about a three-fold approach to enterprise development: training, finance and marketing support. The strategy was developed pragmatically, in response to the needs of huge numbers of economic migrants who were relocating from rural areas to the urban centre, and broke from conventional unilateral approaches. Thomas and his colleagues at TTO recognized that multiple services were required to ensure that would-be microentrepreneurs (MEs) would not only learn an income-generating skill, but would also be able to access markets and to acquire finance to start up small businesses. TTO also realized the importance of employing local trainers in target neighbourhoods, analysing market demand, assessing potential profitability of new business opportunities (e.g. knitting, artificial flower arranging, slipper making), being stringent with quality control and ensuring sound business practices were

2 VALUE CHAINS IN DEVELOPMENT

Defining value chain development

The term *value chain development* is used here in its broadest 'systems' sense and is roughly synonymous with the phrases *(pro-poor) market development* or *making markets work for the poor (M4P when applied to the economic sector)*, and with certain applications of the terms *enterprise development* or *business development services (BDS)*. This usage of the term is diagrammed in Figure 1.1 below which has evolved from various sources including Katalyst, Miehlbradt, McVay, Jones, the Springfield Centre, Action for Enterprise and the SEEP Network among others, and was first presented in this form in 2007 (McVay and Snelgrove, 2007; Miehlbradt and Jones, 2007):

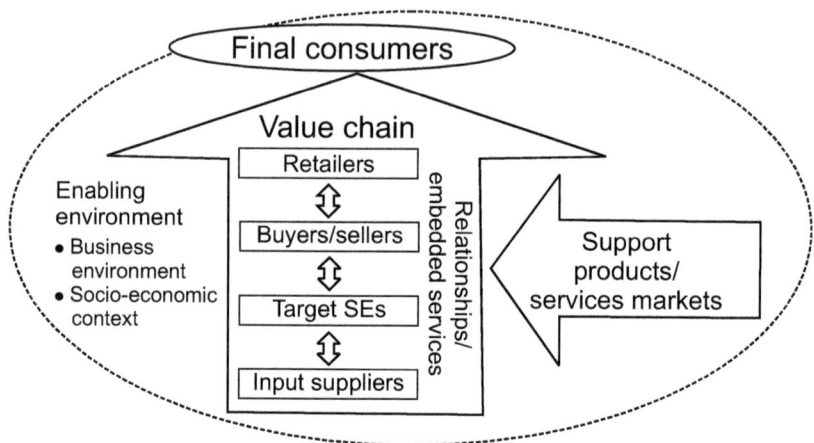

Figure 1.1. The scope of value chain development

As illustrated, the scope of value chain development is a market system; value chain programmes are holistic in their understanding, even though interventions are targeted to benefit microentrepreneurs. Value chain analysis assesses enterprises at all levels in the chain, embedded and external services and products that support the enterprises in the chain, the relationships amongst stakeholders, and the business enabling and socio-economic environments that are the context in which enterprises operate.

adopted by clients. Further, Thomas outlines an exit strategy – 'a progressive weaning' – that was to lead to self-sufficiency of MEs. As such, this forerunner to market development programmes embodies many of the elements of a successful value chain initiative. However, in those early days, without the benefit of hindsight that we have today, TTO and many other organizations inserted themselves into the market system, created new institutions and delivered subsidized services directly to MEs. As experience has shown, this resulted in a relatively low-impact programme (potential of up to 600 trainees per year), and an unsustainable market system that relied on donor funding for its survival. TTO has continued to evolve with the value chain development field, announcing in its 2004 annual report 'we have moved from microenterprise into market development facilitation' (TTO, 2005), and has gone on to implement, for example, a groundbreaking *spaza* shop initiative (Bear et al., 2005).

The following year, 1991, Paul Streeten – a professor at Boston University, and Founder and Editor of the journal *World Development* – published a paper that analysed the informal (microenterprise) sector and made recommendations for the integration of MEs into viable market systems. 'The Judo Trick or crowding in' drew on research from countries across Latin America, Africa, and Asia to discuss the competitive characteristics of small informal businesses as well as the important complementarity between MEs and large formal firms. For example, he highlights an agricultural model that (1) features a 'modern nucleus estate' that supplies services from extension through to credit and market access to smallholder farmers and (2) ensures farmers are properly organized to balance bargaining power and carry out crop production. This parallels the model of the 'lead firm' or 'contract farming' familiar in today's value chain terminology and programmes. Further, Streeten identifies the business enabling environment as a critical challenge for the successful integration of informal enterprises into effective market relationships, and he recommends that changes in government policy, regulation and control are needed to create a supportive milieu. He also touches on concepts of innovation, incentives and information as well as the 'safety net' role of the informal sector, particularly for women. In its comprehensive inclusion of issues pertinent to market development initiatives, not least of which is the systemic lens through which enterprise development is viewed, this paper still remains informative for value chain practitioners. However, his insightful thinking is theoretical, and does not yet offer a platform for analysis or for intervention design.

The first steps towards the codification of market development best practice and the elaboration of an instructional action-oriented approach arrived in the form of sub-sector analysis. A brief article authored by Matthew Gamser, who was the Deputy Director of the USAID GEMINI (Growth and Equity through Microenterprise Investments and Institutions) Project, appeared in the journal in 1992. Sub-sector analysis was presented as a tool for identifying the non-financial services that would have the 'greatest impact on the largest number of firms' and for determining where such support for MEs should be applied. The four primary concepts that constitute the foundation for sub-sector analysis (*and* the basis for market development thinking) are outlined by Gamser: a vertical perspective, competition, coordination and leverage. These concepts are expanded elsewhere – see for example, *A Field Manual for Sub-Sector Practitioners* (Haggblade and Gamser, 1991) and *A Sub-Sector Approach to Small Enterprise Promotion and Research* (Boomgard et al., 1991). Sub-sector mapping – a tool still used widely in value chain/market development approaches – is detailed in the paper, revealing the richness of analysis that is possible as a result of thorough market assessment. Although the term 'systems perspective' is not used, the *Field Manual* emphasizes the need for a holistic lens, and describes the familiar tasks of mapping an industry and determining the most promising market channel for ME involvement based on a series of criteria: for example, market demand, barriers to entry, input supplies, technology, big firm behaviour and government policy.

Moving from academic theory to practical application, by means of sub-sector analysis, was a huge step forward for the emerging value chain approach. But later papers in the journal reveal that analysis without guidelines for programme execution are not enough – indeed, the *Field Manual* is 85 pages long and reserves just two pages for the section 'From Analysis to Action'. Without an intervention lens, sub-sector analysis does not offer implementation tools to practitioners, highlight the critical difference between 'facilitator' and 'provider', stress the importance of sustainability based on market based solutions, or underline the need for viable exit strategies. The 1993 paper by Sen and Mahajan (reprinted in this volume), while based on and supportive of the sub-sector approach, reveals multiple difficulties in designing and implementing effective sub-sector programmes without adequate guidance and tools. In the two cases summarized by Sen and Mahajan – wild silk and poultry – the implementing organization, Pradhan, intervened directly in the market system and achieved limited results by the time of publication. In the silk sub-sector, for example, Pradhan subsidized the cultivation of host plants, established grainages for production of insects, introduced new technologies, supplied marketing services, and lobbied the government on behalf of the producers. A later paper (see Van der Land and Uliwa, 1997, not included in this volume) explicitly adapts the methodology 'to be more practical and focused on output' in the furniture, horticulture and dairy sub-sectors of Tanzania. Van der Land and Uliwa recognize the need to go beyond analysis in a framework to 'initiate' and 'undertake' action.

In tandem with the mainstream development of value chain approaches, there are numerous reports in the journal of interesting models and strategies that had been applied to reduce poverty through enterprise development. These models and strategies are now often incorporated into value chain initiatives, and we can build upon these earlier experiences for the design and implementation of programmes. Two of these papers are reprinted here: an examination of trade associations in transition economies in Eastern Europe (Levitsky, 1994) and the utilization of franchising as a way to promote ME development in South-east Asia (Henriques and Nelson, 1997). Trade associations and franchising are especially interesting models in that they hold promise for deep market sustainability and massive scale-up as we move to next generation value chain development programmes. Scale-up initiatives that have been recently launched by Entrepreneurship and Community Development Institute, Pakistan, and SDCAsia, Philippines (seed money made available by the Gates Foundation and the SEEP Network) are specifically looking at leveraging these two models to achieve their ambitious programme impact targets. We hope to report back to the journal on these topics in a later issue.

Following sub-sector analysis, the next clear stage in market development programmes was known as Business Development Services or BDS. BDS is a term that can be narrowly used to mean non-financial services such as business management and marketing training for MEs (often the sense implied by microfinance professionals), or can be applied more generally to denote a host of support services along with a systemic viewpoint. The expanded usage of the term won widespread favour when, in 2001, the Donor Committee for Enterprise Development (http://www.sedonors.org/default.asp) published a pivotal position paper *Guiding Principles for BDS* (World Bank, 2001). This document elaborated the BDS programming paradigm that had been evolving through the 1990s and was characterized by two primary themes: the importance of non-financial services to the growth of MEs, and the need to sustainably reach larger numbers of MEs with these services (Jones, 2008). The recognition that BDS programming can and should be sustainable, that initiatives need to rely on local commercial suppliers, and that implementers must become facilitators of service development and not providers of services was a critical turning point for the enterprise development industry in general and the BDS approach in particular.

The first two BDS papers in this volume were authored by leaders in the BDS and market development arenas, both of whom have had considerable influence in the overall advancement of the field. The first of the two articles, by Jim Tanburn (1996), describes the experience of FIT Kenya in facilitating the development of affordable, demand-driven services for smallholder farmers. The FIT programme concentrates on a few specific service markets – e.g. appropriate technology and business networking – and does not intervene in response to other smallholder farmer constraints. As long as the entire system is understood, targeted service interventions can achieve excellent results; the successful Katalyst programme in Bangladesh is a case in point (see for example, Miehlbradt, 2007). Tanburn also emphasizes the importance of impact assessment that informs future action, an area that is having an increasingly higher profile amongst donors and executing agencies.

The second paper 'Business development services: core principles and future challenges' (Gibson, 1997) delineates a general framework for BDS interventions, and raises unanswered questions. The 'good practice' defined herein stands the test of time enumerating familiar guiding principles such as: business-like, demand-led, financial sustainability, tailored services, systemic approaches, and maximizing outreach. Like Tanburn, Gibson underlines the need to prioritize rigorous assessment to understand what has and has not worked, resulting in increased innovation in the field.

Several years later, a richer and more nuanced BDS market development approach is evident in a number of field-based papers. Tomecko (2003 – not included here), for example, draws on three cases from Nepal to illustrate how well-designed BDS programmes can be effective in even very weak service markets. The article goes beyond private-sector service provision, and examines how business chambers, associations, government agencies and others can play a role in ME promotion and poverty alleviation. Dawson (2003 –included in the collection) employs four BDS initiatives in Kenya, Uganda and Sri Lanka to demonstrate the efficacy of BDS for integrating MEs into high value markets including lucrative export opportunities. Dawson proposes that only 'star' producers can easily take advantage of the new markets and associated BDS services, since limitations of geography, culture and logistics impede the participation of other MEs. However, he suggests that through combining BDS with sub-sector analysis, implementers can 'give greater consideration to the different characteristics and needs of growth sectors, in which large numbers of enterprises – both stars and smaller, less sophisticated producers – are active.... [to] deliver benefits more widely throughout.' This proposed merging of BDS strategies and sub-sector analysis forms the foundation of current best practice in value chain initiatives.

Three years later, Kula et al. (2006) refined this blended strategy, with a new emphasis on industry competitiveness (USAID, 2003) drawing on the work of well known figures such as Michael Porter. The paper offers a practical step-by-step guide for selecting competitive industries that incorporate substantial numbers of MEs, and devising programmes that enhance the equitable integration of MEs into competitive value chains. It includes a diagnostic framework for analysing constraints and opportunities with the goal of improving the competitiveness of value chains, and details a six-step value chain assessment approach from industry selection through to performance measurement. Based on theory reinforced by experience, the authors give useful guidance to other practitioners in value chain development.

The final papers published between 2006 and 2009 take this blended value chain approach as more or less a given; no longer struggling to define the methodology, the articles examine specific subjects that fall within its boundaries. Jones and Snelgrove (2006) present the case of ECDI and MEDA in Pakistan that reaches downmarket to extremely marginalized rural women who are disadvantaged by geographic isolation, abject poverty and social segregation. The case illustrates that the trend toward focusing on macro-level issues – e.g. business enabling environment and trade agreements – is not necessarily conducive to high-impact value chain programmes for disenfranchised communities. Rather, as the case demonstrates, more narrowly targeted interventions that concentrate on the micro- and meso-level constraints of producers and their value chain can produce excellent results for the very poor. This begs the question: is there a logical ordering in development programming that may need to start at the micro level and eventually graduate to a stage in volume or complexity where macro-level concerns predominate?

In 2007, Miller and da Silva describe and analyse the emerging area of value chain financing. Their paper contributes to the growing body of literature on the topic, with a focus on agricultural value chains and agrifood systems – taking into account and describing financing within the value chain (e.g. advance credit from buyer to seller) and financing from external agencies such as microfinance institutions to value chain actors. The authors also offer an interesting typology of value chain finance approaches, analysing the advantages and disadvantages to producers/borrowers and companies/lenders. They conclude with a discussion of moving forward – gaps, opportunities, areas of innovation, and the role of policy makers to adapt regulatory frameworks to the changing environments. This paper served as the launching pad for a comprehensive book on agricultural value chain financing (Miller and Jones, 2010).

The next two papers, from the Making Markets Work for the Poor issue of the journal in 2008, deliver further guidelines and frameworks for market development practitioners – strategies that are still relevant as we move into the future of value chain development.

Bekkers et al (2008) analyse the internal monitoring system of the Katalyst programme that develops support markets for improved sector competitiveness in Bangladesh. The analysis reveals that private-sector development projects can provide concrete evidence regarding their level of impact on poverty reduction, a growing requirement of donors, governments and other stakeholders. The authors describe a specific intervention (in the fish pond sector) and its 'logic,' and outline how an impact assessment measured key links in that logic. A critical element of the analysis is the evaluation of a treatment (project) group versus a control (non-project) group. Building on this concrete example, the paper then details the overall Katalyst monitoring and impact assessment system with information on how to keep the system simple yet meaningful. A section on challenges and a conclusion that discusses benefits of the system to managers are worthwhile additions to our corpus of value chain knowledge and practice.

Bear and Field (2008) contribute to the volume with an insightful and thought-provoking paper that includes two frameworks for managing the process of change in value chain development programmes: an industry pathway and a knowledge management process. The tools reflect the fluid environment of market development initiatives through the stages of analysis, demonstration and scale up/exit, and delve into complex issues of benefits, relationships and learning, taking into consideration not only financial but also cultural incentives for change. These complex concepts receive practical interpretation in the presentation of the PROFIT programme's Zambia beef industry veterinarian case description. It concludes with comments on scale-up, facilitation, sequencing, the need for failure in market systems, and knowledge management.

Reforming the business environment has moved up on the agenda of donor agencies, and this is reflected in the article by Altenburg and von Drachenfels (2008). They describe 'Doing Business' reports that illustrate how excessive regulation is a key obstacle to private sector development. These reports recommend the simplification of regulatory business environments as the most important reform for private sector development and claim that countries achieve the greatest success if they do not regulate at all. This article argues that the Doing Business reports ignore important benefits of regulation and underestimate the difficulties and variability in the requirements for institutional change across countries, regions and sectors. They advocate defining appropriate levels of regulation and the accountability of governments for related services.

Daniels and Jeans (2009) conclude the volume, applying market development thinking to vulnerable populations through the examination of two cases: people living with disabilities in Uganda and those affected by HIV/AIDS in Kenya. The authors take the position that even when markets become more accessible to poor people (note that even this outreach is subject to ongoing debate with regard to value chain development more generally), wealth differentials occur and vulnerable communities are still often excluded. They propose that an integrated approach can take multiple dimensions of poverty suffered by the most vulnerable into account, and address deep levels of poverty through employment and enterprise. Daniels and Jeans describe entry points and key services required to facilitate and sustain participation of the vulnerable as employees and enterprise owners, emphasizing the roles of attitudinal change and creation of a more level playing field. This paper is a fitting conclusion to the volume, reminding us that a full life includes productive participation, and empowerment for all is both a fitting and realistic goal for our field of practice.

We hope that this collection of papers opens the door to the next generation of value chain development theories and practices as well as frameworks and tools – articles that deal with the challenges of scale, sustainability, equity and inclusiveness in deep and enduring ways. An early version of this introduction was expanded and published in the anniversary issue of the journal, including references beyond the journal and offering deeper analysis of the recent history of enterprise development (Jones and Miehlbradt, 2009). The journal will continue to seek out and publish leading edge articles to keep theorists and practitioners up to date on the state of the art.

References

Altenburg, T and C. von Drachenfels (2008) 'Business environment reforms: Why it is necessary to rethink priorities and strategies', *Enterprise Development and Microfinance*, Vol. 19. No. 3.

Bear, M., P. Bradnum, S. Tladi and D. Pedro (2004) *Making Retail Markets Work for the Poor – Why and How Triple Trust Organisation Decided to Intervene in the Spaza Market in South Africa*, Practitioner Learning Program in BDS Market Assessment, Case Study #1, Small Enterprise and Education Promotion Network and USAID, Washington, DC.

Boomgard, J., S. Davies, S. Haggblade and D. Mead (1991) *A Sub-sector Approach to Small Enterprise Promotion and Research*, GEMINI, Bethseda.

Daniels, A. and A. Jeans (2009) 'Integrated approaches to enabling the most vulnerable to participate in markets', *Enterprise Development and Microfinance*, Vol. 20. No. 2

Haggblade, S. and Gamser, M. (1991) *A Field Manual for Sub-Sector Practitioners*, GEMINI, Bethseda.

Jones, L. (2008) 'Editorial', *Enterprise Development and Microfinance*, Vol. 19. No. 2.

Jones, L. and Miehlbradt, A. (2009) 'A 20/20 Retrospective on Enterprise Development: In Search of Impact, Scale and Sustainability', *Enterprise Development and Microfinance* Vol. 20 No. 4.

Miehlbradt, A. (2007) *Developing the Advertising Market for SMEs in Northern Bangladesh*, The Katalyst Cases, Case Study Number 3, Katalyst, Dhaka.

Miehlbradt, A. and Jones, L. (2007) *Market Research Toolkit*, Information to Action: A Value Chain and Market Development Toolkit Series for Practitioners, L. Jones (ed.), MEDA, Waterloo.

McVay, M. and Snelgrove, A. (2007) *Program Design Toolkit*, Information to Action: A Value Chain and Market Development Toolkit Series for Practitioners, L. Jones (ed.), MEDA, Waterloo.

Miller C. and Jones, L. (2010) *Agriculture Value Chain Finance*. FAO, Rome/ Practical Action Publishing, UK.

Tomecko, J. (2003) 'Case Studies of BDS Market Development Interventions in Weak Markets' *SED*, Vol. 14 No. 4.

Triple Trust Organization (2005) *TTO Annual Report 2004/2005*, Cape Town.

USAID (2003) 'Promoting Competitiveness in Practice: an Assessment of Cluster-Based Approaches', prepared by the Mitchell Group for USAID.

Van der Land, H. and P. Uliwa (1997) 'Applying Sub-sector Analysis in Tanzania' *SED* Vol. 8 No.4.

World Bank (2001) *Business Development Services for Small Enterprises: Guiding Principles for Donor Intervention*, World Bank Group.

CHAPTER 2
The Triple Trust – a three-fold approach
James Thomas

This article was first published in March 1990.

Abstract

The Triple Trust Organisation (TTO) is a South African not-for-profit organisation committed to the alleviation of poverty in South Africa through making markets work for the poor. At the time this article was written, it was an autonomous, independent body in the private sector that was formed in September 1988 in response to the need for self-employment opportunities in the fast-growing black community in the area immediately surrounding Cape Town, South Africa, where the problems of unemployment were particularly acute. The vision was to help people to help themselves by means of a threefold approach – training, financing and marketing support – working through existing community organizations.

There have been no new employment opportunities created in the formal job market in Cape Town in the last ten years. In the past six years Khayelitsha (a huge new shanty town of about half a million people) has mushroomed because of the relaxation of influx control legislation which for many years prevented the natural migration of people from rural to urban areas. The problem continues as every month thousand of people are coming into the greater Cape Town area – all of them looking for some way of supporting themselves.

Leaving rural areas, they arrive on the periphery of an urban area without sufficient land for subsistence. They expect to find employment, but possess no skill that is useful to the urban economy (even if jobs were available).

The Triple Trust Organization provides people with the skills needed for self-employment, recognizing the importance of people achieving personal dignity through the control of their own economic destiny. This organization's pragmatic approach has not been based on any theoretical framework, but rather on practical experience. Having had no role model to follow, the programme has developed by trying new ideas, adopting those which have worked well and scrapping anything that has not! The Triple Trust is comprised of three non-profit-making trusts: the Neighbourhood Training Trust, the Self Help Financing Trust and the Africa Trading Co-operative Trust.

Under the Neighbourhood Training Trust, all skills training is conducted through existing community organizations in the neighbourhoods where trainees live. Structures such as community centres, churches and even shacks are used. No sophisticated training facilities are provided as it is important that the training environment resembles the eventual workplace (people's homes) as closely as possible.

People are only trained in economically viable skills suitable for profitable self-employment, requiring minimal capital input. Before a new skill is introduced, a carefully researched viability study is conducted. This is to ensure that the product can be made at home without sophisticated equipment or electricity, that all the raw materials are readily available at reasonable prices and that channels for the marketing of the product exist or can be set up.

At present people are being trained in the following skills: sewing, sheepskin slipper making, knitting, artificial flower arranging. New courses which are in the process of development are: machine knitting, garment applique, soft toy making and selling skills, which will train unemployed people to sell the produce of existing producers.

Unemployed people are selected by community organizations and are required to undergo simple basic testing which checks their ability to be trained for the particular skill. People are trained in their own language by members of their own community. All training is based on the finest competency-based methods which enables each person to progress at his or her own rate.

Training is conducted full time over a period of eight weeks. The first four weeks are spent mastering the basic skill – the next four weeks concentrate on making a profit out of the newly acquired skill as well as developing speed, quality and creativity. During the second four-week phase, the trainees are required to pay R15 (USD $4) per week for the rental of their space and equipment, thereby learning to take responsibility for the costs of operating a business from the earliest stages. Spread over the eight weeks, training in basic business procedures is included which assists trainees in areas such as cash-flow management, costing, pricing, market investigation, merchandizing, etc. (These self-instructional business training modules have been nicknamed the 'Township MBA' and are now in great demand by other development organizations.)

After people have left the full-time training phase they are visited at their place of work by trained mentors who will evaluate their progress and help to iron out any problems.

Under the second trust, the Self-Help Financing Trust, it was hoped initially that only training would be needed, but it was soon found that there were very few financial institutions which were prepared to make credit available to those whom they perceived to be high-risk clients. Also, some of the referrals to these funding sources took over three months to process. We soon realized that instant access to finance was required if these small businesses were to get off the ground.

The Self-Help Financing Trust was set up to provide mini-loans of up to R500 ($200) in the form of equipment and materials to qualifying trainees. The only qualifications required are reasonable stability within the community, complete mastery of the skill, reliable attendance and payment of a weekly rental during the training period. The loan, which is issued when the full-time training finishes, is repayable in twelve equal installments over a period of one year. The rate charged covers interest, administration, collection charges and provision for bad debts, and is consequently high at 44 per cent. (The current prime rate of interest in South Africa is 22 per cent.) There has been no community resistance to this high rate (for which we have been criticized in some 'First World' circles) since immediate access to credit is viewed as far more important than the rate of interest charged.

Most of these small businesses have a return on investment in excess of 500 per cent within the first year and as such, the cost of capital is easily affordable.

South Africa is in the unique position where apartheid legislation has over the years resulted in a polarized dual economy with a strong, sophisticated, white-controlled First World economy running side by side with a struggling Third World economy. Although it is relatively easy to train people to produce goods, it is very difficult for them to gain access to raw materials at reasonable prices, and to break into markets tightly held by highly competitive First World businesses.

Africa Trading Co-operative Trust was set up to 'build the bridges' between the fledgling producers and the First World suppliers and markets. The Trust buys in bulk and passes on the savings when supplying to the new producers. Attempts are made to source raw materials to the producers in the most convenient forms – for example, designer garments are pre-cut and packaged with all the trims made available to those who wish to buy. This service is welcomed by the producers as it is very cost effective, saving time and cutting down on wasted fabric. (The producers do, of course, pay the full costs involved in providing the service.)

Africa Trading offers to buy back specified items from producers at pre-determined prices, if they wish to sell through this route. It is always emphasized that people selling items for themselves will make more than by selling through Africa Trading.

High-quality standards are insisted upon. They are actually quite simple to control as everybody knows that Africa Trading will only buy back products that meet 100 per cent quality standards.

Because of economies of scale, Africa Trading can act on behalf of a number of producers when negotiating with potential markets. For example, sheepskin slippers made by a number of producers are now sold to a large supermarket chain. It is not intended, however, to set up a permanent channel that producers will become solely dependent upon. Rather, Africa Trading provides a structure which will enable new producers to gain confidence in buying and selling as well as boosting their productivity in the initial stages of their business.

The overall aim is a system of 'progressive weaning' in which the producers' dependence on the Triple Trust Organization steadily diminishes until they become totally self-sufficient. Africa Trading will introduce producers to the market contacts, enable the transactions to happen between them until the link up is well established and then step out of the picture.

The Triple Trust has been criticized for being involved in too many aspects of development for an organization whose primary involvement is training. However, it is precisely the integrated approach of addressing three major components (namely training, financing and marketing) which enables new businesses to become rapidly established without having to lurch from organization to organization re-establishing their bona fides each time.

The Triple Trust started with dreams and very little funding. This has forced it to be very creative with meagre resources and has resulted in a streamlined 'lean-and-clean' administration. A full-time staff of 20 starts 600 unemployed people on the road to self-employment each year. At present the total cost per person is R800 ($320).

Experience has shown that a new entrepreneur can easily increase his or her income by R500 ($200) per month. This represents a return on the cost of the service that Triple Trust has provided to the new business of 750 per cent in the first year. As the whole programme gains momentum, it is intended to become increasingly self-regenerating. Profits from Africa Trading Co-operative Trust will be ploughed back into Neighbourhood Training Trust so that people will pay back the cost of their initial training out of profits from their operations.

About the author

At the time of publication, James Thomas was the Director of the Triple Trust Organization, Cape Town, South Africa.

CHAPTER 3
The Judo Trick, or crowding in
Paul Streeten

This article was first published in June 1991.

Abstract

Businesses in the informal sector have often provided a safety net for people who cannot find employment elsewhere. They also thrive better than large-scale formal sector firms in some settings. This article describes the circumstances in which informal sector firms perform best. It suggests that there can be a complementarity between the formal and informal sectors through sub-contracting, such as between importing houses in advanced countries and informal sector firms in developing countries. Successful relations of this kind would require an encouraging economic environment provided by the government. A positive model for the role of the informal sector in developing countries is already seen in the 'flexible specialization' of small-scale firms in many industrialized countries.

The recent emphasis on the role of private enterprise and free markets has been useful. It has been partly a healthy reaction against excessive early faith in the power of governments to direct the economy, to manage businesses, and to correct market failures. Unregulated markets can, however, be both inefficient, and cruel. Joan Robinson once said that the 'invisible hand' can work by strangulation. We know that both markets and governments may fail, and that the failure of one does not automatically constitute a case for the other. It is now widely accepted that market failure is not necessarily a case for government intervention. It is less generally realized that government failure does not necessarily constitute a case for private enterprise. There is no *a priori* presumption as to which is preferable.

The fact of government and bureaucratic failure suggests that it is important to concentrate the activities of the government on areas in which private efforts fail even more. Government activity is often complementary to private enterprise and efficient markets. The aim should be to avoid crowding out, and to achieve 'crowding in'. Government intervention should provide the conditions in which markets and enterprise can flourish. Market-orientation and state minimalism, far from going together, are incompatible. A well-designed policy calls for interventions to maintain competition and to prevent restrictive practices, monopolies and cartels, to provide physical and social infrastructure, and some research efforts. It may also require new types of institutions, about which more later. Governments should also take care of the victims of the competitive struggle, both for humanitarian and for efficiency reasons. The informal sector can play an important part in providing a safety net. However, the policy of looking after the victims of the competitive struggle by encouraging the informal sector to provide a safety net (and it should not be a safety hammock) can be carried beyond this point and can make a substantial contribution to production and productivity growth.

Distinct groupings within the informal sector

The informal sector has been much discussed. It comprises four quite distinct groups. First, there are the self-employed, sometimes with unpaid members of their families. They are a heterogeneous group, ranging from shoeshine boys, street vendors, garbage collectors, petty thieves, prostitutes, drug traffickers, smugglers, self-appointed tourist guides and bag carriers to jobbing gardeners, and small-scale producers such as blacksmiths, carpenters, sandal-makers, lamp-makers, bricklayers, bus and taxi drivers, seamstresses, repairmen, cobblers, bakers, shopkeepers, auto mechanics, and builders who sometimes earn more than workers in the formal sector. Some formal sector workers use their savings to set up such enterprises for themselves in the informal sector.

Second, there are the casual workers, hired on a day-to-day basis in the docks, in construction, transport, and services. If the criterion for being in the informal sector is the method of hiring, then some workers hired casually by quite large firms should be counted as being in the informal sector.

Third, there are workers employed on a regular basis by small-scale, labour-intensive, not bureaucratically controlled firms outside the formal sector. Fourth, there are the 'outworkers', working in their homes under the 'putting-out' system.

Another distinction to be made is between three quite different kinds of informal sector firm. First, there are the productive, entrepreneurial, often rapidly growing firms. They often graduate to middle-sized, and occasionally to large, firms. Second, there are the viable family firms, neither dynamic nor lame ducks, who stand midway between the first and the third category. Third, there are the absorbers of the lame ducks thrown out of the formal sector, or incapable of entering it: small family firms of infirm, old or otherwise unemployable people, such as an elderly, infirm couple who live above their small grocery store, but are not bound by the laws about closing hours, and who might be entirely unemployable elsewhere. If their receipts exceed their costs, they earn a small producer's rent. Businesses such as these constitute the safety nets for personal incapacities and the misfortunes that befall people, and the shifts in demand or technology that occur in the formal sector.

The second type has been swollen in recent years by declining aggregate growth rates and austerity programmes that have thrown people out of employment in the formal sector. The activities of these firms are anticyclical, swelling with a decline in aggregate demand, and declining with its growth. At the same time, the crisis also provided opportunities for some firms who belong to this group to move into the first category, although if they are linked, say through sub-contracting, to the formal sector, their behaviour will be pro-cyclical. Nevertheless, they benefit from fluctuations, for they will receive excess orders in booms, when the large firms run into capacity limits, and in slumps, when these firms wish to convert fixed into variable costs by hiving off employees and transforming them into sub-contractors.

Informal sector firms, in the right setting, thrive on certain advantages more than large-scale, formal sector firms. These advantages may be:
- locational, when raw materials are dispersed and the enterprise processes them, or when markets are local and transport costs high;
- relating to the process of production or the product, when the work requires simple assembly, or other activities that are best carried out by hand or with simple tools;
- relating to the market, when operating on a small scale for a local market has lower costs than larger-scale, more distant operation, or when the service has to be rendered where the customer is;
- relating to adaptability and responsiveness to changing demand or technology, because of the absence of high fixed costs.

Characteristics of the informal sector

In the informal sector employment is largely supply driven, fairly easily absorbing additional entrants (although there are some barriers to entry into some informal sector enterprises, particularly the need for some capital, and employment is offered by small businessmen *demanding* labour), whereas in the formal sector employment is largely demand driven (although in the public sector there is a *supply-driven* component). There is also the work of women in the informal sector, until recently invisible in some cultures, who perform hard work without being counted as members of the labour force because their product is often not sold for cash.

According to an ILO Kenya report (1972) informal sector activities are a way of doing things, characterized by: ease of entry; reliance on indigenous resources; family ownership of enterprises; small-scale operations; labour-intensive and adapted technology; skills acquired outside the formal educational system; unregulated and competitive markets.

It is easy to dismiss the informal sector as a useless concept (Peattie, 1987). It is equally easy to romanticize it and to think of it as having potential for high productivity, for competitive capitalism, harassed and discriminated against by mercantilistic, predatory and interfering bureaucrats. At the time this was written, the Mayor of New York was driving street vendors off the streets of Manhattan.

The informal sector is certainly a very heterogeneous collection of people and activities. There are some whose marginal productivity is zero or negative, because their activities only take away from the sales of others, or because they only create nuisances and then extract payment for their removal. Beggars, petty thieves, small vendors, providers of unwanted services are manifestations of disguised unemployment. Even genuinely productive firms often break the law and evade taxes. Many informal sector employers exploit their workers at least as much as formal sector employers. There is no point in glamourizing them, or in overstating their contribution to production.

Another way in which the informal sector has been misleadingly romanticized is by holding it up as a splendid example of entrepreneurial competition and free enterprise capitalism. The informal sector has its peculiar modes of behaviour and formalities. As the studies of Hernando de Soto (one of the leading proponents of this form of activity) and of Judith Tendler have shown, relations between firms in the informal sector are sometimes characterized by a striking degree of co-operation (de Soto, 1989, and Tendler, 1987). They share inputs when these are in scarce supply; when one firm has a large contract and its neighbour does not, it shares the contract with the other firm by sub-contracting or by hiring out its owner as a temporary worker; there is work-sharing not only between firms, but also when the demand for labour is reduced. Not much attention has been paid to this fact, partly because it contradicts the idealized individualistic picture of firms in active competition.

While, on the one hand, the informal sector should not be glamourized, there are, on the other, actually or potentially highly productive small enterprises, some of whose owners earn more than some workers in the formal sector. They tend to use more labour per unit of capital and per unit of output, and often use it intensively, remuneratively, and highly efficiently (Liedholm and Mead, 1987).

In Peru some informal sector firms absorb those who wish to, but cannot, enter the formal sector. In Argentina, on the other hand, people with secure but ill-paid jobs in the formal sector opt to earn extra income and gain additional mobility in the informal sector.

Some people who work in the informal sector also work in the formal sector. Sometimes members of the same family are engaged in both. Some characteristics of the informal sector can be found in the formal sector, such as the casual hiring of labour. Some firms are informal with respect to some of their activities (not paying certain taxes, working without some licences, or casually hiring some of their workers), and formal with respect to others. We have seen that some informal sector incomes are higher than some formal sector earnings. It is impossible to count and record the informal sector, because, by its nature, no official records exist. (Since less interventionist governments will tend to include in their national accounts activities that more interventionist governments do not count, because they are illegal, it is easy to overstate the growth performance of countries that have followed the World Bank's advice to rely more on markets. World Bank reports have not always paid attention to this distortion of growth figures in comparing good and poor performers.) In spite of these obstacles to a clear and neat definition, however, the concept meets a real need and I shall not abandon it.

The importance of the informal sector

There are those who believe that the informal sector is entirely the creature of mistaken government policies. 'Get the prices right, deregulate, decentralize, liberalize and privatize, and the informal sector will disappear.' The evidence does not show, however, that modern technology, even with the most 'realistic' equilibrium prices for labour, capital and foreign exchange, can absorb the numbers of workers who will be seeking jobs at wages that can support them.

There are four reasons for paying attention to the informal sector. They arise from the triple needs to increase production, employment (for the sake of recognition and self-respect), and incomes, and the need to avoid rebellion.

To expand upon the first, the informal sector represents a potentially large reserve of productivity and earning power. Although not all informal sector activities contribute potentially to productivity and earnings, some do.

Second, the labour force in low-income countries is likely to grow rapidly in the next fifteen years, and neither agriculture nor the formal industrial sector is capable of absorbing even a fraction of these additions, to say nothing of the large number of already unemployed or underemployed people. Workers seeking remunerative employment are likely to grow at a rate of 2–3 per cent per year in Africa. The labour surplus economies of Java and Bangladesh represent the future for Africa, where at this time there are still relatively few landless workers seeking jobs in the towns. The situation is further aggravated by low world growth rates. The combination of population growth, urbanization and recession has swelled the informal sector, which presents the only hope for jobs.

A third reason is that, although the informal sector should not be equated with the poor (we have seen that some members of the informal sector earn more than some in the formal sector and many poor are outside the informal sector), it is in the informal sector where many poor people are to be found. By harnessing its potential for generating incomes (and self-respect), not only is efficient growth promoted but also poverty is reduced. If its productivity and remunerativeness can be raised without depriving the high-productivity sector of resources, and hence without preventing not only more production but also the opportunity of future employment, there is no conflict between efficiency and equity.

A fourth reason is that prolonged unemployment leads to alienation and a sense of worthlessness, and can be a source of rebellious instead of productive activity. Governments in power in particular have an interest in not upsetting the existing order and peace, and in using the informal sector as a vote bank.

Complementarity between large and small firms

Normally one would wish the informal sector neither to be subsidized at the expense of the high-productivity formal sector firms, nor to be squeezed out by privileged formal sector firms. The task then is to make these informal sector enterprises complementary to the larger-scale, formal sector firms, including foreign multinational corporations. At present the two sectors are often competitive, and, aided by the government, the large firms often drive out the small ones. Both Mao's declared strategy of walking on two legs and the success of the Japanese in combining a modern and a small-scale industrial sector illustrate the possibility of successfully combining the two sectors. The East Asian success stories illustrate how the marketing of manufactured exports can be undertaken by foreign firms. In Singapore, it was transnational corporations that marketed the output of wholly- or majority-owned local subsidiaries. In other countries it was the importers in the advanced countries, retail and department stores, wholesalers or trading companies who performed these functions. The Koreans used foreign buyers in the early stages of development not only to sell their goods but also to acquire knowledge about styles, designs, and technologies. The current trend towards modular manufacturing, according to which some quite small firms produce components for assembly in large firms, also encourages the growth of informal sector firms. All these are illustrations of ways of using the power of the large firms, the Goliaths, in their self-interest, for the benefit of the poor, the little Davids, rather as a judo fighter uses the power of his opponent for his purposes. Let us call this the judo trick, partly because it uses the leverage of an initially antagonistic force with multiplied effect, and partly because it uses the force of what is usually regarded as a powerful, strong opponent for the benefit of the weak.

One model for such a symbiosis in agriculture has been pioneered by the Commonwealth Development Corporation first in the Kulai Oil Palm Project in Malaysia and then in the Kenya Tea Development Authority. A modern nucleus estate does the management, the processing, the exporting, the marketing, and provides the extension services and the credit for a group of smallholders clustered round the estate. The activities best carried out on a large scale, with modern techniques, are done by the nucleus estate, while the growing of the crop is done by newly settled smallholders. This type of project has proved highly successful, although it is rather management intensive and the calls on skilled professional management, and extension services would have to be reduced if it were to be replicated on a large scale in labour-surplus economies, such as those of South Asia. Another model is the National Dairy Development Board in India. The production of milk, largely by women, remains traditional and informal, while processing, credit and marketing follow modern, formal sector lines.

A similar model has been followed by private foreign agro-businesses. It has been called the 'core-satellite' model, or contract farming, or the smallholder outgrower scheme. Companies like Heinz, Del Monte, United Brands, Nestle and Shell, provide marketing, equipment, technical assistance, credit, fertilizer, and other inputs, as well as ancillary services, and smallholders grow fruit and vegetables. In order to balance bargaining power in drawing up contracts, the smallholders have to be organized. Then they can use their power both directly and indirectly on the government to give them political support. The high fixed costs of a processing plant make it important for the company to secure an even and certain flow of inputs, which is ensured by the contract. It is preferable either to open market purchases or a plantation with hired labour, though contract farming is sometimes supplemented by these other forms. The smallholders, in turn, acquire an assured market, credit and inputs at low costs. I do not advocate the replication of these schemes, for too little research has been done on the precise division of gains and conditions for the optimum smallholder benefit, but these are worth exploring.

This type of institutional arrangement can combine some of the advantages of plantation farming, such as quality control, the co-ordination of interdependent stages of production, and marketing, with those of smallholder production, such as autonomy, keener incentives and income generation for poor people. However, the possibility of abuse of its monopsonistic power by the private company against the smallholders makes it necessary to have either smallholder organizations with countervailing power or public regulation.

No similar type of arrangement exists as yet in manufacturing. One can easily imagine a large, modern manufacturing plant round which are clustered informal, small enterprises doing repairs, manufacturing components and spare parts, and providing anciliary services such as transport, handling, cleaning, packaging, catering, and so on. The nearest thing to such an arrangement is the system of modular manufacturing. It has, for example, replaced or perhaps complemented the assembly line as a method of manufacturing cars. It involves designing and assembling an entire motor car as a series of sub-assemblies, or modules. Suppliers of these components (e.g. dashboards, sunroofs or doors), with their lower labour costs, could concentrate on the nuts and bolts, leaving to the large firms styling, packaging, marketing and distribution.

Implications for government policy

Such a project, to make use of informal sector enterprises, would require changes in government policies. The first step would be to stop repressive regulation, harassment and discrimination against the informal sector; to stop, for example demolishing informal sector houses, subject, of course, to some urban planning for open spaces. In Peru a union of *formales* and *informales* has been formed to reduce government regulations and bureaucratic meddling. It is an interesting example of a reformist alliance, in which formal sector enterprises make common cause with informal ones, sharing with them their experience and uniting in exercising political pressure. The next step would be to adopt policies and to create institutions with respect to the provision of credit, information and imported inputs (for example, tariff remission for the informal sector). As to credit, innovative steps are needed for small loans and new types of collateral, such as inventories, or an unlicensed bus, or plots of land in shanty towns. Another option is the mobilization of peer pressure, as in the Grameen Bank in Bangladesh. A third step would be to remove legislation that gives the formal sector special advantages in buying from or selling to the informal sector.

The implications of this proposal for policy are quite radical. For example, the common prescription is to lower real wages in order to raise employment. In this model, however, a rise in real wages may increase employment and incomes in the informal sector. The production of spare parts, repairs, and ancillary activities, such as cleaning, transport, packaging, are carried out inside the firms in the organized sector while wages are low. When they are raised, these activities become worth contracting out to small informal sector firms not subject to minimum wage legislation. These firms carry out these activities in a more labour-intensive way, and benefit from the new contracts. Even if the workers previously engaged on these activities inside the formal sector firms were to be dismissed (rather than redeployed), and were to add pressure on incomes in the informal sector, the savings in capital and profits may be enough to produce higher incomes as well as more jobs for the sub-contractors. This would be the case, for example, if the self-employed small entrepreneur works harder than the same man as paid foreman or manager. A similar effect is produced by legislating for a shorter working week, to which the informal sector firms are not bound. Higher taxes, avoided or evaded by these enterprises, work in the same direction.

It is true that, for such efficient and income-raising sub-contracting to occur, the initial in-house production by the formal firms may have been sub-optimal. For, it may be argued, if it pays to sub-contract at the higher wage, it would have done so also at the lower wage. In this case stubbornness, inertia or ignorance stood in the way, and the rise in the wage wakes up the businessman. There may have been non-pecuniary offsetting advantages in in-house production, however, which are more than offset when costs rise. These may be the result of transport, communication or transaction costs, or high training costs with a greater probability that the trained sub-contractor may leave than the in-house worker.

Other linkages between formal and informal sector firms affecting competing and complementary inputs and products should be carefully traced. If high and modern growth rates in the formal sector are not to be impeded, it is important not to deprive it of scarce factors, such as capital, management or wage goods, in order to benefit low-productivity activities. This implies that the capital and organizational capacity should be recruited from within the informal sector. At the same time, it is also important that the expansion of the formal sector should not raise the prices of goods necessary for production in the informal sector. This appears to have happened in Colombia, where a housing project for the rich was intended to generate incomes for workers.

The resulting price increases in concrete and steel, however, led to price rises in sheet metal and cardboard, jeopardizing the building efforts of the poor (Peattie, 1987).

The 'putting-out system'

A second illustration is to be found in a modern version of the eighteenth-century putting-out system. Sub-contracting by large firms to small, sometimes informal sector firms or cottage industries is quite common in the developing world. There is still much scope, however, for importing houses in advanced countries or retail chains independent of developed country producer interests to apply the putting-out system to informal sector firms in developing countries. The large firm provides the materials, the designs, the credit and the marketing, while the informal sector firm produces the clothes, the sports equipment, the electronic components, the cloth and woodwork for handicrafts, or the crops. The British retail chain Marks and Spencer have employed this modern putting-out system not only in England but also in some developing countries.

There opens up another use for the judo trick. The political power of these retail chains, such as Atlantic and Pacific Stores or Safeways in the USA, can be used to counteract the pressures for protection of the producer lobbies in the developed countries. Their interest in low-cost, labour-intensive imports coincides with those of the poor producers in the developing countries. If institutional safeguards are adopted to prevent exploitation and sweated labour, firms such as Marks and Spencer can do more for the poor of the world than Marx and Engels.

In addition to new institutions, policies will have to be revised. Thus, many economists have opposed minimum wage legislation on the ground that it prevents higher employment. As we have seen, however, if a higher wage level or a shorter working week, applied only to organized sector firms, forces them to contract out to the informal sector activities previously carried out inside these firms, this can be a gain in employment and earnings. For these activities are likely to be carried out in a more labour-intensive way in the informal sector than they were inside the large firms. One characteristic of the distinction is the flexibility of incomes in the informal sector compared with rigidity downwards in the formal sector. Therefore the absorptive capacity of labour in the informal sector is higher, and policies that make it worth while to give more business to the small firms are to be welcomed.

The measures needed to implement such a policy can be summarized as follows:
- A more favourable economic environment for the informal sector should be created. At present, macropolicies tend to discriminate against it. For example, investment incentives confine tax concessions to formal sector firms. Overvaluation of the exchange rate combined with import

restrictions and undervaluation of the interest rate handicap the access to inputs and credit of informal firms.
- It is necessary to design new institutions of the kind indicated above. The access of the poor to assets should be improved. In agriculture this policy has worked. It is more difficult to apply it in urban industry. Steps are being taken to provide these small entrepreneurs with credit. The Grameen Bank in Bangladesh is finding many imitators in other countries. The Inter-American Development Bank wants to establish itself as the bank for Latin America's informal sector. The International Fund for Agricultural Development has successfully provided credit lines for businesses without collateral. Pressures for repayment can be exercised by peer groups, and by making small loans for short periods. Loans should be primarily for working capital. Judgement of the borrower's reliability can replace conventional collateral requirements.
- Returns to these enterprises must be raised. It is not enough, as is often said, to raise their productivity, for productivity gains can be passed on in the form of low prices to often better-off buyers in the formal sector. It is the earning power, the remunerativeness of the enterprise, that matters.
- Employment opportunities must be improved. Even though the informal sector is often defined as supply-driven, there are obstacles to entry and to employment, which can be reduced.
- The demand for their production should be raised. Since poor people tend to buy the goods produced by the poor people in the informal sector, policies that generate incomes for poor people will also raise the demand for their products (Sinha *et al.*, 1979; Liedholm and Mead, 1987).
- Access to education, training and health services must be improved, both as an end in itself and in order to raise the productivity of the poor. Technical training and instruction in simple managerial techniques, such as accounting and bookkeeping, marketing and technical know-how are important. The identification and provision of missing components, such as market information, infrastructure or technical know-how can yield great benefits at little cost.
- Transfer payments out of public funds are also required to provide a safety net, not only for the 'unemployables', the disabled, the sick, the old, but also to tide people over periods of no earnings, of failure of their enterprises or of temporary inability to work.

It is customary to distinguish between primary incomes, earned through production and sales for the market; secondary incomes as a result of access to the sources of improved earning power, such as education, training and health services; and tertiary incomes which are pure welfare payments. Another way of categorizing the necessary public-sector measures to make the symbiosis between multinational corporations and the informal sector successful can be summarized with a mnemonic device. it is the seven 'Ins' or 'Instruments':

- Incentives: prices of both inputs and outputs must be right.
- Inputs: both imported and domestic inputs, including credit, must be available.
- Institutions: access to marketing and credit institutions and a noncorrupt, efficient administrative apparatus must exist.
- Innovation: the right small-scale technology, appropriate for small enterprises often does not exist, and research should be provided to create, find, and adapt it.
- Information: a knowledge bank for technology should provide the means of spreading the results of research among the firms. Instruction in management, bookkeeping, and recording should also be provided.
- Infrastructure: roads, communications, harbours, and utilities must be available if the output of the informal sector is to be sold in national and international markets.
- Independence: to permit and encourage self-reliance and freedom from excessive regulation and harassment.

In the manner described above, the informal sector can be made complementary to the formal with respect to access to markets, inputs, information and technology; the small-scale firms complementary to large-scale firms, domestic to foreign firms, public to private firms, and non-governmental organizations to governments. The putting-out system of foreign retailers or importing houses is an example of the symbiosis between large foreign and small domestic enterprises. Similarly, private voluntary organizations engaged in helping informal sector projects should find ways of co-operating with government departments and multinational corporations, which are often in a better position to finance and replicate successful projects.

Our knowledge of the informal sector in most developing countries is still rudimentary. What we need is both time-series and cross-country studies of informal sector activities to show at what income levels, with what policies, which activities, actually or potentially, there is a contribution to employment, productivity, earning power, production, and growth. It has been emphasized that the encouragement of complementarities should not be done at the expense of the growth of the high-productivity, modern sector. On the contrary, the small units should contribute to raising the productivity of the large ones. According to S.P. Kashyap (1988), handicaps for large firms and biases in policy against them are largely responsible for the growth of small-scale enterprises in India. Nor should there be any form of exploitation, such as child labour, inhuman working conditions, sweated labour, or monopsonistic depression of the prices at which outputs are bought. Fears have been expressed that informal sector enterprises have been reduced to a state of 'peonage' by their formal sector principals. Nor should there be monopolistic overpricing of the intermediate products supplied by the formal sector as inputs to the informal enterprises. Such overpricing could be the result of import restrictions or other barriers to entry. In Sierra Leone large-scale flour mills, which supply flour to small-scale bakers, are protected by an exclusive import licence, and therefore can sell flour at prices over twice those of potential imports (Chuta and Liedholm, 1985).

Policies must be designed to mobilize the energies of small-scale firms, and to make use of their lower costs, more labour-intensive techniques, greater employment creation, and wider dispersion of technology, without, on the one hand, sacrificing efficiency and innovation, and, on the other, depriving the informal sector, by underpricing outputs or overpricing inputs, of adequate rewards and humane working conditions.

Flexible specialization

Encouragement that the informal sector, or at any rate the sector containing small-scale firms, can be the dynamic sector of the future comes from an unexpected source: the literature on 'flexible specialization', mainly applied to trends in the advanced, industrial countries (Tendler, 1987, Sabel, 1986). The move from standardized, large-scale mass production to small-scale, flexible firms is the result of changes in demand and in supply. On the demand side, the mass consumer has been replaced by a more sophisticated person with higher purchasing power and more differentiated tastes. On the side of supply, the technology for energy and information has encouraged the decentralization of production and the smaller size of firms. 'Mass production is the manufacture of standard products with specialized resources ... flexible specialization is the production of specialized products with general resources' (Sabel, 1986).

In Mexico the large number of small, decentralized workshops *(maquilas)* and household units are sub-contractors for the large firms. The uncertainties of the 1980s have encouraged the rise of these units which produce specialized products with a broadly skilled and weakly specialized labour force. The division of labour resembles the Japanese *kanban* where many small suppliers and sub-contractors are clustered round a large firm. Similar patterns are to be found in northern Italy (the so-called 'Third Italy') and other parts of Europe, with their regional clusters of small, co-operating, flexible firms. As demand and technology changes, skills and products can be easily switched and adapted to the new situation. The shoe industries around Novo Hamburgo in Brazil and Leon in Mexico are organized on this basis and have encouraged the growth of rural industries.

As Judith Tendler has pointed out, there has been a role reversal, and in this literature the formal sector firms, interpreted as the traditional, largescale, fixed-cost, mass-production firms, are seen as 'sick', whereas the flexible, small firms are capable of responding dynamically to changing demand and technology. Not only have they taken over the function of leadership, but they are also more humane and responsible in their work relations. There is also a new form of co-operation between the small firms, and the old confrontation between labour and capital is replaced by one between the managers, owners and workers in the small, subcontracting firms, on the one hand, and the large buyers of their output on the other. In addition, supportive local institutions evolve that provide information, technical know-how and training. All this holds out great productive and social promise for the informal sector, especially if supported by the right social policies.

Reference

Chuta, E. and C. Liedholm, (1985), *Employment and growth in small-scale industry,* London, Macmillan.

de Soto, H., (1989), *The Other Path: The invisible revolution in the Third World,* New York, Harper and Row.

ILO, (1972), *Employment. incomes and equality: A strategy for increasing productive incomes in Kenya,* Geneva, International Labour Office.

Kashyap, S.P., (1988), 'Growth of small-size enterprises in India: Its nature and content', *World Development,* Volume 16 Number 6.

Leadholm, C. and D. Mead, (1987), 'Small-scale industries in developing countries: Empirical evidence, and policy implications', International development paper Number 9, Department of Agricultural Economics, Michigan State University, Michigan.

Peattie, L., (1987), 'An idea in good currency and how it grew: The informal sector' in *World Development,* Volume 15, Number 7.

Sabel, C., (1986), 'Changing roles of economic efficiency and their implications for industrialization in the Third World' in *Development, democracy and the art of trespassing: Essays in honor of Albert O. Hirschman,* edited by Alejandro Foxley, Michael S. McPherson and Guillermo O'Donnell, Indiana, University of Notre Dame Press.

Sinha, R., Po Pearson, G. Kadekodi and M. Gregory, (1979), *Income distribution growth and basic needs in India,* London, Croom Helm.

Tendler, J., (1987) 'The remarkable convergence of fashion on small enterprise and the informal sector: what are the implications for policy?', mimeo.

About the author

Paul Streeten was at the time of writing Professor Emeritus at Boston University, was founder and editor of the Journal of World Development, and established the World Development Institute.

CHAPTER 4

Sub-Sector Analysis – a macro-analytical tool for microenterprise support

Matthew Gamser

This article was first published in March 1992.

The vast majority of small enterprise development programmes seek to deliver credit, training and technical assistance directly to a community of firms having less than a ceiling number of employees, amount of capital or both. These multi-input, direct-assistance efforts have generally reached only a limited number of firms, and have proven very expensive per beneficiary. This has given rise to a new generation of assistance efforts, the so-called 'minimalist' programmes, which concentrate on the provision of short-term working capital at market interest rates. These programmes are seen as more cost-effective.

Despite the important achievements of minimalist programmes, they do not address all small enterprise development needs. Enhancing the productivity and competitiveness of small enterprises to capture market opportunities often requires more than short-term, working capital infusions. Sub-sector analysis provides a means for specifying these other needs, for identifying what types of assistance can have the greatest impact on the largest number of firms, and for pin-pointing where this assistance can be most effectively applied.

Sub-sector analysis starts from the recognition that small firms operate within a larger production and distribution system. Understanding the opportunities and constraints facing small firms and developing sensible policies for their promotion requires looking not only at the small enterprises but also at the larger firms that compete with them, supply them with inputs, and market their output. Focusing on firms of all sizes concerned with the production and distribution of a specific range of products (wood furniture, agricultural machinery, or edible oils, for example) provides the framework for examining these critical inter-firm relationships.

Sub-sector analysis relies on four key concepts, which together lead to a systematic search for growth opportunities for large numbers of microenterprises.

Vertical perspective. Many small businesses work in vertical supply chains. They purchase inputs and market output through others, often through larger firms.

Competition. Small firms compete among themselves. They also compete with medium and large firms using different technology. Understanding this competition helps to determine where small firms have an edge, and how they can develop this advantage.

Co-ordination. This describes the linkages among firms active in the subsector. It examines how policies and regulations influence market access and interaction, and how insiders regulate product flows within the system.

Leverage. One-on-one assistance to small enterprises is expensive and rarely cost-effective. Because target firms are small and dispersed, individual contact costs are high. Benefits per firm, even if projects double incomes, are small in absolute value. Sub-sector analysis starts from the premise that interventions most likely to be cost-effective are those that influence large numbers of small firms at a single stroke. With the benefit of this type of leverage, small focused project inputs can generate large output, just as a small person using a lever can lift a large mass. Leveraged interventions multiply benefits and reduce per-firm contact costs.

Sub-sector analysis uses a schematic map that summarizes the economic relationships between small enterprises and other actors in the system. The sub-sector map traces system flows and, within them, the options available to small enterprises. It serves as a focus for discussion and as a basis for displaying key information.

Looking at the problems and prospects of a system containing firms of many sizes, as opposed to those of a cross-section of firms of like size, brings a new perspective on the types of assistance that might be most useful. Opportunities for indirect measures, which do not involve working directly with small entrepreneurs but which change the system in which they operate, are revealed. These include introducing technological change to make production viable on a smaller scale, improving information flows to facilitate new marketing linkages, and changing a specific policy to reduce production costs for all small firms in a sub-sector. Where opportunities for firm-level interventions emerge, they tend to focus on larger firms, where changes in production or marketing patterns can benefit a number of smaller firms.

For example, an examination of rattan furniture production in Indonesia showed that export markets held great potential, but that small producers in central Java could not export by themselves. Helping a larger exporter firm to assemble production from artisan producers opened up a new market opportunity for hundreds of rattan craftsmen in the villages of central Java.

This poses a challenge for small enterprise support programmes and institutions. A different set of skills and resources may be necessary to provide such indirect support than that required for intensive, small firm support. Should institutions devote scarce resources to activities that do not directly touch small enterprises, but that can alter the larger business environment in a way that may open up substantial opportunities for these enterprises? The GEMINI project is working with a few institutions to examine the risks and the rewards of such a change, and will be reporting on this experience over the next three years.

About the author

Matthew Gamser was at the time of writing Deputy Director of the GEMINI Project, USA. He is now Principal, Advisory Services, East Asia–Pacific Region, IFC.

CHAPTER 5
A sub-sectoral approach to small business and microenterprise development

Biswajit Sen and Vijay Mahajan

This article was first published in September 1993.

Abstract

A sub-sectoral approach to enterprise development has the capacity to identify particular factors limiting the incomes of poor producers in the manufacturing chain of a particular item. In dealing with such bottlenecks it is sometimes possible to have a much wider impact upon poor people's incomes than other approaches to poverty alleviation, which may be limited to a geographical area. A further advantage of the sub-sectoral approach is that rapidly growing sub-sectors may be identified and poor producers enabled to take over more profitable elements of the manufacturing chain, so as to benefit from the growth. This article describes the work of PRADAN in north India, and gives case studies of how a sub-sectoral analysis of production has enabled disadvantaged groups to increase their skills or change their working patterns and to sell higher-value produce, thereby earning a better income.

Interest in promoting small business and microenterprise development as a strategy for poverty alleviation has come from two apparently opposing ideological streams for bringing about development in Third World countries. One stream, concerned primarily with issues of *growth*, finds that the model of industrial development based on large industry not only has inherent constraints in a capital-scarce economy, but also seems to have reached its limit in terms of growth. On the other hand, small-scale industry and the informal sector have shown robust growth in terms of both output and employment. This has attracted the interest of international institutions such as the World Bank and public sector promotional and financial institutions towards the field of small business and microenterprise development.

The second ideological stream, essentially concerned with issues of *equity* finds that the typical 'integrated' rural development efforts, with an area-based, multi-activity, service-delivery, or awareness-building approach has limitations in terms of achieving significant impact on the income of the poor, which to a large extent determines their quality of life. Hence many public and private, non-profit sector enterprise development organizations (EDOs) have started looking for ways of raising the income levels of the poor through promoting small businesses and microenterprises (MSEs).

Institutions operating at both ends of this ideological spectrum have until recently been concentrating on promoting a variety of enterprises, through providing specific inputs such as training, credit, marketing and entrepreneurship development. In this strategy, which has been called a missing input or minimalist strategy in the literature (see, for example, Mahajan and Dichter, 1990), the promotional agency focuses on the missing input rather than on a specific economic sub-sector. This approach, while successful in some situations, has limitations because of the problem of handling the diversity of needs across many sub-sectors, each with its own dynamics and complexity.

Interestingly, the only institutional actor who has traditionally adopted the sub-sectoral approach is the individual entrepreneur guided by the profit motive. While certain lessons can definitely be drawn from his or her experience, it is one thing to run a business for one's own profit and another to promote it for others, specially those who are less skilled and privileged. Keeping this difference in mind, what is needed is to analyse systematically the logic of the sub-sectoral approach to MSE development as a strategy for poverty alleviation, especially in underdeveloped rural locations. For this, it is necessary to define the sub-sectoral approach to poverty alleviation, delineate its logic and historical position, build up a conceptual framework to study its application and implications, document a range of live experiences where this approach is being applied in different contexts, draw lessons from this experience and finally convert these on-the-ground lessons into models for strategy formulation, institutional development and policymaking.

This article will not cover the whole range of issues, from building a conceptual framework to evolving policy guidelines, in depth. It focuses on documenting the field level experience of one organization, PRADAN, which has been implicitly following the sub-sectoral approach, and drawing lessons from it. PRADAN is an Indian enterprise development organization (EDO) primarily involved in rural development, with projects spread over seven different states in India. As each of its projects is unique in terms of the context, region and sector, an analysis across projects would throw up some possible generalizations having implications for enterprise promotion strategy, institutional development and policy.

The logic of a sub-sectoral approach

Traditionally, economic sectors such as agriculture, forestry and manufacturing industry, are regarded as quite large. A sub-sector is a smaller slice of the economy: technically, a row or a column in a detailed input-output matrix of an economy. The definition of a sub-sector is flexible in terms of the level of detail: for example, food-processing may be a sub-sector in one context, whereas it may be too general for another, requiring further breaking down into sub-sectors such as fruit preservation, or even, pineapple canning.

A sub-sectoral approach to MSE development may, therefore, be defined as a co-ordinated strategy to work at multiple levels – policies, programmes, projects and institutions – related to a specific sub-sector. Normally, this kind of strategy is used for promoting growth in a sub-sector. For our purposes, however, the relevance of the strategy is in using existing growth in the sub-sector to benefit those groups of the population who, under existing socio-economic conditions, would have been excluded from the sub-sector's growth process. Under circumstances where the sub-sector in question is itself underdeveloped, it may be necessary to develop it simultaneously. The primary goal of the approach, however, is to ensure that the poor also share proportionately in the rising size of the cake. Hence the key is utilization of an ongoing growth process rather than promotion of the sub-sector itself.

The rationale for the adoption of a sub-sectoral approach for rural MSE development is based on four factors: the ground situation in the rural areas of several developing nations; the experience of other approaches to rural development; the trends in certain sub-sectors in modernizing market economies and the practical question of the EDOs' institutional capabilities. Each of these is briefly explained below.

The context. Most developing countries today are characterized by widespread poverty and unemployment. The poor are less skilled and quite powerless to enter the relatively small modern sector. They also have limited and often dwindling access to productive natural resources such as land, water and livestock on which agricultural livelihoods can be created. The development of the modern sector taking place in many developing countries also seems to be creating enclaves and bypassing the poor. Under such a situation, creating what has been termed non-farm rural employment has become a key goal. Such a goal, however, is only achievable through a dispersed, small-scale, labour-intensive, low-capital and easily assimilated industrial growth pattern.

Other approaches. Traditional approaches to rural enterprise development, while keeping the above scenario in mind have adopted different strategies for tackling the problem. From the experience of various EDOs we have the following approaches: the *welfare approach* of providing essentials, such as a production shed or equipment, free or at subsidized rates; the *service delivery approach* of providing key inputs such as raw materials supply, credit, or marketing; the *educational approach* of providing skills and entrepreneurial ability training; and the *organizing approach* of taking up issues jointly for change in policy or laws.

Even though these approaches differ, two common factors stand out. First, they cut across sub-sectors or occupational groups. Second, they usually concentrate on a specific location. This has had both advantages and disadvantages. While allowing for a wider local reach, many of these experiments have failed to spread horizontally across a particular region. Even within the location they have arrived at an impasse where larger doses of subsidies have been required to prop up the employment generated. Looking back, EDOs providing only one kind of input at one extreme, and at the other, EDOs providing a dispersed set of subsidized services in a specific location, have both failed to understand and capitalize on the growth potential in selected sub-sectors of economic activity.

Growth in sub-sectors. The third factor which characterizes the enterprise development scenario is remarkable growth in certain sub-sectors, even as the overall economy may be growing sluggishly. Over the last two decades many developing countries have experienced rapid industrial growth in a wide variety of sub-sectors, such as food-processing, garment manufacture, leather manufacturing and electronic consumer durables. Further, even though this growth has been concentrated in selected urban areas and has generally used capital-intensive technology, economic logic and comparative advantage is not always in favour of such a growth pattern.

Simultaneously, there is an expanding consumer base consisting of the urban middle class who have been the beneficiaries of this growth process. Looking at this lop-sided growth positively, we see that it has opened up a large domestic market and possible production bases for a variety of final and intermediate products, many of which are agriculture and rural based. In fact, in many sub-sectors, the demand far outstrips supply, and given appropriate incentives, training and the removal of institutional bottlenecks, the poor can become key producers of these goods and services.

Institutional capabilities. Finally, given the magnitude of the problem, the past experience of well-meaning EDOs and the present opportunities, the question of the relevance of an approach needs to be tested against institutional capabilities. It is obvious that equitable development will not occur automatically, so institutions have to promote it. But what strategy will allow individual EDOs to achieve significant impact? Given the macro-economic growth pattern of sub-sectoral development, it may be worthwhile to align oneself to it but with a strong equity agenda, rather than choose an approach contradictory to macro trends and thereby become marginalized. Further, managing multi-sectoral services that are contradictory to macro trends requires a level of clarity, integration, and effectiveness beyond the capacity of most EDOs.

Keeping in mind the two sets of factors – mass unemployment and the limited results of other approaches to rural enterprise development on the one hand, and growth in selected sub-sectors and the need for building institutional capabilities on the other – we have a strategic pairing that seems to point to the sub-sectoral approach as a valuable and timely strategic choice for EDOs interested in equitable growth.

This rationale, however, in no way reduces the complexity or difficulty in pursuing this approach. It only points to an appropriate strategic choice that can have significant impact on poverty alleviation and generate synergy for institutional learning and development.

Conceptual framework

To study the sub-sectoral approach to rural enterprise development, it is necessary to delineate certain key variables which influence the pattern of development adopted within the sub-sectoral approach. The variables can be divided into two broad sets – the situational variables which determine the context within which such an approach is adopted and the policy variables which in some way lay down the basic goals adopted by the implementing institution. These two sets will determine the strategic choices that need to be made for effective performance and growth in the sub-sector.

The critical policy variable is the choice of the target group in terms of income. We will take as given that the policy goal is raising the income level of the poorest sections of society, i.e. those who are below the poverty line. This is a flexible definition depending on the nature of society, but in general, it concerns the lowest 20 to 30 per cent of the people in any society.

The second policy variable is the extent of control by the target group over the enterprises: it can vary from them being just wage-earners in EDO-run enterprises to being full owners and managing all operations themselves. Again, we assume the desired goal will be to build up the self-managing capability of the poor who participate in any programme of sub-sectoral development. Although this goal may be relegated to the background in the initial stages for strategic reasons, it implies that just ownership without management control in the long run has limited value.

The third related policy variable is the level of sustainability of the enterprise. In their anxiety to create livelihoods for the poor, many EDOs end up subsidizing operating costs. This may be a necessary phase in the initial stages in some cases, but long-term dependence on subsidies is not sustainable. Similarly, sustainability could be threatened if the resource base for the enterprise is non-renewable and likely to deplete very fast. The desired policy goal will be to promote permanently sustainable livelihoods within the chosen sub-sector.

Taking these policy variables as given, we have a variety of contextual or situational variables that will determine the boundaries within which a specific programme will function. These are:

community related:
- extent of poverty,
- present occupational structure,
- extent of available skills,
- extent of entrepreneurship,
- integration into the market economy;

political economy related:
- availability of infrastructure,
- presence of consumer markets,
- nature of finance markets,
- overall development of the region;

38 VALUE CHAINS IN DEVELOPMENT

sector related:
- type of activity chosen *vis-a-vis* community,
- range and level of technology available,
- scale of operations required for viability,
- extent of centralization required for viability,
- control of key input resources,
- nature of markets for inputs and outputs,
- maturity of the sector,
- growth rate of the sector;

legal and policy framework:
- extent of policy support available,
- nature of ownership structures.

Many of these variables have been delineated and discussed in Mahajan and Dichter (1990). Each field situation and sub-sector chosen will have a specific configuration of the variables listed above which will determine the strategic choices in each chosen programme.

PRADAN's experience

PRADAN is an Indian EDO having several field-based projects in different regions of the country where the explicit goal is the creation of sustainable livelihoods for the poor. Four of its projects, located in different states of the country, have implicitly adopted the sub-sectoral approach to promoting rural livelihoods. These projects have been under implementation for between three and five years. Two of these projects are briefly described below, keeping in mind the conceptual framework developed in the previous section.

Tasar sericulture with tribals in Godda, Bihar

Tasar is a form of 'wild' silk, in which the insect feeds on the leaves of the *Terminalia* species of trees to spin a cocoon, the filament of which is reeled into silk yarn. Traditionally, tasar cocoons were gathered by tribal people living in India's forest heartland. Tribals constitute nearly 8 per cent of India's population, and until recently had a subsistence economy based on gathering various produce from natural forests and selling it to a network of traders who usually pay very little for the raw produce. With their tradition of a forest produce-gathering economy they are not practised in business entrepreneurship. They are skilled, but primarily in traditional activities related to a subsistence economy.

The regions where the tribal population is concentrated are generally underdeveloped, with little infrastructure, urbanization or industrialization, other than enclaves of forest- or mineral-based extractive industries. Local demand for modern consumer goods is limited. Even though the government has a wide variety of programmes directed at tribal development and an extensive network of banks, the tribals have limited access to them. Thus financial markets are restricted to petty traders doubling as moneylenders, who advance both consumption and production loans but at exorbitant rates of interest. Loans are usually tied up with forward buying up of harvested forest produce at low prices.

With most of the natural forests coming under the ownership and control of the state, the tribals do not have free access to the forests but do enjoy certain traditional rights such as limited collection of minor forest produce. The policy framework, while being favourable in theory is in reality not supportive. Land ownership is largely individual today, though tradition and kinship bonds have enabled the tribals to maintain collective ownership of part of the land in almost every village.

It is in this overall context that PRADAN decided to promote tasar as an activity that could generate livelihood for the tribals. The process of producing tasar silk fabric follows the following stages.

- Establishing plantations of the tasar host plant *Terminalia arjuna*. Natural groves of such plants already exist in the area.
- Rearing tasar silk worms on these host plants and harvesting them.
- Using part of the cocoon harvest for producing layings (eggs) for the next generation of tasar insects.
- Spinning the harvested cocoons into tasar silk yarn.
- Weaving the tasar yarn into silk fabric.

The activity chosen was a traditional one for the tribals, especially in the Santhal Parganas region of Bihar where the programme was initiated. Tribals were already skilled in many of the sub-processes required. Significant changes were, however, introduced in each sub-process from the traditional practice. While traditionally tasar cocoons were reared only in natural forests, the project introduced a more intensive way of doing this. It involved systematically planting Arjuna seedlings in private uncultivated lands. Similarly, while the tribals just saved a part of the previous year's harvest of cocoons as seed for the following year, the project established grainages, or facilities for the production of high-quality seed of the tasar insect. This increases the productivity significantly.

In the spinning stage, the project introduced improved *charkhas,* or devices with elementary forms of mechanization in spinning the yarn. These technologies had been developed by the Central Tasar Research and Training Institute (CFRTI), a government research institution. The technologies, however, had not earlier been tried in the field within a community setting. One of the major modifications of the project was to decentralize the production package developed by the CFRTI. Results show that with the given technology it was possible to do so without any decline in productivity.

As tasar was a traditional product, existing trade channels for cocoons were well established, even though exploitative. Further, while the sub-sector had not grown over the years, this was not because of a lack of demand but because of a shortfall in cocoon production. Hence all the cocoons produced by the project had a ready market. The reason for the failure of the sub-sector to increase the production of cocoons seemed to be related to the fact that the key actors, the tasar rearers, traders and the technology researchers belonged to very different strata and had little interaction. The rearers were poor, illiterate, tribals living in remote areas. The traders operated from cities such as Chaibasa or Bhagalpur and, as they could not own the natural groves for tasar rearing, had no incentive to invest in increasing production. They concentrated on squeezing as low a price from the tribals as possible. The researchers were institution-bound government employees, with little interest or incentive to extend the modern technology to traditional tasar rearers. Absence of entrepreneurial skills in the region, and a lack of host plants in the natural forest combined with restricted access to the forests for the tasar-rearing community.

Even though tasar was a known activity for the tribals, substantial investment had to be made in convincing them of taking up plantations as against rearing in the dwindling natural forest. In fact, the plantation activity had to be subsidized and many small innovations, such as intercropping with food crops, had to be tried for them to gain interest in maintaining the plantations' growth. This investment had to be made since the other option of growing tasar in natural forests seemed incredibly difficult in view of the forest access policy.

Since 1987, PRADAN has promoted tasar plantation by over 500 farmers in nearly 85 villages of Santhal Parganas. In addition, around 300 traditional rearers are provided with disease-free layings for rearing in the existing natural forests. To produce the layings, PRADAN established a central grainage and helped set up two village-level grainages run by the rearers. PRADAN also assists the rearers in marketing the cocoons. Finally, a group of 60 women have been trained to spin yarn from the tasar cocoons locally. Weaving the fabric has been tried on an experimental basis and will be taken up as a fully fledged activity in the coming year. At the policy level, PRADAN has lobbied for greater attention to the tasar sector, and established the precedent of raising funds for plantations from the national Wasteland Development Board. Once the economics of the plantation are firmly established, PRADAN hopes to convince the National Bank for Agriculture and Rural Development to lend to tasar planters.

Poultry-rearing in Kesla, Madhya Pradesh, and Kishangarh Bas, Rajasthan

Kesla is a tribal area in central India; poultry rearing was initiated here and in Kishangarh Bas block of Rajasthan, just 150 kms from Delhi, in 1988. Poultry rearing is a relatively new and growing industry in India. The stages involved in poultry rearing for meat purposes are as follows:
- the production of selected-breed day-old chicks (DOCs);
- feed production;

- the brooding of DOCs up to three weeks of age;
- the rearing of three-week old birds up to eight weeks;
- poultry dressing.

The structure of the industry that has emerged is centralized, capital-intensive poultry farms. The technology of producing DOCs requires a high degree of biological cleanliness and control over feeding and environmental parameters for the parent stock. As a result, hatcheries for DOC production are highly capital intensive. Feed plants are relatively easy to establish and manage, but these also require a minimum scale to be viable. Only brooding and rearing can be decentralized. After that, the birds may be either sold live, or, for greater value addition, after dressing. The dressing plant also requires a certain degree of sophistication and capital inputs. Thus the established model of poultry rearing seemed unfeasible in a remote tribal area with little infrastructure, such as Kesla, or for poor people in a relatively developed area, such as Kishangarh Bas. To overcome this, once again experimentation had to be done to descale the available production model and to go in for small brooding and rearing units, with DOCs and feed purchased from the outside, and the centralized marketing of live birds.

Even though PRADAN has been able to promote some 50 odd poultry producers in the two locations, the activity has yet to take root unlike the other sub-sectors undertaken. One of the main reasons has been that at the descaled level, the project has not been able to get the poultry rearers to control critical production parameters such as bird mortality, feed conversion ratio, weight gain and disease outbreak. In addition, though marketing has not been a problem, the margins are highly variable and the production base is too small to act as a significant player in the wholesale markets for the birds. To counter this, the project has tried to sell directly as many birds as possible, and has more recently diversified into producing chicken pickle. The results have at best been mixed and tend to show that poultry rearing is only viable at a certain minimum scale of operations. (See PRADAN, 1990).

In the poultry sub-sector, our approach has been the least sub-sectoral, in the sense that neither of the key inputs, DOCs and feed, have been established through local sources, nor have other linkages such as veterinary care, bird dressing or marketing, been adequately controlled. The production preformance, therefore, has not always been competitive. Again, at the policy level, with the exception of convincing local commercial banks and development agencies to include poultry rearing as a valid activity, we have not been able to make much headway.

Lessons from experience

The experience gained from implementing these projects where the sub-sectoral approach to poverty alleviation is being applied has enabled PRADAN to draw certain lessons about the approach as applied to different sub-sectors and contexts.

Design variables. There is a whole range of variables that need to be aligned complementarily for the sub-sectoral approach to be effective. Some of these variables are externally determined and will have to be taken as given constraints, at least in the medium run. These include the level of development of the specific region, the socio-economic status of the people there and the overall trends in the chosen sub-sector.

In most cases there will be one set of constraining variables that must be overcome before any development can take place in promoting sub-sectoral enterprises. In the case of tasar it was the need to provide subsidized plantations and provide quality layings to convince the farmers to shift from the traditional practice of rearing tasar in the wild; in the case of poultry, we suspect the critical variable is feed supply, as it accounts for over 70 per cent of the cost. Our inability to control this may partly be responsible for the poorer performance in poultry.

Occupationally traditional vs. new sub-sectors. There are two kinds of sub-sectors that can be chosen for development. One, in which earnings from traditional occupations are raised through various interventions, such as tasar. Two, where completely new activities are introduced, such as poultry production. The dynamics of promoting each is very different. The former has the advantage of people having the basic skills, hence once the activity is organized with a little training the business is run directly by the beneficiaries. The latter being a completely new activity, the business has to be run by the promotional agency for an intermediate time period. While in a traditional activity the role of the promotional agency can be limited to that of being a social entrepreneur in the latter it has to be combined with that of being a foster entrepreneur.

Growth and extent of the sub-sector. The maturity of the sub-sector determines how a project can be integrated into the existing industry. In tasar, because of the strong base of the sub-sector, little investment had to be made to develop the sub-sector. In the case of poultry, the sub-sector is in fact too well established in the centralized, capital-intensive mode, and unless the decentralized model can become cost-competitive, it may not be possible to piggy-back on the robust growth of this sub-sector.

Even in a growing sub-sector there is one key resource that needs to be controlled for the programme to be initiated at a viable level. In the case of tasar, it was the processing and supply of high-quality seed cocoons, in the case of poultry, DOCs and feed.

Scale. Given the dispersed nature of producer households in rural areas combined with a lack of infrastructure, the greater the extent of decentralization possible, through smaller scale but viable operations, the more the chances of spread through the adoption of simple individually owned units. We have attempted to do this by decentralizing those stages of production which are scale neutral. Thus, in tasar, rearing plantations have been decentralized, whereas grainages have been descaled. In poultry, brooding has been decentralized to the village level, whereas rearing is done at the household level. Our inability to compete with larger units has largely to do with our failure to scale up the number of poultry rearers in one location so that they can afford a feed plant, and later a hatchery.

Technology. There is often a contradiction between centralized models of technology available and the simplicity of individual ownership. There is a dearth of available technologies that allow for intermediate scale. A certain amount of work needs to be done with respect to breaking down the production process in such a way that at least parts of it can be descaled and decentralized, to the village or household level if possible. This allows for greater flexibility in the choice of social models of ownership.

An EDO rarely has the capability to do technology intermediation by itself. In poultry production, which was the first sub-sector PRADAN began work in, very little input was taken from any outside agency to descale the technology or adapt it to the constraints of the village situation. Nor was any poultry expert hired in the team at the start of the project, though we did have veterinarians. The result is that we are still unsure of a production model, nor have we been able to match the organized sector's performance in crucial parameters such as feed conversion ratio and bird mortality. In tasar, we began by taking a close look at the technologies developed by the CTRTI and also the team leader recruited was a qualified tasar expert.

Policy. An appraisal of the policy framework pertaining to the sub-sector and working to bring about desired changes in it is very much a part of the sub-sectoral approach. For example, in tasar, the appraisal indicated that changing policy related to access to existing tasar groves in state-controlled forests would be very difficult, and this led us to promote private, tribal-owned plantations. In the case of poultry, the present policy framework, by default, is favourable to large, capital-intensive units, for a livelihood which is eminently suited for decentralized production by the poor. We have only recently understood this and are yet to work at the policy level.

Conclusions

It becomes obvious that there is a series of strategic choices that need to be made, having adopted the sub-sectoral approach. The first strategic choice the EDO has to make is the choice of the community, the region and the sub-sector. The second strategic choice it has to make is determining which key input bottleneck needs to be removed before proceeding further. The third strategic choice it has to make is within the sub-sector: how much should be internalized within a single institution.

Working with an extremely poor, marginalized community in a remote region with a hostile policy environment, in a non-traditional sub-sector is possibly the most difficult scenario. In such a situation the EDO has to have a wide variety of capabilities ranging from community organization, establishing infrastructure, intermediating technology, developing new markets, to influencing policy. All these functions have to be managed by the

EDO simultaneously during the course of the programme. In other situations, some of these inputs may be readily available and it may be possible to focus on the other inputs required. In both scenarios, however, there will be one key input whose supply needs to be assured before the other inputs have any relevance at all.

This brings us to the question of the absence or presence of relevant EDOs required to pursue this approach to development and their effectiveness. It is obvious that for a single institution to have all the capabilities is a difficult situation. This points to a network of inter-related institutions. In many developing countries, EDOs are either absent, thinly spread, ineffective, or directed towards large-industry development. Under such circumstances a single institution has to build up all the capabilities required to promote the sub-sectoral agenda. Under such a situation it is necessary for a single institution to limit the choice of sub-sectors that it will work in to just a very few. It is only by doing this that the institution can gain from its experience over time and cumulatively build up its capabilities.

References

Mahajan, Vijay and Thomas W. Dichter, (1990) 'A contingency approach to small business and microenterprise development', *Small Enterprise Development* Vol. 1, No. 1.

PRADAN, (1990), *The potential of poultry rearing as a livelihood for the rural poor*, New Delhi.

Sen, Biswajit, (1989), *Rural industries development: dilemmas in implementation.* PRADAN Occasional Paper, New Delhi.

About the authors

Biswajit Sen was formerly the Programme Director of PRADAN and is now a rural Development Specialist at the World Bank in Delhi before launching BASIX, an institution of which he is currently the Chairman. Vijay Mahajan was Founder and formerly the Executive Director of PRADAN.

CHAPTER 6
Business associations in countries in transition to market economies

Jacob Levitsky

This article was first published in September 1994.

Abstract

The establishment of strong, representative private-sector organizations is important for protecting the interests of the small business sector in any economy seeking to develop along market lines. With this in mind, the Organization for Economic Co-operation and Development (OECD) commissioned reports from Poland, Hungary, the Czech Republic, Slovakia and the Russian Federation to review the state of business associations in these countries. This article, based on these OECD reports (produced in 1993), evaluates the development of such organizations, examining issues of advocacy and political influence, voluntary or compulsory membership, the provision of services and financial independence. Comparisons are also made with the experience of business associations in other free market economies.

There has been virtually an explosive proliferation of business associations of different types in the former communist countries of eastern and central Europe since 1989. This may be partly explained as a reaction to the many years of communist rule when the government claimed that it would deal with all matters appertaining to economic activities and would take all the needed initiatives in this field. Associations of businesses, in the limited situations where private business was allowed in those days at all, were prohibited other than the few government-controlled organizations in which membership was obligatory.

Not surprisingly, when it became possible to form associations, a large number was set up quickly. Business associations may be defined as organizations set up as 'self-help' bodies by groups of businesses and individuals to further the interests of, and respond to the needs of, member enterprises and of the private sector as a whole. Generally these consist of federations, chambers of commerce and industry, as well as sectoral and small business associations, but in the former communist countries the range of associations that have developed has been wider. They also include foundations; chambers of economy; craft and traders' chambers; associations of entrepreneurs and craftsmen; local business clubs; religious groups; and economic societies (as in Poland), just to mention a few.

It is difficult to quantify and categorize the very large number of business associations of the types referred to that have developed in the former communist countries as they seek to make the transition to a market economy. One estimate puts the figure at 5000 associations in Poland (many of them with restricted local and sectoral membership) and 3000 in Hungary.

Apart from the sudden newly found freedom to form associations which provided an impetus to the creation of this very large number of new business organizations, another factor stimulating this grouping together in associations was a belief - presumably a legacy of the past - that political influence-peddling was virtually a precondition for business success.

Small business associations in Poland

Poland is perhaps the most interesting example. The first type of association to be established was the Economic Society set up in 1984 (still in the communist period) in Krakow, by a group of intellectuals, professionals and academics. This was proclaimed as having the goal of fostering private economic initiatives and generally of working to counter government efforts to impede the growth of the private sector. Within a few years, as the communist government adopted a more tolerant and liberal attitude to private enterprise, 15-20 such economic societies were quickly set up in the major cities of Poland, but although more businessmen joined the societies, it remained primarily a forum for economists, journalists and politicians engaged in 'opposition' activities to the economic policies of the then government. Most meetings were devoted to an exchange of information on new regulations, on business problems and on laws that were being introduced on taxation and labour controls. A great part of the activities of these societies was based on developing foreign contacts, and inviting speakers from other countries aimed at identifying sources for financial support for possible joint ventures, as well as gaining information on how the private sector operated in other countries.

The economic societies were very popular associations in the main cities of Poland in the late 1980s, and after 1989 they became legally registered associations. After the change of government, however, many of the leading figures became ministers, senior officials, Members of Parliament and generally active in political life, so that interest in the economic societies declined, since these were no longer the only forums for the expression of free market ideas.

By 1993 there were 17 regional economic societies with about 4000 members. Several of them are relatively inactive, and in general they play a less effective role in providing active support for private business than they did in the earlier period.

The story of the 'economic societies' – a Polish phenomenon – is illustrative of the general trends and character of business association growth in the former communist countries.

Although the large number of sectoral, regional and local associations still continue to struggle on with meagre resources and limited influence, in most of these countries the major membership private-sector organizations that have emerged are the chambers of commerce and industry or of economy, and the various associations of entrepreneurs. The latter have developed as the most important organizations in the Czech Republic, Slovakia and Hungary. The union of entrepreneurs has also become the largest and most influential industrial organization in Russia, although it includes both representatives of state-owned and private enterprises and of joint venture firms with partial foreign ownership.

The Czech Entrepreneurs Association (CEA) founded in December 1989 claimed by mid-1993 to have 220,000 members. The CEA has both individuals as members and also collective groups of craftsmen. CEA is really an 'umbrella' organization comprising various regional entrepreneurial associations in Moravia, Silesic, Prague, and so on, and also different professional, sectoral and craft organizations.

Like its counterparts in Slovakia, Hungary and Russia, the CEA has concentrated until now on presenting its proposals for changes in laws and in the regulatory structure. It has also transmitted the views of its members on all types of legislation with relation to chambers, privatization, taxes, social security, the restitution of property and procedures for initiating different types of private-sector activities. In Slovakia, the entrepreneurs association with 15,000 members attempts to do the same.

All these associations of entrepreneurs have also put great emphasis on foreign links and have looked to external donors both to provide funding and to offer guidance and assistance in carrying out programmes and activities. The European Community's Phare programme, CIPE (Centre for International Private Enterprise) of the US and the German Craft Chambers *(Handwerkkammer)* have all provided help to these agencies. IPOSZ (the Hungarian chamber of artisans), which claims around 130,000 members in 296 branches, and was founded in 1989, has received German aid to try to introduce the type of training programmes run by the crafts chambers in Germany with responsibility for the certification of craftsmen. Although started in 1990, this aid programme has been confined to arranging training for Hungarian craftsmen in Germany. The Hungarian Government has failed to provide finance for IPOSZ's training activities and to approve fully its status as responsible for such artisan training and certification. IPOSZ relies mainly on membership fees, as do similar organizations in the other countries, apart from some limited external donor support. As in the case of most of the business associations in the former communist countries, IPOSZ is actively looking for additional funds overseas.

Lobbying and politicization

All these associations (IPOSZ, CEA, and the Slovakian Entrepreneur Association) have become heavily politicized. Viewed objectively, the lobbying efforts have borne some fruit in that legislation and regulations have been adapted somewhat to meet the needs and concerns of private entrepreneurs, but the associations (and presumably their members) seemed to have had exaggerated expectations as regards the outcome of their lobbying efforts, and are accordingly disappointed in that the government has not fully taken account of the views of the associations and their members.

As has happened in other countries, the associations may have been manipulated by people with political ambitions, and this could prove counter-productive in the long run as regards the effectiveness of the 'lobbying' effort. A leading figure and former president of VOSZ, the important Association of Entrepreneurs in Hungary, has now formed a political party and it is reported that VOSZ and the new party will work closely together. This development reflects, one assumes, the frustration among VOSZ management and membership at the lack of consultation between those making laws and the interested groups, such as private entrepreneurs. While increased consultation is without doubt a legitimate and important central objective of business associations, these organizations will need to recognize the responsibility of governments for all sectors of the economy and of society. Taxation is a prime example. Business organizations have every right, and even a duty, to their members, to prevail on governments to introduce a reasonable taxation regime to permit the proper financing of businesses, but full account must be taken of the problem of budget deficits and chronic tax evasion encountered by governments.

There is also a danger in any over-politicization of advocacy efforts. Business organizations that convert themselves into political organizations or have too close a relationship with any specific political parties can create a situation where some major political movements become estranged or even develop opposition to this overly political manifestation of business interests. In most democratic societies, small business enjoys a wide range of support on both the left and right of the political spectrum. It is in the interest of small business in the private sector to seek co-operation with, and support from, different political movements that may aspire to power.

Business associations aimed at small enterprises

Small companies have interests and concerns that often differ from those of large businesses. In European countries, as in North America, Japan and elsewhere, there is a strong movement within the small business community to create small firm representative bodies which are distinct from the larger business associations, and this situation has already developed in eastern and central Europe.

In most countries there are benefits both in developing organizations for large and small enterprises together, and on the other hand for maintaining separate small enterprise organizations. Associations that cater for both large- and small-scale members, have more resources and have more suitable candidates for leadership positions. Such organizations can usually attain a higher profile and status in the community and more power in relation to the government. Furthermore, common membership of large and small-scale firms in a single organization can often lead to beneficial linkages and even result in useful advice and assistance from larger to smaller businesses. Unfortunately, experience also shows that in a number of cases such organizations are taken over by the larger and more powerful members and the smaller firm members begin to feel that the organization does not respond to their particular problems nor cater to their needs. This situation is particularly acute where many large enterprises are still in the public sector. This understandably creates a rationale for setting up separate small business associations.

Business chambers of commerce and industry

The most active representative bodies of private firms are local chambers of commerce usually affiliated with a central federation of chambers, headquartered in the main commercial city of the country. These chambers are set up with the purpose of promoting and protecting the interests of commerce and industry and usually they perceive their main function to represent the interests of the business community to the governing authority at the local, regional and national levels.

Chambers have developed throughout the former communist countries. In Poland, the National Chamber of Commerce and Industry established by a special Act of 1990 has local chambers throughout the country affiliated to it. The law allows any group of 50 companies – state-owned or private – to establish a chamber, which has led to small unrepresentative chambers being set up in different cities, sometimes two or three in the same town. Although the law does not oblige businesses to be members of a chamber, the National Federation of Chambers has a close relationship with the government.

In the Czech Republic, the Czech Chamber of Commerce and Industry (COPK) has become part of the newly created Chamber of Economy which also seems to have a close relationship with the government. It is unclear as yet whether the Chamber of Economy will adequately represent the interests of all sectors of private business.

Some of the chambers in these countries are not business associations of the private sector only. State-owned and publicly owned companies are also members, and as such the relationship of the chambers with the government and the private sector can at times be confusing. The presence of representatives of the large and powerful public-sector enterprises, with their very different interests, in most such chambers in the former communist countries, has raised serious questions as to whether these bodies can really be expected to respond to the concerns of the smaller private businesses. The case is strong at this stage for independent representative organizations of private small enterprises.

Voluntary and obligatory membership

Chambers of commerce and business associations operate differently in the various countries. In European countries such as France, Germany, the Netherlands and Italy membership of a chamber is obligatory. These bodies have 'public law status' and are financed by a levy or tax on all businesses. In these countries all new businesses are required by law to register and become paying members of their local chamber and thus coverage of the business sector is complete. In the English-speaking world of USA, UK, Canada and Australia, chambers have developed as voluntary associations, and there has been strong opposition against imposing obligatory membership.

In an effort to enhance the status and power of representative business organizations, there has been, and still is, considerable pressure in the countries undergoing transition to market economies for legislation to be introduced to require all businesses to be members or to register with specific representative bodies. A law was introduced and actually approved in the Czech Republic in 1992 imposing obligatory membership in the chamber of economy, in order to prevent the chambers becoming too powerful. A similar law is in preparation in Hungary to require all businesses to register with a business chamber. The belief in most of these countries that obligatory membership in specific representative organizations could raise their political status and help solve the financing problem is possibly influenced by the experience of the years of a strong government role.

There are strong arguments for and against obligatory membership. Voluntary membership creates a problem in building up a viable size of membership, sufficient to finance an organization able to provide an adequate representation of the sector and useful services for its members. Furthermore, the 'public law status' of representative private sector organizations such as the chambers in European countries obliges governments to consult with representatives of the private sector before enacting legislation and regulations. This status can ensure the designation of a single comprehensive strong organization as representing the sector, whereas voluntary membership can lead to fragmentation into a number of small ineffective bodies.

On the other hand, there have been indications that in some European countries where there is a representative organization to which businesses are legally obliged to become members, there is a tendency to look upon the administration of such organizations as part of the public bureaucracy and not as of an independent self-governing institution truly representing the private sector. While obligatory membership can ensure a more adequate representation of the sector and the capacity to deliver effective services, there can also develop an 'alienation' of the leadership from the members who may feel resentment that they are forced to belong to an organization from which they may feel they are deriving little benefit. This may be a particularly sensitive issue in countries that have lived through long periods of centralized government and authoritarian rule.

In general, it might be advisable in most developing countries, or those in transition to a market economy, to postpone consideration of obligatory membership in a representative body such as a chamber, until a suitable relationship has been built up between private sector business organizations, and the government, and where the former have built up a substantial membership, and have attained recognition and authority both from the membership and from outside. This should result from a proven ability to represent the sector and to provide quality services to members.

In the stages of build-up of the private sector as in the former communist countries, probably the most effective approach is for the government:
- To recognize and accept the role and status of the private sector organizations as partners in economic development, and as the spokesmen of private enterprises to be consulted on all major issues and policies affecting businesses.
- To transfer some statutory obligations, such as the authentication of the origin of products when needed. Private sector organizations may also play a limited role in the processing of taxation assessments of small enterprises and in the registration of new small firms.
- To channel through the private sector organizations various promotional and procedural activities, such as the screening of suitable government suppliers; preparing and certifying lists of qualified subcontractors; the organization of groups for industrial estates, clusters and incubators; the arrangement of bulk purchasing of materials and equipment and of collective marketing; credit guarantee schemes; export promotion, and so on.

In Japan, chambers have a half-way status between the voluntary character in the English-speaking countries and the 'public law status' of mainland Europe. Membership is not a legal obligation, but because of strong social pressures from the societies of commerce as they are called, about 95 per cent of all small firms are members. This high membership is mainly due to the great deal of assistance given by government through these bodies to smaller businesses, such as loan guarantees, special financing, preference in government procurement and the promotion of sub-contracting arrangements and industrial estates. So many projects are implemented through these organizations as to make it highly advantageous for small businesses to become members.

Advocacy ('lobbying')

The term 'advocacy' used in the USA, which is recognized as the prime role of private sector representative membership organizations, refers to the lobbying activities on behalf of small business members to improve the economic and legal environment in which they have to operate. This means the transmission of the concerns, opinions and needs of members to the government through consultations on policy, the enactment of legislation and the design and implementation of the regulatory framework.

As already stated, in the countries of eastern and central Europe, 'lobbying' activities are considered the major 'raison d'etre' for all business associations. As the private sector is still developing in these countries, such activities of necessity have a wider significance. For example, business organizations feel they should have an important say in how the economy is privatized and how business activities are transferred from the public to the private sector. The privatization process has become a central focal point of the 'lobbying' activities of the CEA in the Czech Republic and of the similar organizations in Slovakia, Hungary and Poland. CEA has played a significant role in the so-called small privatization programmes, whereby smaller retail outlets, catering establishments and service organizations were 'auctioned' off to the private sector, both in the planning and implementation of the process. The CEA has also involved itself in the privatization of larger state-owned enterprise to ensure that more time was given for the consideration of various alternative proposals on how the privatization of these firms might take place.

Both the private sector and the government must understand that consultation cannot be left to *ad hoc* arrangements. In the USA there is an Office of Advocacy in the Small Business Administration, a federal government agency set up in 1953 to help small firms. Although enjoying no public law status, the US chamber of commerce and industries manages to exert substantial influence on policy makers through its well-organized and wide spread lobbying efforts. The business communities of eastern and central Europe also have to accept that the basis of successful 'advocacy' in representing the interests of the small business sector requires a responsible approach to the situation of society and the economy as a whole.

The fledgeling associations in the countries in transition have already registered some achievements. The entrepreneurs' association in Slovakia carried out a successful campaign to modify the new legislation with regard to social insurance to meet the concerns of private businesses; IPOSZ in Hungary has had some success in lowering the tax burden on enterprises; the CEA in the Czech Republic also managed to change the onerous tax and social security law of 1993 to alleviate the burden on private firms, as well as influencing the process of privatization; Polish business associations have also achieved concessions from the government in the field of taxation. These may be modest accomplishments, but they indicate that policies can be modified through a concerted 'lobbying' effort. The 'lobbying' efforts in these countries would probably be more effective if the representation of the private sector was not so fragmented and if the private business community could speak with a stronger more unified voice.

The government and the private sector

The relationship between the government and the private sector can be decisive both in the creation of a conducive environment for the operation of small business and the provision of the services and support needed. This relationship between the private sector and the government need not be based on ideological or political considerations on either side, nor become excessively confrontational.

An important factor influencing the organization of small enterprise support will be the geography of the country. A vast country such as the Russian Federation will necessarily require a different organizational structure for small business support than a small country such as Slovakia. In all cases, however, it is desirable to have the maximum decentralization, as services delivered locally by those integrated into the local scene generally evoke the most positive response from local businesses. Where countries are divided into regions, provinces, states or localities this will inevitably affect the organizational breakdown and location of support arrangements.

Another factor must be the degree of development and size of the small industry sector and the strength of the private sector in general. Not surprisingly, in the countries building up a free market after years of centralized state control, the private sector is still relatively weak and the business associations accordingly will reflect this weakness for a prolonged period of transition. The types and numbers of different enterprises and their distribution into sectors and sizes will influence the type of associations and institutions to be created.

The relationship between the government and the private sector will be decisive in determining the role that each of these will play in providing the services and support needed by the small business sector. In the countries changing to market economies this relationship may be particularly sensitive. Undoubtedly some in these governments cling to ideas of the former regime and are hesitant to hand over too much of the economy to the private sector too quickly. On the part of the private sector there may be exaggeration regarding how much help they can expect to receive from the government and how much freedom from taxation and regulatory control they can reasonably demand. More dialogue, consultation and negotiation between governments and private sector representatives are needed to reach a suitable understanding and relationship.

Services provided by the government

The government provides the legal and fiscal framework in which small enterprises operate, and which is a basic factor in determining the economic and financial well-being of small enterprises. Basic education and skills training are also best left to governments, so as to establish and operate an educational and vocational training network to guarantee an adequately trained and skilled labour force to meet the need of the various sectors of the economy.

Beyond the need to ensure adequate training in technical and management skills, governments, usually through their public agencies, disseminate information on programmes and schemes for regional development, on efforts and schemes to promote more exports and incentives and assistance for enterprise development. Some more enlightened governments may help to forge links between business enterprises and the research and technological development being undertaken in institutions of higher learning and publicly financed research centres.

Services provided by organizations

While advocacy may be the prime role of private sector organizations, these bodies can also provide some direct help to members. They may keep them informed on all legal and taxation matters relevant to their operations and on the availability of assistance being offered from all sources. They may also provide information on new technologies and data that could be of help in the manufacture and marketing of products and services. Private sector organizations would also be expected by members to help in the provision of training opportunities in the *upgrading* of technical skills and management techniques, basic training schemes which more appropriately would be left to governments. Limited direct counselling and consultancy for small firms could also be within the programmes of private sector organizations.

The degree to which organizations are able to offer such services effectively at an acceptable quality *level* would differ according to the circumstances and resources available. In the eastern and central European countries, it could not be expected that private sector organizations would be able to offer all such forms of direct help to its members in the early stages of their development. But organizations and associations could also help to forge sub-contracting links between small enterprise members and public procurement and larger firms, or links with overseas partners for joint ventures or for obtaining technological or marketing help.

The provision of finance

Some business associations in former communist countries have become more directly involved in business ventures. Frustrated by the lack of access to finance for private smaller businesses and the reluctance of banks to lend to these enterprises, some associations have participated in setting up financial institutions or have close links with such organizations. Some associations have even set up subsidiary businesses.

The CEA in the Czech Republic is closely associated with a new private bank which it hopes will be more amenable to lending to private small businesses. IPOSZ in Hungary, following the German example, is working to develop a loan guarantee scheme to overcome a lack of collateral which is considered to be a major constraint for private members obtaining loans from banks. The Russian Union of Entrepreneurs (RUIE) has among its objectives the development of joint business ventures, leasing companies and credit guarantees. It is not clear how realistic such plans are at the moment, although the RUIE does reputedly have some limited involvement in the implementation of the large loan for small businesses in Russia provided by the European Bank for Reconstruction and Development.

Well-organized private sector organizations have in some countries become involved in the provision of direct financial and business support, such as helping create new banks, business incubators, industrial estates, credit guarantee schemes, leasing companies, bulk purchasing and marketing centres, the exhibition of products as well as investment funds and insurance schemes. However, business associations still building up membership with limited resources and less-experienced staff need to be cautious in embarking on such ventures too quickly.

In the countries under consideration the availability of suitable premises to carry on small businesses is a major constraint. In Poland, some business organizations have focused on this problem in particular. The chamber of traders and entrepreneurs has sought to negotiate agreements with the city council of Warsaw to ensure that members are given information on the availability of space for rental and preference on the renting of former state premises. Various business organizations in the Czech Republic and Poland have helped promote and implement business incubators which can provide both space and support services for small businesses. In the course of time, business associations in these countries will become more involved in assisting enterprises to resolve their difficulties in obtaining suitable physical facilities.

Although finance is usually the help most sought-after by small enterprise, it is difficult for private sector organizations to provide such assistance directly, although they may be able in some circumstances to arrange financial help through co-operation with financial institutions or through assisting in the provision of guarantees. More generally, such organizations offer training and technical and management advice.

Service provision – the example of NEA

An interesting and innovative example of the provision of services by a private sector organization in Eastern Europe is the case of the Nogradi Enterprise Association in Hungary (NEA). The NEA, founded in 1990 as a partnership between a small group of businesses and the local government, has managed to obtain funding from the national government for carrying out training courses. From the start NEA has charged for services, such as preparing applications for government grants. NEA is probably the most active of Hungarian associations in offering direct support services. Its small staff includes a lawyer, accountant and financial specialists, and so is in a position to provide direct business consultancy and training, even though in a limited capacity.

From its inception NEA has preferred to offer support services rather than concentrate, as the other Hungarian associations do, on advocacy. Located in a poor region of the country – Nogradi region – NEA has utilized its limited resources, mobilized from the localities and the central government fund for less developed areas of the country, to promote small businesses in the district, rather than relying mainly on foreign assistance. Unfortunately NEA has been hampered by the restriction imposed on non-profit organizations in Hungary of being limited to obtaining only 10 per cent of its revenue from charges for services. This unusual restriction runs counter to the laudable objective of an organization, such as NEA, of trying to expand its activities through earnings from payment by users of its services. This limitation on earnings may help in the short term to protect business consultants from competition, but will do little to make services more available to small businesses at costs they can afford.

Although NEA has preferred to focus on technical assistance and training it has operated a small micro-credit programme giving new 'start-up' business loans from 50,000 to 500,000 florints (US$600 to $6000). NEA is now considering extending its services beyond the Nogradi region.

The financing of operations

Finance is always one of the main problems of private sector organizations and it affects their ability to engage in effective 'advocacy' and to provide quality support services. Even under conditions of obligatory membership and levies, private sector organizations are rarely able to cover more than 50 per cent of their expenses and maintain an adequate staff solely from membership fees. In conditions of voluntary membership, fees have to be set at a reasonable level so as not to deter prospective members, and this can only further reduce the income available for operating expenses.

Several business associations in former communist countries rely mainly on membership fees to finance their activities. In the difficult economic conditions of these countries this will for some time to come be a limited source of funding. In some cases – Hungary in particular – some help is available from the government and from donations, but in these countries, with their past history, over-reliance on government support can be even more sensitive than in other situations. External donor support has been available to some of the associations in these countries, but usually in the provision of advisers, financing of training programmes or visits overseas but little towards operating expenses. Most business associations should be selective in receiving external donor funding, especially if this is linked to advice or assistance in replicating systems from other countries which may or may not be applicable to the situation prevailing in the countries of the recipient organizations.

Apart from membership fees, finance may be obtained from users of the organizations' services, such as participants in training courses, recipients of consultancy or of information, or from any other of a wide range of services from which income can be generated. This may include, for example, accounting help, office facilities (copying, faxing, computer services, translations, typing, document distribution, and so on), bulk purchasing of materials and the procurement of equipment. More enterprising organizations in some European countries have hired qualified staff and have offered insurance, investment promotion services, mutual funds, legal assistance, export promotion, industrial premises, publications and directories, product catalogues, the organization of exhibitions or fairs, and travel facilities. This assistance, if delivered efficiently and at reasonable cost, can generate significant income and would be much appreciated by members in countries where such services are not readily available. Training and consultancy cannot be expected to produce large revenues, but neither should they be provided entirely free. Although some income has been derived from this source by the associations in the countries under consideration, notably in the case of the Nogradi association, so far the services have been limited and the revenue derived not very substantial.

However, some countries – Hungary in particular – have imposed restrictions on the proportion of income a business organization, as a nonprofit organization, may earn from fees for services. The limited capacity of all such associations to provide training, consultancy or information will not seriously impede the development of a commercial consultancy business. On the contrary, the provision of some consultancy and training by non-profit business organizations will help both to raise interest and understanding of the value of such services and will also provide some healthy competition to ensure that that business consultants do not charge excessively for limited services. Business associations should be encouraged to charge for services to cover more of their expenses in this way: possibly up to 30 per cent or more.

Efforts should also be made to keep expenses at a reasonable level and to avoid extravagance in office accommodation, salaries, expense accounts, excessive travel by elected officials, and so on. Apart from posing financial problems they may contribute to the alienation of members, who may regard this as mis-use of their membership fees or of grants made available for their benefit.

Conclusions

Successful small business associations and representative bodies will always be organized so as to maintain a consistently democratic framework. This means that the leadership must be responsive at all times to the concerns and interests of member firms and submit itself regularly to election by the members. This also means providing services and support in a way and at a cost which answers to the needs of small enterprises, and in a manner to satisfy the reasonable expectations of the members as regards the role and behaviour and activities of the organizations and its elected leaders.

About the author

The late Jacob Levitsky was at the time of writing an enterprise development consultant, a founder of the Donor Committee for Enterprise Development and the Small Enterprise Advisor to the World Bank.

CHAPTER 7
Using franchises to promote small enterprise development

Michael Henriques and Robert E. Nelson

This article was first published in March 1997.

Abstract

Franchising has been an extremely popular means in the developed world, expanding the geographical coverage of successful businesses, often in the retail sector. This article identifies the factors that make franchising a potentially useful tool for small business promotion in developing countries, including the existence of large numbers of unemployed people with training but not necessarily entrepreneurial experience. It describes some indigenous franchises that have been a success, and suggests ways in which governments could promote franchising.

A new approach to indigenous small enterprise development based on franchise principles could radically improve survival rates among business starters and contribute to the cost-effective creation of large numbers of quality jobs. In the US, according to statistics from the Commerce Department, less than 5 per cent of franchises failed on an annual basis from 1971 to 1987 (International Franchise Association, no date).

Franchising may be defined in the following manner. Franchising is a way of doing business whereby the owner of a proven business system (the franchiser) grants the right by contract to an entrepreneur (the franchisee) to establish a similar business. In exchange for franchise fees and the obligation to adhere to strict quality standards, the franchisee acquires the right to use the franchiser's trademark and receives marketing support, detailed manuals on how to operate the business, start-up assistance, staff training, equipment, raw material procurement, and regular visits by a representative of the franchiser (see Figure 7.1).

The following statistics indicate the impact of franchising on economic development. In 1992, it was estimated that franchises in the US accounted for $803.20 billion in sales and that figure represented 40.9 per cent of all retail sales. In 1991, there were 542,496 franchises in the US and a new franchise opened every 8 minutes of each business day. In terms of employment creation, more than 10 million people are employed by franchise establishments, with

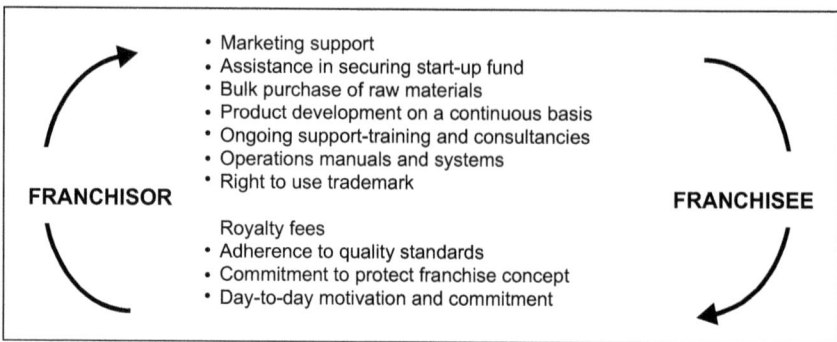

Figure 7.1 Flow of services and support

an average of 8 to 14 employees per establishment. In a 1991 study by Arthur Andersen and Company of 366 franchise companies in 60 industries in the US, it was reported that nearly 86 per cent of all franchise operations opened in the previous five years were still under the same ownership; and only 3 per cent of these businesses were no longer in business (International Franchise Association, no date).

In Western Europe the trend in small enterprise development focuses on franchising as one of its basic components. There is a trend for franchisors in the United States to expand their operations to other countries in Europe and to other developing countries on a highly selective basis (Frauen huber, 1993). In 1990, 374 franchising companies in the US were operating 35,046 franchise outlets overseas. A breakdown of the overseas franchise outlets includes: 2,854 in Australia, 2,097 in Asia, 8,975 in Japan, 584 in Mexico, 579 in the Caribbean and South America, 9,544 in Canada, 2,843 in the United Kingdom, and 4,975 in Europe (US Department of Commerce, 1990, p. 99). A survey found that an estimated 20 per cent of US franchisors operate internationally by means of company units, master licenses, individual franchises, or joint ventures (Steinberg, 1992, p. 5).

The franchise approach effectively combines many of the most successful features of traditional entrepreneurship development programmes, such as: an emphasis on small business expansion rather than start-ups, mutually beneficial large-small enterprise linkages, highly focused and sustained training and extension support to the entrepreneur, improved access to capital, and collective purchasing and marketing arrangements. At the same time, franchising can also be considered as an innovation which combines the advantages of a large business (economies of scale in purchasing, advertising and product development, experience and track record, and specialized in-house expertise) with the strengths of the small-scale entrepreneur (a high level of commitment and motivation, and knowledge of the local area). It is this unique blend of features which allows the franchise-based approach to reduce dramatically the risk involved in small business creation.

The essence of franchising

Essentially, franchising is a marketing system and method for distributing goods and services to consumers. Through franchising, a successful business can be replicated in other locations within a country as well as internationally. If the franchising concept is not used, each new business is created according to what the entrepreneur believes is best for that individual business. Many of the business decisions will be made on a trial-and-error basis. If 15 small businesses were initiated relating to appliance repair, for example, there would be 15 different types of business, even though the services they provide were similar. Although some of these businesses might be successful, it might be expected that 80 per cent of these independently owned businesses would fail within the first eight years of existence.

By using the franchising concept, a model business might be developed based on an existing successful appliance-repair business. The business procedures would be carefully examined and the operations of the business would be determined in a logical manner. Operating manuals would then be prepared to provide step-by-step instructions on starting and operating an appliance-repair business. In a vehicle-repair business, for example, techniques for repairing cars would not be needed since most car mechanics would already have the requisite skills. However, the managerial and operational aspects of the vehicle-repair business would need to be identified and prepared in a logical sequence.

Although there are numerous benefits to both the franchisor and the franchisee (Table 7.1), there are also disadvantages to the franchising concept which need to be identified (Table 7.2).

Table 7.1 Potential franchise benefits

Franchisor	*Franchisee*
• Rapid expansion of business.	• Use of a proven business system.
• Business growth facilitated through capital inputs from the franchisee.	• Business risks greatly reduced because franchise has proven track record.
• Financial and manpower resources provided by the franchisee.	• New product development and quick response to competition by franchisor.
• Few permanent staff required by franchisor.	• Can devote full attention to day-to-day operations.
• Broader and more rapid market coverage by the franchise.	• Provision for staff training and continuous support from franchisor staff.
• Bulk purchasing of inputs is greater because of financial inputs of franchisee.	• Requires less capital than an independent business.
• Involvement in day-to-day operations of business outlets are limited to monitoring.	• Benefits from franchisor advertising, brand name, and promotions.
• Capital risks are shifted to the franchisee.	• Bulk purchasing and negotiating power of franchisor.
	• Easier access to bank loans and start-up capital.

Table 7.2 Potential disadvantages of franchising

Franchisor	Franchisee
• Constant monitoring of quality required to maintain franchise reputation, conformity and integrity. • The franchise is a complex business system to manage. • Long-term relations with franchisees may be difficult to maintain. • Fees based on franchisee income may be misrepresented (understated).	• There is usually strict adherence to quality standards. • Initial financial inputs and continuing royalty fee may be substantial. • Previous business success record of franchiser may be difficult to assess. • Detailed contractual arrangement may restrict creativeness of franchisee. • Sale or transfer of the franchise may be highly restricted. • Dependency on franchisor and franchise name. • Franchisor policies may adversely affect franchisee operations. • Franchise may have a limited product line. • Franchisor may lack initiative and flexibility in reacting to local market changes. • Franchisee position weak relative to franchisor.

The franchising approach can overcome many of the negative barriers affecting the initiation of new businesses. Franchising can foster rapid growth and can be focused on business sectors which can provide the desired economic stimulus for development. For example, franchises can be particularly successful in providing the infrastructure needed in the tourism sector. Potential franchises in this sector include hotels, car rentals, tours, restaurants, and various leisure activities. In countries such as Tanzania, the franchise method might promote rapid growth and provide a wide range of tourism-related activities and services.

Tourism can attract the influx of foreign currency to offset the balance of payment deficits in many developing countries. Employees hired within a franchise may not need specific qualifications or skills since they will receive much of their training as part of the franchise package of services. The specialized training and experience gained by the employees of franchises will help to create a pool of skilled personnel, and once employees have gained business experience, they may initiate their own businesses based on the work skills developed while they were employed in the franchise.

In many developing countries, retrenched civil servants create a pool of potential entrepreneurs. They may have the management skills and startup capital, however, most do not fit the full entrepreneurial profile. One of the major concerns of small enterprise development programmes for retrenched civil servants is the fact that they may start independent businesses without having the necessary background or experience. This approach will often lead to failure. Under a franchise approach to small enterprise development, however, the chances of success for retrenched civil servants are much greater as there will be less reliance on the entrepreneurial aspects of the owner of a new business.

It is important to understand that when a franchise is being developed from an existing business, there will be two businesses in operation: (a) the business that is currently operating and (b) the business as it will operate as a franchise. It is also important to understand that a franchise needs to have a minimum number of franchisee operations in a fairly limited geographical area to be successful. The franchisor will need to support the franchisees to make their operations efficient and profitable. The idea of franchising allows a business to expand fairly quickly and allows the franchisor to expand its coverage using capital raised by the franchisee.

The decision to run a franchise requires a great deal of knowledge concerning legal and accounting aspects, management, and marketing information. Without the right information, the potential franchise will be greatly at risk.

Implementing franchise-based programmes can incorporate environmental issues as well as occupational safety and health concerns by building appropriate measures into the structure, organization and training system of the business which is being franchised.

Franchising principles might be applied to enterprises in the informal sector with the objective of upgrading them. The franchising system can be applied to areas such as village blacksmithing, push carts, and sheetmetal enterprises.

The government can play an important role in influencing standards for initiating franchises and through the establishment of franchise associations. This concept also fits in with the current privatization activities which are often an important part of the structural adjustment process in many developing countries.

Many developing countries experience capital flight because of a lack of credible investment opportunities within their home countries. A successful franchise requires local capital and can provide the credibility needed to encourage people to invest their capital locally. Franchising may also be a means of controlling the movement of profits out of a country if the franchisor is an international company.

Initiating a franchise-based assistance programme will have a multiplier effect. If such an assistance programme works with franchisors only, there will be a multiplier effect when these franchisors assist their franchisees. A franchise-based small enterprise assistance programme will be able to leverage available resources devoted to the promotion of the small enterprise sector.

Government strategies for promoting franchises

Governments wishing to introduce franchise-based approaches to small enterprise activities into their overall development plans have a number of potential strategies for doing so.

Overseas franchisors. They may rely mainly on attracting overseas franchisors. This process will happen more or less automatically, but may need monitoring to ensure that the interests of local franchisees are protected. The process might be accelerated by the government playing an active role in facilitating contacts between overseas franchisors and potential local franchisees. In January 1994, for example, the Malaysian Government organized an International Franchise Conference. The conference provided a forum for franchise experts and franchisors from a range of countries to interact with potential Malaysian entrepreneurs and investors who were made aware of opportunities in regional and area franchise investments and joint partnerships.

Indigenous franchises. They may decide to embark on a programme to foster indigenous franchise systems. This could involve various measures to raise awareness of basic franchise principles and, possibly, the establishment of local support structures capable of identifying successful local small businesses with the potential for franchising. The provision of training, consultancy and other services would be made available to potential entrepreneurs who embark on the process of expanding their small business through the creation of a franchise. Various types of institutional structures might be established to facilitate such an indigenous-based strategy.

A combination of the two approaches could also be adopted, by both actively attracting overseas franchise systems while providing support measures aimed at creating a competitive local franchise community.

If it is decided to rely primarily on attracting overseas franchise systems, this is likely to lead to a relatively elite group of franchises, since most international franchises require high levels of investment and their products are typically aimed at the high-income urban consumer. An indigenous-based strategy is likely to result in the creation of more affordable franchise opportunities, and products and services more in line with traditional tastes and income levels. An indigenous strategy is, however, likely to require considerably more support and nurturing by government during the initial periods.

If an indigenous-based strategy is adopted, it should be viewed as one element of the country's overall strategy for promoting small business to ensure that synergies and linkages with other programmes and local resources are carefully considered. For example, the Malaysian Government has recognized the potential of franchising and included franchising as one of the strategies to develop local entrepreneurs in the distributive trades under its National Development Policy (1991–2000). This includes the establishment of a 'one-stop' franchise agency under the Implementation Co-ordination Unit within the Office of the Prime Minister. In addition, a Franchise Development Division was established to provide a range of direct support to franchisors.

Indigenous franchises

Several indigenous franchises which have achieved success in developing countries highlight the fact that dependence on international franchises is not the only way to promote business development through franchising. In Thailand, Big Seven is a convenience store franchise which closely resembles the American convenience store 7–11. The first Big Seven store was opened in 1988. This was one year before 7–11 entered the Thai market. Currently, there are more than 22 Big Seven branches and 8 of them are owned by franchisees. The remaining stores are operated by the Cathay Department Store Group, one of Thailand's largest department store chains.

Another example of an indigenous franchise is the Jollibee Foods Corporation which began in 1978. Since that time, it has become the number one hamburger fast-food business in the Philippines. In 1989 it achieved the distinction of being the first fast-food chain in the country to reach the 1 billion peso sales mark. By 1990, it had 53 branches around Metro Manila, five in the provinces and two each in Taiwan and Brunei. Of the 62 branches, only 11 are company-owned and the other 51 are franchised. The Filipino-Chinese owner indicated that the success of the franchise is based on an original recipe of his mother. He claims that his hamburgers cater to the Asian palate. Jollibee employs over 3,000 people, most of whom are students. The company is known to offer the highest employee compensation and benefits package in the total food industry in the Philippines (World Executive Digest, 1990).

Whatever strategic option is followed, it will be necessary for the government to conduct a review of the legal and regulatory requirements as they relate to franchising, particularly in such areas as trademark legislation and copyright. Adequate protection for potential franchisees could be ensured through such measures as prior disclosure regulations and access to adequate information on the franchise opportunities being offered by franchisors.

Private sector support

A few international companies focus on the promotion of small and medium businesses through franchising. One American company, Sibley International works with the following aspects of the franchising industry.
- Helping entrepreneurs turn their businesses into franchises.
- Preparing franchisors to enter international markets, and helping them find suitable master licensees in their chosen markets.
- Assisting master franchisees in the choice of a franchise, in the process of starting their new business and in the ongoing relationship with the franchisor.
- Assisting private institutions and aid organizations dedicated to the development of the small and medium business sectors, by providing franchising expertise, and by building a business environment in which franchising can flourish.
- Assisting non-US franchisors who wish to enter the US market to prepare their franchise for such an entry, to find prospective master licensees and to assist in their launch in the US.

- Helping foreign governments who see franchising as an important development strategy for their economy, to help them educate the business, financial, and legal communities, to introduce the concept through the import of franchises and to develop an indigenous franchising industry, including the privatization and restructuring of government-owned businesses.

USAID has funded the promotion to promote franchising in both Russia and South Africa. In South Africa, the project was instrumental in establishing franchise businesses owned by members of the formerly disadvantaged community in South Africa. The project personnel packaged the following existing indigenous businesses as franchises for rapid expansion: a hair salon, an automobile repair business, a brick and tile business and a cinema. They organized and conducted the first international franchise conference on the continent of Africa in 1992 which led to subsequent conferences in 1993 and 1994. Franchises that participated in these conferences and subsequently identified master franchise partners included: Professional Carpet Systems, Baskin Robbins, Coverall, Futurekids, AlphaGraphics, Mail Boxes Etc., and Robo Clean.

In Russia, the project worked with the owners of Blue Kristal, a self-serve and full-service laundry in Moscow, to refine and package the business as a franchise. Blue Kristal is currently establishing franchises in St Petersburg. From August 1995 to May 1996, a team of Sibley consultants travelled to 10 cities throughout Russia including Moscow, Ekaterinburg, Novisibirsk, Vladivostok and Nizhny Novgorod, conducting franchise education and training workshops. The workshops were attended by: university representatives, Russian business owners, representatives of local financial institutions, and government officials. A total of 2,130 delegates attended the programme. The consultants assisted: a construction materials company interested in forming a franchised distribution chain, a large insurance company interested in a franchised drug store and the city administration of Ekaterinburg who wanted to select a portfolio of franchises to pilot in their city.

Support measures and institutional capacity building

Experience from various countries indicates that a number of institutional structures can have a positive impact *on* the development of a competitive indigenous franchise community. Franchise associations can play an important role in providing a forum for the exchange of information between local franchise operators, and can also represent the interests of its members to the concerned government agencies in such areas as legislative issues and other regulatory matters. In the early 1990s the ILO, as part of its small enterprise development programme in Indonesia, worked with the Ministry of Trade which had recognized the potential of indigenous franchising in expanding employment and raising efficiencies in the retail sector of the economy. As a result of this collaboration, the recently established Indonesian

Franchise Association (IDA) received the services of an experienced manager and specialist from a European franchise consultancy organization in the development of a detailed short-term plan for the work of the IDA.

In many developing countries such an association may not exist because the indigenous franchise communities are very small and do not have the time or resources to take the initiative to organize themselves. Initial government support and encouragement for the establishment of a local franchise association can be an important first step in an effort to facilitate the expansion of an indigenous franchise community. The main services of the franchise association would initially be to provide a forum for the discussion of common problems, establish a code of ethics to protect the reputation of the franchise community, identify policy and regulatory concerns which can be raised with government agencies, distribute general information on basic franchise principles and franchise opportunities, and publicize successful franchise experiences. Such an association might also provide information and guidelines on how potential franchisees might evaluate the various franchise opportunities which are available.

Franchise Resource Centres (FRCs) are institutional structures which can provide a range of services in support of the emergence and development of an indigenous franchise community. Such FRCs may be established to achieve the following objectives:

- To stimulate interest in franchising by promoting its concepts through the distribution of information and materials through workshops and meetings.
- To support the growth and development of indigenous franchising through the provision of a range of practical technical support services.

While such centres may be initially supported by government subsidies, they should be established independently of government structures to give the flexibility and demand orientation which is required if they are to be truly responsive to the needs of their clients. One possibility is to establish the FRC in close collaboration with the franchise association so that their relationships can be mutually supportive. In the medium term, it might be possible for the local franchise association to take over the management and resourcing of the FRC, which would provide services on a fee basis.

On an experimental basis, one Asian country has decided to take an equity position in the franchise systems which were established. This approach might be found to lead to sustained subsidies, inefficient programme management, and conflicts of interests which make it difficult to terminate involvement in unsuccessful investments. It is recommended that government involvement be in the form of indirect support through subsidies (preferably on a declining basis over time), the establishment of a franchise resource centre or the strengthening or establishment of a franchise association.

Future action

Franchising is a concept which is currently being implemented on a limited basis in some developing countries. There is a need to monitor these initial experiences and to develop a means of exchanging information between countries. An international franchise clearing-house might be established to facilitate the exchange of information between countries, and to conduct research on the impact of franchising on small enterprise development. The clearing-house may also serve as a resource for international franchises which are interested in expanding their operations to other countries, and it might also match franchisors with franchisees in developing countries.

Given the lack of published information on franchising in developing countries, and specifically on the multi-national dimension, international comparative studies might be conducted in co-operation with governments and franchisors to identify potential multi-national franchising arrangements. Possible roles for multi-national franchisors in encouraging indigenous franchising development might also be investigated.

The World Intellectual Property Organization has prepared a *Guide to franchising in developing countries.* Its purpose is to provide information about franchising that would not otherwise be available. In most countries where regulations do not exist, government may want to introduce some form of regulation and monitoring of franchising as a new form of business organization. However, too much regulation might prevent the growth of franchising before it has an opportunity to become established.

Franchising has become part of the national small enterprise development strategy in newly industrialized countries such as Malaysia and Indonesia. It would be very useful to monitor the impact of franchising as it relates to economic development in these two countries.

Franchise resource centres might be established in developing countries with international donor support. To be effective, these franchise resource centres would need the active support of both government and the private business sector. Where the establishment of a franchise resource centre may be premature because of a lack of franchisors, preliminary steps could be encouraged to establish franchising committees or to form task forces with existing foreign franchise associations, indigenous trade associations, manufacturing associations or chambers of commerce.

References

World Executive Digest, (1990) 'Creating your own franchise', June, p. 28.
Dun and Bradstreet Corporation, (1992), *The Dun and Bradstreet business failure record,* p. 17.
International Franchise Association, (no date), *Franchise fact sheet,* Washington, D.C.
Frauenhuber, W., (1993), 'Franchising in Europe: situation and strategy', *Public Enterprise,* 13 (Nos. 1 and 2).

Steinberg, Carol, (1992), 'Franchising: a global concept', *USA Today,* April 9, p. 5.
Timmon, Jeffrey, (1994), *New venture creation: Entrepreneurship for the twenty first century,* Burr Ridge IL: Irwin.
US Department of Commerce, (1990), *Franchising* in *the economy,* Washington, D.C.
Zeidman, Philip, (1992), 'The eye of the beholder', *Franchising World,* (November–December), p. 37.

About the authors

Michael Henriques was at the time of writing Director of the International Labor Organization's Job Creation and Enterprise Development Department in Geneva, Switzerland, and Robert E. Nelson was a Professor of Business Education, University of Illinois, Champaign, Illinois.

CHAPTER 8
Towards success: impact and sustainability in the FIT programme

Jim Tanburn

This article was first published in March 1996.

Abstract

The ILO's FIT programme has been working since 1991 in partnership with existing large, medium and small businesses to investigate and develop business opportunities in providing services to the huge untapped market of the micro and small enterprise sector. At the time of original publication, the FIT programme (Farm Implements and Tools) was working to strengthen local capacity for action research, specifically in the field of non-financial services for micro- and small-scale enterprises (MSEs). High priority was being placed on the development of services which can be self-sustaining in the long term. If the services are self-sustaining, it is argued, then they are presumably in demand by the beneficiaries. They could also achieve considerable outreach in a cost-effective way, if they can be copied by others.

This article gives a brief description of the FIT programme; it then considers the demands of MSEs for services, and the impact achieved by some pilot activities to meet those demands. The needs of the end-users of MSE products, and the situation for the partner organizations, are also discussed. Finally, conclusions are drawn about demand, impact monitoring and the design of future activities.

The FIT programme is a collaborative technical assistance programme between the International Labour Organization (ILO) and TOOL (the Dutch NGO); the programme is funded by the Netherlands Government. FIT aims to strengthen local capacity for the development of innovative 'mechanisms', through which non-financial services can be provided sustainably to MSEs. Local partner organizations, including NGOs and groups of MSEs, are implementing a portfolio of action research activities, in close collaboration with FIT. FIT is currently working in Ghana and Kenya, but this article focuses on FIT's experiences in Kenya, since the author has been working most closely with those activities. In both countries, FIT is working to establish national networks, for the dissemination of the results of pilot activities. It is anticipated that through the exchange of ideas and information, new action research initiatives will result.

'FIT' stands for 'Farm Implements and Tools', since FIT is taking a sub-sectoral approach, focusing on the capacity to meet the needs of MSEs in the metal-working and food-processing sub-sectors. By enhancing the ability of metal-workers to supply appropriate equipment to farmers, it is anticipated that agricultural capacity will be boosted. Similarly, by assisting food processors (and particularly women), it is anticipated that the demand for agricultural produce will rise, stimulating farmers to increase agricultural output. While new approaches are introduced in these two sub-sectors, it is also expected that the lessons learned will also be relevant to MSEs and organizations working in other sub-sectors.

The demand by MSEs for services

MSEs often compete in saturated markets, lowering their prices to gain sales, to the point where profitability is very low. Working conditions may be hazardous, and product quality is generally poor, meaning that customers are not happy with their purchases. The response by development practitioners to this has often been to provide support services which are to some extent scaled-down versions of services designed originally for larger companies. While helpful to the MSEs which benefit, such services will probably always require some external subsidy, and their outreach is therefore limited by the size of the subsidy available.

Meanwhile, the private sector is already providing almost all of the services which MSEs need, such as the provision of raw materials, commercial information and distribution channels, in self-sustaining ways; could these ways be enhanced and made more effective, possibly without the long-term involvement of any of the traditional MSE support institutions? Could new services be provided, which MSEs already want, but have no access to, at present? These questions already imply some important indicators of success:
- the willingness of MSEs or other private sector participants to pay part or all of the costs of the service;
- the willingness of MSEs or others to continue participation after external input has come to an end;
- the interest of other MSEs to participate, or to initiate similar activities.

One such service, which is currently not available in Kenya, is the opportunity to visit other enterprises, elsewhere in the country, and even in neighbouring countries. MSEs would like to be able to visit other MSEs, a facility referred to as 'exchange visits' by FIT; they are also interested in visiting larger enterprises, dubbed 'host visits'. Such visits are sufficiently attractive that MSEs may be willing to pay all of the direct costs, particularly once the new concept has been demonstrated. Thus, in a collaboration with PRIDE (Promotion of Rural Initiatives and Development Enterprises), visiting MSEs paid for about half of the direct costs of the first visit (the total direct costs being about USD $10 per day). After the visit, 85 per cent said that they would pay more next time, covering all of the direct costs, if required.

Similarly, a collaboration with KIC-K (Kisumu Innovation Centre, Kenya) facilitated exchange visits by MSEs from Kisumu to others in Nairobi; the visiting MSEs again paid half of the direct costs. Subsequently, MSEs near the ones which had made the visits saw the effects on the businesses of their neighbours, and organized their own exchange visits, to Eldoret and Kakamega, without any outside input at all. This indicates the delicacy of the process whereby initial demand for a new service is first registered: MSEs are unlikely to ask for (or pay for) a service, until they become aware of it as an interesting possibility.

The format of the service also seems to have a major influence on the willingness of MSEs to pay for all of the direct costs. For example, no subsidy is needed where MSEs can form their own group for the visit, even when the visit is to a neighbouring country (and is therefore more expensive). In contrast, some subsidy may be required, if entrepreneurs are invited to make visits to new places on their own (Craig and Oneko, 1995, p. 22).

It is not always evident why MSEs are asking for a particular service. PRIDE noted that its clients were keen to visit other enterprises, but had difficulty in defining what the objective of such visits would be, for the individual enterprise. PRIDE therefore collaborated with FIT to mount a workshop, the aim of which was to define the objectives for future enterprise visits. The event brought together PRIDE clients from five different branches around Kenya; what emerged was a strong desire on the part of MSEs to broaden their horizons, and specifically to develop networks of business connections. It also became very clear that the participating MSEs had much to teach others, and indeed the workshop became a service in itself, subsequently referred to as a 'brokering workshop'; participants expressed a willingness to pay for at least part of the costs of future workshops.

Another demand for MSEs is for facilitation of more direct contact with the people who ultimately use their products. One format now implemented in Embu and Kisumu has involved the facilitation of a sequence of meetings and exhibitions between groups of MSE metalworkers and groups of farmers, in a process of 'participatory technology development' (PTD). The farmers were initially more enthusiastic than the metal-workers about this facility, paying for their own transport, even from quite remote locations. The MSEs were initially more reluctant, even though participation cost them less, perhaps because they anticipated (rightly) that much of the initial feedback about the quality of their products might be negative. After this hurdle had been overcome, however, the MSEs were very keen to continue the meetings, both to learn from their customers, and to market their products to them.

A related service in demand by MSEs has been helpful in identifying new markets for their products. It has become apparent to some that they have taken a passive approach to market research, often diversifying only after a customer has taken the initiative to ask them to make a new type of product.

In a methodology dubbed 'rapid market appraisal' (RMA), FIT has provided training for MSEs in how to carry out market research (Burger and Haan, 1995). Participants in that course have subsequently trained other MSEs.

Thus, there is evidence that non-financial services can be provided to MSEs, in ways which they perceive to be meeting their immediate needs; they are therefore committed to continue the service in some form, albeit not necessarily the original one. But what impact has been achieved by the provision of these services? The following sections outline the lessons learned in this area, considering both quantitative and qualitative aspects.

Quantitative impact on MSEs of the services provided

Monitoring the impact of pilot activities is incorporated into the activity itself, so that all involved can know what progress is being achieved. At the same time, it has proved valuable to commission local consultants, to evaluate the impact of individual activities; these commissions, often collecting much of the quantitative data, aim to strengthen local capacity in external evaluation. The methodological experiences gained in this way have been presented as guidelines, which include sample questionnaires for the various stakeholders in the activity (Wesselink, 1995). In practice, consultants have used these guidelines as a basis for their work, adapting them to the individual service being evaluated.

One such evaluation, of the enterprise visits facilitated by PRIDE/FIT, found that participating MSEs had each hired an additional three employees, on average. Of those interviewed, 80 per cent felt that their profits had increased by more than 45 per cent, but this was rather a subjective measure, since the MSEs had not kept accurate records. Similarly, an evaluation of the brokering workshop with PRIDE found that, on average, participating MSEs were now employing an additional 0.4 paid employees; relating this to the total cost of the workshop of $89 per participant might indicate a cost per job created of $225. This compares reasonably with the range reported by other projects of $25–$5,500 (Harper, 1995). However, it is not possible to validate it totally, since there was no control group; PRIDE did not have sufficient non-participating clients in the FIT sub-sectors.

An evaluation immediately after the 7-month PTD sequence with KICK in Kisumu found that MSEs had made and sold agriculture-related equipment, to the new designs developed during the PTD sequence, worth an average of $700 per MSE. This may be related to the only input by FIT which could not currently be borne by the participants locally, namely the assistance to purchase raw materials, with which to make prototypes.

Most MSEs felt initially that, despite receiving high-quality information on market potential from the farmers, the purchase of raw materials for the construction of prototypes was too risky for them. FIT therefore provided $70 per participant, and the MSEs decided to form their own group, subsequently investing a further $100 of their own funds, on average; in addition, they contributed their time for design, development and manufacture of the prototypes. Thus, the provision of a small initial amount by RT persuaded the MSEs to invest more, from their own resources; ways should now be explored to make this part of the methodology sustainable, perhaps by offering 'loans for innovation', which could further enhance the group dynamics.

In general, however, FIT evaluators have not placed great emphasis on the quantitative data; participants often seem vague about the financial performance of their business, and a preference for working only with those MSEs which do keep records would presumably exclude the poorer (and less literate) entrepreneurs. There may be data which would be more easily memorable by the MSE, such as working schedules and wage payments, which could subsequently be translated into more reliable income and employment data (Haggblade, 1992); FIT has now drafted a manual to incorporate such ideas. It is anticipated that the manual can now be tested in a future evaluation.

Furthermore, the timescale of the evaluation is often not that of the local economy; MSEs expect a lag of up to three years, between the time when a farmer notes the availability of an improved plough (for example), and the time by which he has saved sufficient funds with which to purchase it. In addition, the MSE metal-worker will probably need some time, even when in good communication with his customers, to develop appropriate implements; in Machakos District, for example, the ox-drawn plough has evolved over a period of about 70 years, passing through many design iterations to reach its current form (Mortimore and Wellard, 1991, pp. 23–5). Thus, it can be argued that any additional sales by participating MSEs during the first seven months after the start of an activity constitute a significant achievement.

Many FIT evaluators have noted a wide variation in impact between different MSEs; some MSE participants have used the experience gained during the pilot activity to expand their business and product range very substantially; others, however, are still hoping for more assistance, before they can realize such benefits. A further obstacle has proved to be the identification of a suitable control group, to isolate the effects of other factors, such as liberalization and seasonality; it is hoped that an approach using the level of economic activity locally as the 'control' (Haggblade, 1992) can also be tried by FIT in a future evaluation.

Thus, while FIT will continue to collect quantitative data, they do at times seem only to prove that pilot activities have not harmed participating MSEs. In the long term, quantitative indicators such as outreach, cost effectiveness and financial sustainability may become important. In the short term, however, it may be concluded that qualitative indicators are probably the most interesting ones to investigate, and these are discussed below.

Qualitative impact on MSEs of the services provided

Qualitative aspects covered during monitoring have essentially included any change in business practice which could be attributed directly to the provision of the new service. Such changes might include improvements in the procurement of raw materials and other inputs, in management or technical skills, and in marketing strategies; they might also include the adoption of new technologies or product designs, or access to new markets. Essentially, the evaluation process required some alertness on the part of the interviewer; however, it was also much easier to attribute a specific change to a specific activity, and the qualitative benefits were often the ones which were perceived by the MSE to be the most important ones. Illustrations of the qualitative benefits could be given at length for each pilot activity, but there is only space in this article for some conclusions about the trends.

In general, MSEs who had participated in visits to other enterprises (other MSEs, or larger enterprises) were found to have benefited particularly in the following ways:

- improved technical skills, and knowledge about improved equipment (having seen them in operation during the visit, many MSEs purchased new tools, such as scales, a thermometer, an improved stove, etc.);
- improved linkages with suppliers (particularly for the supply of spare parts and raw materials);
- ideas for new or improved products (food processing entrepreneurs, in particular, learned many new recipes and techniques of food preparation);
- improved management skills, particularly in customer relations, record keeping and employee relations.

After noting the value of the brokering workshop to participants, FIT sponsored a small evaluation of the impact of other meetings, where MSEs from different locations had had the opportunity to exchange business information informally among themselves. For example, some NGOs bring their clients together from time to time, to give particular training, or to present prizes to the best clients. This study found that MSEs who participated in these group fora (including the brokering workshop) reported the following, particular benefits:

- new product designs (metal-workers learned about new designs for mills, stoves, hoes and water heaters, for example);
- feelings of increased self-confidence, ability and recognition (particularly appreciated by women entrepreneurs, for example when dealing with male customers, suppliers and employees);
- improved management skills, most particularly in the efficient organization of production, but also in the skills listed above;
- improved linkages with existing and new markets.

It is possible that the differences outlined above between the two formats (visits vs. fora) are in some cases a function of the relatively small sample sizes; larger samples may be needed, to draw definitive conclusions about the nature of the potential benefits inherent in each mechanism. Nonetheless, these findings do show that MSEs take every opportunity offered to them to develop their skills and ideas, if the opportunity is in a format to which they can relate. A further illustration of this was provided by a FIT evaluation of the MSE shows in Kenya; this evaluation found that nearly half of the participants had gained new product ideas while at the show, which they had subsequently used in their business (Esbin, 1994, p. 27).

Similarly, the PTD experiences in Embu and Kisumu showed that MSE metalworkers can indeed respond to the needs of their customers, by developing new or improved products. Thus, the range and quality of their products were enhanced, and additional sales resulted. After the course in RMA, the proportion of MSEs who were actively marketing their products increased by 32 per cent; in addition, 27 per cent of the participants introduced new, improved products, as a direct result of improved communication with their customers.

In general, MSEs often described the pilot activity as 'an eye-opener'; it seemed to enable them to move from traditional ways of doing business, to a more modern approach. For example, the traditional marketing strategy was described during one evaluation as 'you either buy or leave'; once the benefits of adopting more modern business methods have been demonstrated, MSEs seldom look back.

However, the demand by MSEs for services is ultimately financed by sales to their customers, and it is the demand and perceptions of these customers which are therefore the origin of all sustainable activities with MSEs. Furthermore, improving the products and services provided by MSEs can generate important benefits for their customers; in FIT's case, the benefits accruing through such linkages are an integral part of the project design. This aspect is therefore considered in the following sections.

The demand for improvements, from the end-users of MSE products

As mentioned earlier, the end-users of MSE products (smallholder farmers, in this case) have demonstrated their interest in providing feedback to MSEs about their products, to the extent that they will pay their own transportation costs, to participate in meetings with MSEs. At one rural meeting where improved implements were displayed by MSEs from Embu, 300 farmers attended; in both parts of Kenya where such meetings were initiated (Embu and Kisumu), they have continued in the subsequent months, without further input from FIT. The additional sales achieved by the MSEs in Kisumu as a result have already been referred to. These indicators show that end-users are very interested in the process, and respond to apparent improvements; however, it is also important to consider the impact on their operations.

Impact on the end-users of the improved MSE products

Ideally, FIT would monitor and quantify increases in agricultural productivity, as a result of pilot activities. Since it is not clear who will choose to purchase the improved implements, however, the final end-users cannot be predicted before the start of the activity. Thus, no baseline data can be collected, for later comparison. Add to this some large swings in climatic conditions, and recent liberalizations in important areas, such as the transportation of maize, and the quantification of impact on the farmer as end-user becomes apparently impossible – at least within the time-frame of the project as it currently stands.

Nonetheless, the opinion and experience of the end-user can still be sought, and representative samples have therefore been traced and interviewed. This is inevitably costly, since it can involve substantial transport costs. Furthermore, it may be time-consuming, when end-users are scattered in remote, rural locations; it has become apparent that MSE products are distributed through wide-ranging networks of traders (Ngau, 1995; Waithaka, 1995).

In general, the end-users' opinion of the improved implement has been very positive, and the farmers are happy that it represents an improvement on what was available before. For example, the recent mid-term evaluation of FIT found, in Embu, that neighbouring farmers had seen the new tools in use, and had purchased them also from the metal-workers who had developed them. Not all of the feedback from end-users has been so positive, however. In some cases, the product which had been 'improved' through PTD or RMA was found not to be very durable, and the customer was therefore quite unhappy. This has raised the issue of tool testing: it seems that MSEs can respond to the needs of the customers for improved technologies, but without achieving 100 per cent success, in the first iteration of development. Options such as product guarantees, and the testing of prototypes in ways which can be self-sustaining, should now be explored.

At the same time, it may be questioned whether a process of technological improvement, which will ultimately rely on local resources, can be expected to satisfy every customer, all of the time. Innovation has historically been a process of success and failure, with entrepreneurs building on the lessons which they have learned from their mistakes. It may also be observed that MSEs tend to appeal to their customers, on the basis that their products are cheaper than the competition; thus, to some extent, the customers should expect to get what they are willing to pay for.

It may also be relevant to wonder whether the end-user has enjoyed qualitative benefits. as a result of purchasing improved products; for example, have farmers been able to adopt new agricultural practices, as a result of improved access to equipment? In practice, this has apparently not yet occurred. As with tool testing, the MSE does not generally have the resources to demonstrate the application of new or improved tools in any detail. Where farmers felt that the tools should enable them to adopt new practices, they tended to be waiting for further demonstration and adaptation, perhaps by extension officers. Again, FIT is interested in exploring ways in which new tools could be demonstrated, sustainably, so that their potential can be fully realized.

Since the majority of smallholder farmers and food processors in Kenya are women, it is also particularly important to consider the involvement of women in the process. In Kenya (and apparently also in Ghana, where participatory technology development sequences are currently running), many of the farmers participating in meetings with MSEs were men, even when women farmers had been specifically and individually invited. This trend was most apparent when the meeting was advertised as relating to tools, probably since the man in a couple is generally the one responsible for tool purchase; this tends to be the case, even for tools which will subsequently be used by women (e.g. weeding tools). Some steps have already been taken to address this situation; at PTD Shows where improved tools have been judged by a panel of farmers, for example, FIT has ensured that 50 per cent of the judges were women farmers. Further work is needed, to involve women farmers and food processors more in the process of developing appropriate equipment.

The providers of support services

The experiences outlined above indicate that local organizations can develop innovative mechanisms for providing non-financial services to MSEs, in ways which could become self-sustaining. Through such experiences, it is anticipated that this capacity is being strengthened, and one indicator of that would be the ability of local partners to replicate and expand on the pilot activities. Here, there are some promising signs; PRIDE, for example, is now working to facilitate the concept of enterprise visits throughout East Africa, and other organizations are also interested in incorporating it into their SED programmes in Kenya. Similarly, a local consultant is offering courses in rapid market appraisal, in both Kenya and Tanzania.

Another important indicator for each mechanism is the extent to which pilot activities are scaled up, so that they achieve national outreach; this would ultimately imply that the service becomes available to any MSE in the country, at least in principle. Development agencies, however, tend to focus on their own clients and areas of geographical concentration; they may not aim to provide a service nationwide. Many development agencies do not currently consider 'innovation' as part of their core mandate, although this may now be changing, partly as a result of the activities of FIT and others. Furthermore, development agencies tend to rely on external funding, while the ultimate goal is for service provision to be internally self-sustaining (i.e. with all of the costs being met from local, commercial sources).

For these reasons, FIT is continuing to explore the potential for the provision of new services through the private sector, perhaps with no formal partner agency at all. For example, could larger companies which supply MSE inputs be assisted to meet the needs of MSEs more effectively? Indeed, one could hope to monitor the impact of MSE promotion on those suppliers. In practice, however, it may be difficult to measure this impact in the short term;

even in scrap steel, for example, MSE metal-workers form only 10–15 per cent of the total demand in Kenya, and substantial increases in overall demand will appear, therefore, only in the long term. Nonetheless, many suppliers may see MSEs as an important source of future demand; some are sufficiently interested to pay for advertising in bulletins, aimed at MSEs, currently being 'test-marked' by FIT. Indeed, there seems to be a great potential for the promotion of such linkages, since the possibilities extend far beyond the sub-contracting mode which has tended to be the favoured format of many development initiatives to date (Mead, 1994).

The development of individual services is only one objective for FIT, however; a major indicator of success in the long term is whether the mode of 'action research' in this important field is continuing and expanding. Are more 'mechanisms' being developed, to provide non-financial services to MSEs in sustainable ways? Essentially, it is too early to say whether this has yet been achieved. FIT is currently working to establish a National Network of collaborators and partners in Kenya; this network will bring together people from a wide variety of backgrounds, who are enthusiastic about the potential. It is anticipated that, during the next two years, their common interest will enable them to form a self-sustaining stimulus for local innovation through action research.

Some initial conclusions

It is widely accepted now that services for MSEs should be demand-led; it is also increasingly acknowledged, by both development practitioners and by the MSEs themselves, that the most important demand, in this context, is the demand of the final customer of the MSE. The money paid by the final customer enables the MSE to pay for services to improve his or her business, and the MSE generally provides the most accessible entry point for such interventions. Nonetheless, the final customer may also be willing to contribute to the costs of activities, which will ultimately lead to improvements in MSE product quality. This willingness to pay for the service, is one of the most important indicators of achievement.

It is also apparent that services may not be self-sustaining, because a small adjustment is needed in their format. For example, MSEs may be reluctant to try a new service, at full cost, if they must apply as individuals; however, if they are allowed to try it as a group, they may be willing to pay the full costs. Similarly, MSEs which did not participate in the pilot activity may nonetheless benefit, through spontaneous replication of what they have observed.

Efforts have been made to quantify the impact of FIT activities on MSEs, and some promising data have been collected, for example indicating that additional employment opportunities have been generated. Improved methodologies for collecting data are being developed. There are, however, considerable obstacles to ensuring that these data are totally reliable, and qualitative indicators have therefore been given greater importance; in addition to being valued by the MSEs themselves, they can often be directly linked with the individual services which have been provided to the MSE. Qualitative evaluation has shown that MSEs have benefited in many areas of business operation, from the services provided.

The response of MSEs to FIT's pilot activities has been very encouraging, as have the signs of replication by development agencies; however, FIT has not yet achieved extensive, private-sector replication of those services which have now been demonstrated on a pilot basis. Finally, it is too early to tell whether the local capacity for innovation in the provision of new services for MSEs has yet been strengthened; the initiation of a network of such organizations is a significant step to meeting that challenge.

FIT is keenly interested to hear from any other organization working in similar or related fields elsewhere in the world, so that experiences may be exchanged in more detail.

References

Burger, Kas, and Hans Haan, (1995), *Rapid market appraisal for MSEs,* FIT/TOOL Amsterdam, FIT manual.

Craig, Kim and Mike Oneko, (1995), (ed. Hileman), 'Strengthening the Kenyan informal sector through exchange forums', PRIDE Nairobi/FIT working document.

Esbin, Howard, (1994), 'Marketing channels for MSEs in Kenya: analysis and strategic plan', Nairobi/FIT working document.

Haggblade, Steven, (1992), 'A proposal for monitoring small enterprise promotion,' *Small Enterprise Development Journal,* Vol. 3, No. 4, London.

Harper, Malcolm, (1995), 'Small enterprise development: value for money?' Cranfield School of Management, for ILO Geneva.

ILO, (1981), *Procedures for the design and evaluation of ILO projects,* Geneva.

Mead, Donald, (1994), 'Linkages within the private sector: A review of current thinking', Michigan State University/FIT working document.

Mortimore, Michael, and Kate Wellard, (1991), 'Environmental change and dryland management in Machakos District, Kenya, 1930–1990: ODI Working Paper No. 57, London.

Ngau, Peter, (1995), 'A study of traders servising MSE metal-workers of farm implements and tools in Kenya: a case study of Kisumu and Vihiga Districts', University of Nairobi/FIT working document.

Tanburn, Jim, (1995), 'Pointers to success: A framework for evaluating the impact of the FIT programme', FIT/ILO Geneva.

Waithaka, Daudi, (1995), 'Thika town SME metal-working and services study', Matrix consultants, Nairobi/FIT working document.

Wesselink, Bert, (1995), 'Guidelines for evaluating FIT activities, including Evaluation Forms', F1T/ILO Geneva.

About the author

Jim Tanburn was at the time of writing employed by the ILO to work on the FIT Programme, was the founder of the ILO BDS Seminar Series and is currently an independent consultant, based in the UK. The views expressed are those of the author and not the ILO.

CHAPTER 9
Business development services – core principles and future challenges
Alan Gibson

This article was first published in September 1997.

Abstract

Business development services (BDS) have not been subject to the same degree of comprehensive, systematic analysis as microfinance, a fact now recognized by many development agencies. Although there are difficulties in defining precisely what is meant by 'good practice' in BDS, examination of the experience of BDS donors and practitioners suggests that there are a number of core principles which underpin the current state of the art of BDS. These form a general framework to guide interventions. However, there remain many unresolved questions in BDS. Future priorities for action should seek to answer these questions, focusing in particular on more rigorous assessment of current practices, the development of benchmarks of performance and greater innovation.

There is now considerable experience among international development agencies of interventions aimed at the development of small and medium size enterprises (SMEs). Indeed, there has been a discernible trend in recent years to devote a greater proportion of aid resources towards SME development. While donors support SME development in a variety of ways, since the early-1980s most attention has focused on support for financial services reflecting widespread agreement that significant progress has been made in how to design and deliver this kind of intervention.

Donors' experience in supporting SME development through non-financial services – business development services (BDS) – stretches over several decades. However, unlike financial services, this broad experience has not been assessed in a comprehensive or systematic manner. Recognizing this gap in the development community's understanding, the Committee of Donor Agencies for Small Enterprise Development recently commissioned a report to assess donor experience with this type of intervention. Researchers were able to draw upon donor documentation and other sources to provide a brief summary of the collective experience of BDS, concentrating particularly on emerging underpinning principles in good practice and future challenges.

This article summarizes some of the main findings from the above report. It does not concentrate on the detailed issues and lessons pertaining to individual micro, meso and macro-level BDS instruments. A considerable amount has been written on these elsewhere (for example, CEDEFOP and Durham University Business School, 1993; Humphrey and Schmitz, 1995; Grierson and McKenzie, 1996; and Mead, 1994). Rather, the priority here is to look at the general situation relating to BDS, with the intention of:

- describing 11 core principles of good practice which apply across all (or most) BDS instruments and which constitute a set of principles embodying the *current state of the art* of BDS; and
- summarizing the key challenges facing BDS organizations (donors and practitioners) stemming from current unresolved issues and which outline a *future agenda* for BDS activity.

What do we mean by 'good practice'?

'Good practice' in BDS refers to approaches which deliver the most beneficial outcomes. One of the key reasons for the rapid ascendance of microfinance is its apparent, intrinsic measurability in relation to performance. The strong numerical base to microfinance and often strong similarities between programme approaches has allowed the development of common indicators in performance assessment. These are concerned mainly with operational performance (rather than external impact) but are nonetheless a useful tool in aiding the design, management and assessment of microfinance interventions. Where values can be given to these indicators, so creating benchmarks of good practice, they are especially useful. Despite considerable reservations on issues associated with impact (Johnson and Rogaly, 1997), many donors and practitioners alike have a strong sense of what good practice means.

Relative to microfinance, in BDS there has been relatively little attempt to develop a similar tight definition of good practice. In some senses, this is not surprising. 'Business development services' is a catch-all phrase for a diverse collection of activities (including training, counselling and advice, developing commercial entities, technology development and transfer, information and business linkages – and this is not an exhaustive list) and is not conducive to neat standardization. Except in the training field, where there are some semi-generic training products, there is relatively little standardization in BDS instruments. Moreover, the difficulty of measuring performance in BDS appears, in some cases, to have been compounded by a reluctance to attempt rigorous measurement. While a limited amount of benchmarking may be possible in relation to basic performance indicators related to training and consultancy (such as the percentage of direct cost recovery and start-up and survival rates), in general, there is no existing strong consensus on what good practice means in BDS in terms of results. The following analysis of good practice in BDS is therefore based both on qualitative analyses of *what works* in BDS interventions as well as quantitative assessments of performance.

(1) BDS should be business-like and demand-led

This is the fundamental principle for good practice in the development and delivery of BDS. It shapes decisively all the main instruments of BDS and its influence is felt in the other general principles examined here. It emerges both from theory and hard experience (Gibb and Manu, 1990) and its esstential message is inherently simple: the best BDS organizations for supporting SMEs are themselves like those SMEs in terms of their people, systems and values. This principle is manifested in numerous different ways but the following are some of the more important. For donors:
- BDS partner organizations should be selected which are able to develop in a business-like way (donors and governments should generally not be deliverers of micro-level services);
- BDS organizations should be developed with a vision, culture, motivations and attitudes which reflect a commitment to business-like behaviour; and
- BDS organizations should be encouraged to take ownership and responsibility for their work and, similarly, within these organizations, individuals should be given an opportunity to develop personal ownership.

The principle as it applies to BDS organizations means:
- those who 'receive' BDS instruments should be regarded not as beneficiaries but as discerning clients or customers, with whom transactional relationships may be developed (i.e. on the basis of exchange not charity);
- instruments should be designed on the basis of a sound understanding of the needs of clients and a comprehensive knowledge of their situation;
- instruments should be regarded as 'products', and a rigorous and transparent approach to their measurement adopted, both in terms of costs and income; and
- close contact should be maintained with clients so that the demand-driven impulse is not weakened.

The business-like and demand-led principle does not require the abandonment or dilution of social objectives. Being business-like is *not* about the objectives *per se;* rather, it is concerned with the manner in which objectives are pursued. While there will be differences in practice between interventions focused at different groups of SMEs, the essence of the overall approach should not be different.

(2) Sustainability

For every donor agency this is always an issue of key concern. Every BDS intervention has to address sustainability issues from the outset. However, the meaning of this in practice is far from clear. Sustainability can be assessed at

86   VALUE CHAINS IN DEVELOPMENT

> **Box 9.1 Extending the business-like principle to donor-counterpart relations**
>
> The Swiss Agency for Development Co-operation (SOC) has pursued an approach to SME development in Ecuador and Peru which is based around a business-like relationship with BDS providers. BDS organizations are invited to bid for particular contracts such as investigating and monitoring service markets and the provision of services to SMEs. Payment for these contracts is performance-based with agreed incentives for good performance according to defined criteria (similarly, institutions which do not meet agreed targets receive no more contracts). The purpose of these contracts is to try and develop improved offers of services from BDS providers to meet the demands of SMEs and actually to stimulate this demand in the long-term. Early evidence suggests that the offer of services has been upgraded by the stimulus from SOC.
>
> In each case the programme is administered by Swisscontact. Their involvement as a second-tier institution is important; it would be extremely difficult for a donor (with all its attendant rigidities and lack of closeness to the SME situation) such as SOC to develop the kind of relationship with BDS providers (first tier) which is necessary for the business-like basis to be established.

two levels: the level of impact (in relation to the SME), and the level of the BDS provider.

In the case of sustainability of impact of SMEs, all the principles of good practice mentioned in this guideline are aimed at this objective. It is the latter issue where most debate arises (and clearly impacts on SMEs themselves may not be sustainable if BDS capacity is not sustained). What should donors' commitment to sustain ability mean at this level?

There is no consensus emerging from current practice on the specific meaning which should be given to sustainability in terms of BDS capacity. There is agreement on the value of charging fees and on being business-like. There is also agreement on the different dimensions of sustainability: organizational, managerial, technical and financial. There is an acknowledgement of a degree of awkwardness in promoting BDS instruments which did not really exist in industrialized nations in the early days of industrial growth and which are significantly subsidized in industrialized countries currently. Certainly, it is pointless believing that the full panoply of subsidy-supported BDS infrastructure which has developed in wealthy countries can be sustained (internally) in economies with per capita incomes perhaps less than 10 per cent of those prevailing in industrialized economies. This means that the types of BDS which develop have to be appropriate for local conditions rather than imported for wealthy donor countries. There is a clear and relevant comparison here with the origins and evolution of microfinance organizations which owed little to the influence of practice in industrialized nations.

At this stage of understanding of BDS, two points can be made in considering how the sustainability principle should be applied:
- The priority in BDS should be to support interventions which appear to offer a credible path to sustainability, through, for example, incorporation

into private learning mechanisms or the commercialization of services; i.e. which are *finite,* offering a realistic end to donor involvement.
- Interventions which do *not* offer a finite end need to be clear about their rationale and have a realistic strategy for long-term support.

(3) Tailoring: relevance through focus

SMEs exist in complex and variable situations; generalizing about needs can over-simplify a situation and lead to inappropriate interventions. Knowing specifically what an intervention is trying to do and with whom is an essential feature of BDS interventions; i.e. in this sense being 'tailored' means being specific and relevant.

This tailored approach has been dominated in recent years by an increasing use of sub-sector analysis. The essence of this is that SMEs have to be viewed within the economic context of their work, which means the input suppliers, manufacturers, distributors, retailers, customers and supporting government and private institutions which constitute their particular sub-sector. It thus enables BDS organizations to understand the totality of potential clients' situations. Many current BDS interventions which appear most interesting have begun with a sub-sectoral tailored approach.

A sub-sectoral approach does not preclude targeting on a socioeconomic basis. It *may* make it more difficult, since economic systems do not confine themselves to one social group or another. Moreover, it is clear that interventions which do not target a group directly may still benefit it considerably.

(4) Participatory approaches

The advantages of pursuing participatory approaches to planning interventions are now well documented and can be grouped under three related headings:
- greater knowledge of SMEs' situation (understanding needs);
- greater ownership among BDS organization staff, clients and other participating organizations, such as business associations; and
- a greater possibility of longer-term sustainability (ownership leads to greater responsibility and to a commitment to maintaining services).

In practice, more emphasis on participation has questioned the value of some 'classic' social science approaches to needs assessment and planning (such as large surveys) in favour of quicker methods which are more integrated with action.

One consequence of accepting a participatory approach is that programmes of intervention should allow some flexibility in their design. Clearly, this has to be a matter of negotiation and reasonable limits have to be set. However, it is contradictory for interventions to be, on the one hand, demand-led and participatory and, on the other, inflexible.

> **Box 9.2 Developing services at the Chambers of Commerce and Industry in Brazil**
>
> This GTZ project was conceived as an intervention at the micro level: SMEs would receive training and advice from German artisans, who would come to Brazil or receive trainees in Germany. Chambers of Commerce in Germany and Brazil were considered appropriate intermediaries. However, the project developed into a meso-level intervention, as it found that institutional change was required to enable the chambers in Brazil which functioned as an interest group for larger enterprises only, to provide need-based services to SMEs in a sustainable manner. An orientation phase at the start of the project made this redirection possible. Introducing participative approaches to planning, decision-making and training, without infringing on the organizations' autonomy, the project allowed a new sense of mission to develop with regard to SMEs, which resulted in the chambers opening up their membership to SMEs, and offering services specifically aimed at this group. Organizational change happened around concrete activities for SMEs initiated by the project, in a dynamic process. SMEs as well as the Chambers were involved actively in all stages of identification, planning, implementation and the evaluation of services. The organizations have started to view themselves as enterprises which offer advocacy and services as their products, while SMEs have started to recognize them as their legitimate representative and an important source of support.

(5) Maximizing outreach

One of the key problems associated with BDS is that, with some exceptions, it is non-standardized and can seldom be simply replicated. Given this difficulty of replication, there are a number of possible leveraging approaches which BDS organizations are trying in order to increase their outreach:

- *Sub-sector approaches.* Although this is not always possible, in some instances, relatively small and focused inputs can have a significant impact in a whole sub-sector (Chen, 1996 and Lusby, 1995).
- *Supporting indigenous and private systems of learning.* Countries with successful SME sectors usually have well-established private networks of exchange and learning which have become embedded in the local culture. Encouraging SMEs to 'learn to learn' through better exchange, more association and improved information provision may help to develop improved systems of private learning.
- *Macro-level approaches.* Macro-level policies exert a huge influence on SMEs through the economic signals which the system sends them, their specific policies towards business and in their role as key providers of education for children and young people. This last area in particular may be a key influence on cultural attitudes towards enterprise.

(6) Building on demonstrated initiative

Given the commitment of donors to supporting a development process which is both sustainable and owned locally, it is imperative that interventions seek (where possible) to build on what is already there rather than supplanting it with an imported vision or model. This, of course, does not mean that donors

should not seek to influence or that they are passive players in discussions with potential BDS partner organizations. However, it does mean that:
- individual visions are respected and that the large extent to which individuals' egos are tied in with 'their' organizations is recognized;
- the scale of resource commitment – especially if finance or equipment is involved – reflects the capacity of local partners; and
- experiences from the private sector are assessed with a view to learning from them. The microfinance 'revolution' was based on learning from the practices of informal credit sources. Similarly in BDS, some initiatives are seeking to learn from current private sector approaches.

(7) Focus in delivery

BDS can learn from the trend towards minimalist microfinance and implement more focused interventions split from other SME development (or other) functions for two main sets of reasons.

First, it allows a simpler and more effective relationship with clients: SMEs relate to other organizations primarily as transactional agents: their first thought (consciously or not) is: what is your offer? By having a focused intervention and a limited range of instruments to offer, there is more clarity and less chance of sending mixed messages to clients as sometimes happens, for example, when counselling is mixed with credit.

Second, it recognizes capacity limitations: every BDS organization has its strengths and weaknesses and it is extremely unlikely that they will be able to deliver every kind of BDS intervention effectively. It is much better for organizations to focus on what they can do and do this well rather than seeking to diversify into activities where they have less understanding. Similarly, it is important that donor support does not encourage strategic drift among BDS organizations (although clearly there is a balance between strategic certainty and listening to one's stakeholders).

(8) Systemic approaches and programme integration

Donors clearly need to have knowledge of the overall environment within which BDS exists. This means not simply being aware of the links between micro, meso and macro levels, but also between BDS and financial services.
- *Co-ordination between donors.* This should prevent clear conflicts of interest developing between programmes. However, as important as liaising over what donors are doing is consensus on how they are doing it.
- *Networks between different providers.* In spite of the competition between BDS organizations, it is important that providers have a wider sense of their clients' needs beyond what they can deliver, and are prepared to refer people to the appropriate place.

- *Joint venture/sub-contracting arrangements.* There are nascent signs that these kind of relationships are developing between organizations, for example between 'generalist' development agencies and specialist BDS providers.

(9) Renewed focus on costs analysis

Cost analysis has historically been a neglected discipline with BDS. Of course, BDS organizations have budgets and maintain accounts. However, until recently, most BDS organizations did not seek to use financial analysis as a tool for improved management and the delivery of instruments. The main problem has been a reluctance or inability to allocate costs to different activities so that it is difficult to relate the outcomes of BDS interventions with the input costs. This is a problem for four reasons.
- It means that BDS managers do not have the right kind of information on which to make decisions about what they should and should not be doing. Within an organization it encourages a culture which divorces inputs from results and removes costs from staff's awareness.
- It makes BDS organizations less financially transparent (especially in relation to microfinance) and more open to accusations of wasteful consumption of resources.
- It does not allow any progress with comparability and benchmarking, since many of the key measures here have a cost base.
- It offers a misleading picture of what a BDS instrument actually is, implying it does not cost anything.

None of the above imply that costs should be seen as more important than BDS outreach and impacts. However, it is the case that the neglect of costs has often distorted BDS organizations' analysis of their performance.

(10) Continued importance of impact assessment and evaluation

BDS interventions should always have an element of impact assessment built into them as an integral part of the programme. However, two general aspects of evaluation should be stressed which underpin its importance. First, benchmarking and the ability to compare organizations needs to be improved.

Second, in order to be responsive to demand pressures from clients, BDS organizations need to review their performance regularly with a view to making changes for the future. Combining retrospective and prospective analysis – evaluation and needs assessment – as part of the normal activity of an intervention, rather than a one-off event, is a new way to think about evaluation. It is important that organizations are able to use evaluation and needs assessment methods for regular market research activity.

(11) Subsidiarity

In essence, this principle enshrines a common-sense idea of who can do what best. In BDS, this means that (usually) responsibility is delegated to the lowest possible level of those who are closest geographically and socially to SMEs themselves. In practice, applying the subsidiarity principle to the role of the state leaves three conclusions.

First, the primary role of the state in relation to SME development is to create a conducive environment for entrepreneurship. This means that it creates an environment characterized by sound macro-economic management, including fiscal and monetary control; a relatively liberal economic system in which regulations are not an onerous burden or highly distorting; and competent delivery of public services, especially education.

Second, in the main, the state should not seek to be a direct provider of BDS for SMEs, given the extreme difficulty government agencies have in becoming business-like. BDS providers should come from the private for-profit or not-for-profit sector.

Third, depending on government capacities and wider traditions, the state may be able to play a leading pro-active role (although still facilitative rather than delivery-orientated) in shaping a national framework of policies, practices and institutions to guide SME development (drawing on the East Asian experience).

Beyond these three points, there is less consensus on what the state should do. In particular, there is no widespread agreement over the role of the state in relation to subsidies for BDS, whether delivered to individuals or to the organization. To a large extent this depends on the resources available to it. There are strong general arguments for subsidies on the basis of giving disadvantaged groups access to particular services and there are innovative ways in which state support can be provided which still strengthen BDS providers' responsiveness to demand. However, it is pointless to provide broad principles guiding state spending when the resources available to governments vary enormously.

The key challenges facing BDS organizations: a future agenda

The most realistic assessment of the current state of art in BDS acknowledges that there is a considerable amount which is known, but possibly just as many unresolved questions as definitive answers. While there are a number of specific questions which need to be addressed, there are two main themes which need to underpin future investigation.

More benchmarking: rigorous assessment of current practices. The current weaknesses in BDS data should not be confused with weakness in the *idea* of benchmarking. Yes, BDS analysis is not reducible to a series of boxes and there are limitations to the use of seemingly objective indicators. For example, one indicator of cost effectiveness, 'cost per job' is prone to a variety of interpretations (and manipulations). Nonetheless, there is scope for much greater use of benchmarking. This can most easily start with cost-based measures related to operational efficiency where there are fewer of the methodological difficulties associated with impact and where it is possible to address the historic (and mistaken) separation of costs from outputs in BDS.

Encouragement for more innovation. While there are emerging examples of interesting BDS practice taking place, there is a great need to expand the stock of innovative projects from which donors can learn. On the basis of the framework of principles given above, donors should be supporting BDS organizations who are seeking to develop new approaches and are committed to learning from this experience.

The above two themes – benchmarking and innovation – form the broad challenges for donors and BDS organizations. In more specific terms, there are a considerable number of gaps in our understanding of good practice. Six are identified below.

BDS organizations: creating the business-like (non-profit) organization

In some ways, meso-level interventions have become the core issue for donors. From a donor perspective much of development generally is about finding and developing good partners. SME development is no different. The general message here is clear – the best organizations and people are business-like – but there is a danger that this is accepted as a bland truism only, without thinking about the practical details of its application.

What do we know of the dynamics of creating these organizations, and what actions donors can take to help effectively? For example, is stimulating BDS supply in both qualitative and quantitative terms, as some interventions are seeking to do, also going to stimulate demand for BDS services? Can specific institution-building instruments be identified which show particular promise in developing organizations?

Developing indigenous networks and associations

Successful rapid-growth economies are all lubricated by and driven by private mechanisms of learning, exchange and mutual support. Given the inability or reluctance of the state in many countries to subsidize these, the creation of these institutions of learning is a key priority offering an opportunity to create sustainable learning capacities. There are different traditions associated with business associations and BDS in industrialized nations; in some countries they are of central importance; in others they have a more peripheral role (Havers and Gibson, 1994). Not surprisingly, there is a mixed experience with regard to donor interventions in developing countries.

How can these associations be supported without bestowing on them the 'trappings' and mentality of a dependent bureaucracy? How can genuine capacity be created without raising costs? How can associations be supported, if at all, without undermining the indigenous quality which is their most distinctive feature?

Developing BDS interventions for disadvantaged groups

How will the more rigorous application of the business-like principle affect donors' general concern over distributional questions and commitment to disadvantaged groups? One school pursues the following line of thought.

- Using a more demand-led approach inevitably means that those with more demand (better-off owner-managers) will benefit most.
- The self-selection implied by this approach means that those with most ability, drive and resources will select themselves, with those without these qualities being left behind.
- The self-employment into which many people have fallen in developing countries is a reluctant state. Given the chance, many would gladly go into employment; their businesses are useful in a welfare sense, but are unlikely to contribute significantly to economic growth.
- Most businesses operated by poor people are relatively simple and there is actually little scope for BDS to help them.
- If the poor do benefit from BDS it is primarily as indirect beneficiaries working as employees with larger SMEs.

An alternative view is that, like any product, BDS providers can deliver useful products to disadvantaged groups if they are designed appropriately. The point is to identify a group and find out their needs.

The troublesome subsidy issue

For most donors, subsidies remains one of the most difficult issues associated with BDS. A general position is that interventions which require a relatively short-term period of external intervention to create capacity, and which then appear to have a realistic chance of being sustainable, are a worthwhile investment. Examples of this kind of intervention might include technology development and transfer, developing new market entities and business linkages. In each case, there appears to be a market gap or opportunity. However, what about those interventions where effective long-term self-financing appears unlikely or at least more difficult, for example, types of business training?

In this context, the common practice of industrialized nations may not be hugely relevant. Defining what is a 'legitimate' role for the state cannot be divorced from issues of what the state can afford. Even if there are valid reasons related to wider positive benefits, if there is no significant possibility of government taking on a role of supporting BDS organizations financially, how can donor support for them be seen as anything other than a short-term palliative or as one instalment in a series of donor supports?

This concern seems to suggest two possibilities for future interventions: seeking to minimize or eliminate external financial subsidies; or providing creative, cheaper and less distorting ways of offering state support (for example vouchers).

Developing generic approaches for later adaptation and expansion

The growth of BDS has been constrained by the contradiction between, on the one hand, focusing and developing specialized products to meet particular client needs, and on the other, replicating approaches and realizing economies of scale. Current approaches to leveraging more impact from limited resource interventions are concentrated around sub-sector analysis and networks. However, it may also be possible to develop more standardized approaches which can be adapted and delivered with relatively little development cost. The dangers of the thoughtless replication of 'models' is well known to most donors, but there is also an increasing recognition that, just as principles of intervention may have widespread relevance, so some specific products may be developed which have the opportunity to be scaled up with low-cost adaptation.

Getting the private sector to do more

Many BDS interventions are concerned with highlighting areas where markets have failed to deliver people and SMEs with goods and services. While often this can be attributed to a basic lack of purchasing power on the part of consumers, there are also occasions where this market failure is attributable to the supply side's basic lack of creativity in developing solutions to problems. BDS organizations, with donor support, are sometimes in a position to innovate approaches which may even have the potential to become sustainable from market demand.

Having shown that there can be profitable opportunities in serving SMEs or, perhaps of more relevance here, developing technologies which SMEs can service or manufacture, there may be an opportunity to stimulate the private sector generally into looking at previously unfashionable areas – appropriate technologies – in a serious commercial sense. 'Private sector' here may include self-help groups, microenterprises and businesses at the upper end of the SME range.

Conclusions

On the basis of many years of experience in designing and implementing BDS interventions at micro, meso and macro levels, it is clear that there is a broad framework of principles which underpin good practice. These form a guideline for the design, management and assessment of BDS. However, it is also clear that BDS remains a relatively neglected area of analysis; and there are many unresolved issues. In order to advance collective learning on good practice, donors and BDS organizations must give more priority to the rigorous assessment of current practices and to innovation.

References

CEDEFOP and Durham University Business School, (1993), *Training as an entrepreneurial business,* CEDEFOP, Berlin.

Chen, M.A. (ed.), (1996), 'Beyond credit: a sub-sector approach to promoting women's enterprises', Aga Khan Foundation Canada.

Gibb, A.A. and Manu, G. (1990), 'Design of extension and related support services for small-scale enterprise development', *International Small Business Journal,* Vol. 8, No. 3.

Grierson, J.P. and I. McKenzie, (1996), *Training for self-employment through vocational training institutions,* International Training Centre of the ILO, Turin.

Havers, M. and A. Gibson, (1994), 'The role of small business membership organisations (SBMOs) in small enterprise development', Small Enterprise Development Fund, ODA.

Humphrey, J. and H. Schmitz, (1995), 'Principles for promoting clusters and networks of SMEs', Discussion Paper 1, UNIDO Small and Medium Enterprises Programme, Vienna.

Johnson, S. and B. Rogaly, (1997), *Microfinance and poverty reduction,* Oxfam Development Guidelines, Oxford.

Lusby, F. (1995), *The subsector/trade group method: a demand-driven approach to non-financial assistance for micro and small enterprises,* Gemini Working Paper No. 55, USAID.

Mead, D.C. (1994), 'Linkages within the private sector: a review of current thinking', FIT Working Document No. 3, ILO.

About the author

Alan Gibson is a consultant working for the Springfield Centre for Business in Development. This paper stems from a major review of the donor experience of BDS commissioned by the Committee of Donor Agencies for Small Enterprises Development and supported financially by GTZ. The views represented here are entirely those of the author and do not necessarily represent those of the Committee.

CHAPTER 10
Facilitating small producers' access to high-value markets: lessons from four development projects

Jonathan Dawson

This article was first published in June 2003.

Abstract

Globalization creates opportunities as well as obstacles for small producers in the countries of the global South. This paper describes the attempts of four BDS initiatives – AKILI (Kenya), USSIA (Uganda), SITE (Kenya) and SEEDS (Sri Lanka) – to help small producers exploit emerging opportunities to reach new markets within and outside their countries. Considerable success was achieved in helping client producers access new, higher-value markets and to link up with private sector BDS providers, including packaging firms and standards certification agencies, thus enabling the producers to supply supermarkets and other non-traditional markets. However, such successes were often limited to the minority of more advanced small businesses, the so-called 'stars': more difficulties were encountered when working with the less sophisticated majority of microenterprises and small businesses (MSEs), especially where a significant leap in product quality was required for them to access the new markets. The greatest potential for widespread outreach and poverty alleviation lies in the adoption of sub-sector approaches, where there is greater potential for leverage. There is still an important role for support agencies to identify market opportunities thrown up by globalization, of which small producers are often unaware.

Important changes are taking place in the incentive structure facing small enterprises in the South, driven by the parallel processes of liberalization and globalization. Some doors can be seen to be closing, while others are opening wider. On the negative side, three major trends can be seen at work:
- A lowering of tariff barriers has seen a substantial increase in the import into the South of many goods previously produced by small-scale enterprises, including clothing, food, soap and detergents, simple tools, equipment and so on.

- The austerity measures accompanying structural adjustment have tended to eat into the purchasing power of the traditional clientele of small informal sector producers, the urban and rural poor. Depressed international prices for many agricultural commodities mean that even export crop-producing areas have often not escaped the economic downturn (Meagher and Yunusa, 1992).
- There has been a strong flow of labour (in the form of retrenched workers, rural migrants and new school leavers) into small-scale economic activities, where barriers to entry tend to be relatively low (Grey-Johnson, 1992; Dawson, 1991).

The combined result of these various trends is all too familiar to those working with small producers: a large and ever-growing number of poorly trained and ill-equipped small producers crammed into low-value markets, making the same small range of products and competing primarily on the basis of price rather than quality. This can be characterized as a static (or shrinking) cake being cut into ever-smaller slices. With profit margins squeezed to a bare minimum, the potential for innovation or graduation into higher-value production is limited to those active in markets with higher barriers to entry or with privileged access to equipment, skills, markets or credit.

There is, however, another side to the story. The processes involved in liberalization and globalization are also creating new types of opportunity for small producers. These fall into four main categories:

- Export opportunities for small producers have increased markedly in recent years in product markets including speciality horticultural produce; non-traditional forest products, including seeds, raisins, essential oils, honey and so on; handicrafts and other 'ethnic' goods. As ethical lobbies and consumer niches have developed in the North, so small producers able to meet the quality standards demanded by specific quality seals – such as those of the Fair Trade, Soil Association and other organic produce organizations – have enjoyed spectacular improvements in market access.
- Currency devaluations that most countries of the South have undertaken as part of the process of structural adjustment have created significant import-substituting opportunities in many sectors (King, 1997; Lessard, 1992).
- Liberalization in the South has entailed a shrinkage of the state sector, thus creating market space, some of which small producers have proved able to occupy. Liberalization of the procurement regime in many countries has opened up particularly valuable opportunities for small producers of a wide range of goods (Bagachwa, 1991; Dawson, 1991).
- There has been a parallel trend in the private sector for large businesses to focus on their core areas of expertise, subcontracting out many services previously undertaken in-house to small-scale suppliers (see, for example, de Crombrugghe and Montes, 2000).

The broad picture to emerge from this brief overview is of a high level of polarity within the small enterprise sector. On the one hand, there exists a large number of small producers trapped in low-value, undiversified, saturated markets, unable to escape the 'race to the bottom' with prices, and profit margins dropping ever lower in the face of large numbers of new market entrants. On the other, new market opportunities are opening up that reward small producers able to innovate, diversify their products, produce in larger batches or act as subcontractors, achieve high quality standards and use attractive packaging materials.

A key distinguishing characteristic of these new higher-value market types is that small-scale producers are generally more distant from them – both geographically and culturally – than they are from traditional informal sector markets. That is, while small-scale enterprises have traditionally served the poor communities in whose midst they are located, customers in the new markets are generally not local. Sometimes, as we have seen, they are located

Table 10.1 Background information on four APT-supported projects

Project	Dates	Target groups and project objectives	Services provided	Number of clients
AKILI, Kenya	1997–2001	Nairobi-based metalwork, woodwork and fabrics MSEs; aims to help clients penetrate high-value domestic homeware market	• identify and develop new products and designs • technical training • promote market linkages	310 MSEs (core focus on 17 'star' producers)
USSIA, Uganda	1997–2001	Mpigi district (neighbours Kampala)-based woodwork, metalwork, ceramics and handicrafts MSEs; aims to help clients penetrate high-value domestic homeware and tourist markets	• identify and develop new products and designs • technical training • promote market linkages	778 MSEs (core focus on 37 'star' producers)
SITE (PMTS)	1998–2001	MSEs in Nairobi, Kisumu and Nakuru; food, agro-processing, metal and textile sectors; aims to help clients move into higher-value domestic markets, esp. supermarkets	• business and marketing training • counselling • promote market linkages • promote linkages to other service providers • build capacity of small producer associations	518 MSEs
SEEDS, Sri Lanka	1987– (still on-going)	MSEs nationwide in Sri Lanka; handicrafts, agriculture, agri-business, ornamental fish, cut flowers and textiles sectors; aims to help clients move into higher-value domestic and export markets	• identify and develop new products and designs • technical and business training • counselling • promote market linkages	SEEDS works in over 2,200 villages nationwide; 2,416 MSEs have benefited from market linkages

Table 10.2 Marketing services provided by projects (brackets indicate services provided to a limited extent)

Services	AKILI	USSIA	SITE	SEEDS
Marketing training for client producers	✓	✓	✓	✓
Facilitate client participation in trade fairs	✓	✓	✓	✓
Build linkages with market outlets	✓	✓	✓	✓
Build linkages with other service providers	✓	✓	✓	
Set up retail outlets	✓	✓		(✓)
Help clients set up retail outlets	✓		(✓)	✓
Promote a greater role for 'star' clients	✓	✓	✓	(✓)
Build capacity of associations or groups		✓	✓	✓

overseas. Even where customers are domestic, they often shop in smart high street stores or supermarkets and are generally not prepared to engage in informal sector-style transactions, often involving bargaining on price, providing a deposit and receiving no product guarantee. Moreover, small producers are generally unable to produce goods in sufficiently large batches or to the consistent quality standards required by supermarkets and other large shops.

There are substantial logistical and cultural gulfs to be bridged here for small producers to be able to benefit from the opportunities emerging; they generally have neither the education, the resources nor the working methods required to identify or access the new types of market themselves. Development agencies and projects have a potentially key role to play here, working alone or with other private sector partners, in fostering the development of sustainable linkages between small producers and these markets. But, how can such initiatives most effectively and sustainably intervene?

There is a growing literature that addresses just this question (see, for example, Onvango, 1998; Mikkelson, 1999; Heierli, 1999; McVay, 2000). This paper attempts to contribute to this debate by looking at the experience of four recent innovative market linkage projects associated with the British NGO, APT – Enterprise for Development (APT):

- Advancing Kenyan Industry through Local Innovation (AKILI);
- Uganda Small-Scale Industries Association (USSIA);
- Production and Market Training and Support (PMTS) project, implemented by the Kenyan NGO, Strengthening Informal sector Training and Enterprise (SITE);
- Sarvodaya Economic Enterprise Development Services (SEEDS).

Each of the four profiled projects has faced distinctive methodological problems in tracking impact and none has generated authoritative and comprehensive impact data. All, moreover, have been somewhat experimental and pioneering in nature. The aim here, in consequence, is to present a discussion paper highlighting innovative new approaches and insights that deserve further exploration rather than to draw definitive conclusions on what does and does not work in terms of enhancing market access for small producers in a cost-effective and sustainable manner.

Models of assistance: four small enterprise support initiatives

Table 10.1 provides some background information on each of the projects; Table 10.2 provides a summary of the principal approaches to the facilitation of enhanced market linkages adopted by the four projects. Most of the goods produced by clients of the four projects were not for export. They included, for example, the provision of school furniture and ceramics to hotels in Uganda; foodstuffs sold through supermarkets, household furniture and handicrafts in Kenya; handicrafts and non-traditional foodstuffs in Sri Lanka.

All of the projects have undertaken some level of conventional, enterprise-level marketing training of their client producers to help them reach new markets. However, in every case except SITE, this approach has proved less effective than had been anticipated and did not result in a significant increase in sales volumes. This is primarily for the reasons given above, namely that small producers tend to be at too great a cultural or geographic distance and lack the resources and working methods necessary to penetrate the higher-value markets potentially open to them.

This general point is validated by the experience of SITE, the relative success of whose marketing training is largely due to the fact that it was mostly aimed not at small producers but at either producer associations or food-processors. In cultural terms, these processing enterprises and associations tend to be significantly closer to the final market than most informal sector businesses and much better equipped to gain access to it.

The failure of conventional, enterprise-level marketing training led each of the projects to explore a range of other approaches to facilitating improved market access. Each of the projects, for example, has made extensive use of exhibitions and trade fairs as a way of bringing potential customers into direct contact with small enterprises and their products. In several cases, these were entirely cost-covering and were generally found to be a highly effective and relatively low-cost way of developing ongoing linkages between their client enterprises and larger-scale buyers.

Each of the projects also devoted significant efforts to identifying and brokering linkages with market intermediaries: including high street shops and supermarkets; international and domestic traders; and producer/traders that have contracts with, for example, schools, hotels and restaurants, and that subcontract some of their work to other suppliers.

This proved to be a highly effective strategy. In the case of AKILI and USSIA, the turnover of client enterprises increased sharply following a shift in project strategy to a more market-driven approach that saw the provision of many services transferred from the project itself to market intermediaries. The brokerage of such linkages is also core to SEEDS' strategy: its clients currently supply a range of buyers, including an organic food exporter, an ornamental fish exporter, a cut flower exporter and retailers of coir products, textiles and handicraft items.

SITE additionally seeks to develop linkages between its clients and the providers of a range of services required by those wishing to sell into formal sector outlets, such as packaging, hygiene certification and barcodes. This involved project staff introducing service providers to its clients and persuading them of the economic viability of supplying on a smaller scale than they had done previously. Sustainable linkages have been created for the provision of each of these services, with no ongoing intermediation role for SITE: some 150 of SITE's client producers now purchase packaging and labelling services, while around 50 regularly employ standards certification officers. This has given client enterprises an unprecedented level of access to large-scale, formal sector outlets.

Each of the projects has also been involved in facilitating the opening of specialist retail outlets to market the products of their client producers. This was a key component of the shift by AKILI and USSIA to a more market-driven approach. In both these cases, the shops established by the projects took over from project staff the provision of market information, technical training, quality control and credit (where relations of trust had developed) as well as market access.

In addition to the establishment of shops, three of the initiatives have also facilitated the opening of retail outlets by others as a means of enhancing their clients' market exposure. SEEDS' Banking Division has provided loans to three traders (who are also SEEDS clients) to establish shops in local trading centres. The condition is set on these loans that at least 50 per cent of the stock held in the shops for the first year must come from SEEDS client enterprises. There are plans for the establishment of at least one such shop in each of the 18 districts that SEEDS operates in. AKILI also provided loans to two promising, young entrepreneurs to help them establish marketing outlets.

Each of the projects has additionally encouraged 'star' clients – those that are relatively sophisticated and well-connected or who occupy a key position in the production and marketing chain – to play a greater marketing role. Larger-scale, formal sector buyers are generally reluctant to take part in the time-consuming and often fraught rituals that tend to be associated with sourcing goods from the small-scale sector; they are much more inclined to identify a trustworthy entrepreneur who they know to be capable of producing to order and on schedule. These clients win (often relatively large) orders and assume responsibility for identifying others to subcontract to, training and supervising them and undertaking final delivery of the order.

Several of SITE's 'star' food-processing clients market the produce of other small producers under the brand names they have created with the help of the project. USSIA provides its 'stars' with a training of trainers course and involves them as assistants in technical training sessions taught by its specialists. Several courses have since been taught by the 'stars' unaided by USSIA, with full costs paid by participating small producers. Each of the projects also encourages their 'star' clients to buy mobile telephones as a way of retaining easy contact with their customers, and this has proved hugely effective in the development of buyer–supplier linkages.

For SITE, capacity-building of producer associations is another important strategy for linking up many small producers to higher value markets in a cost-effective way. By the end of the project, assistance had been provided to 11 associations, nine of which were helped to establish marketing committees. Services provided by these associations include:

- organizing trade fairs and exhibitions (undertaken by seven associations);
- opening retail outlets to market the goods of association members (three associations);
- bulk production of promotional materials (one association); and
- joint sourcing of orders through establishing contact with salesmen (one association).

Co-operative marketing facilitated by these associations has been important in helping small producers to meet large orders, beyond the capacity of any individual producer to service. Small-scale furniture-makers and the producers of food products such as fruit juice, dairy products and jam have been helped in this way to win and service orders from schools, restaurants and hotels.

Figure 10.1 illustrates how the various approaches explored by the profiled projects create sustainable linkages between their client producers and 'distant' non-traditional, higher-value markets. For ease of interpretation, the diagram somewhat exaggerates the role of 'star' producers and 'link persons': not all orders and sales pass through them. However, this does serve to highlight the increasingly pivotal role that they play.

Analysis

These various approaches represent not so much 'best practice' in the area of marketing support to small producers in distant markets as interesting and innovative approaches that appear to varying degrees promising, but that need further testing and refinement. The sceptic would be correct in concluding that, with the exception of SEEDS, outreach has been modest and that, were the data available for the undertaking of rigorous benefit/cost analyses, these would be unlikely to be overly flattering for the projects concerned. Nonetheless, a number of interesting themes and findings emerge from these four initiatives that merit further examination.

The role of development organizations

There exists within the private sector strong capacity to deliver services that link small producers to higher-value markets. The projects profiled here deliver substantial evidence that the geographical, cultural and logistical gulfs separating small producers from the new, non-traditional, higher-value

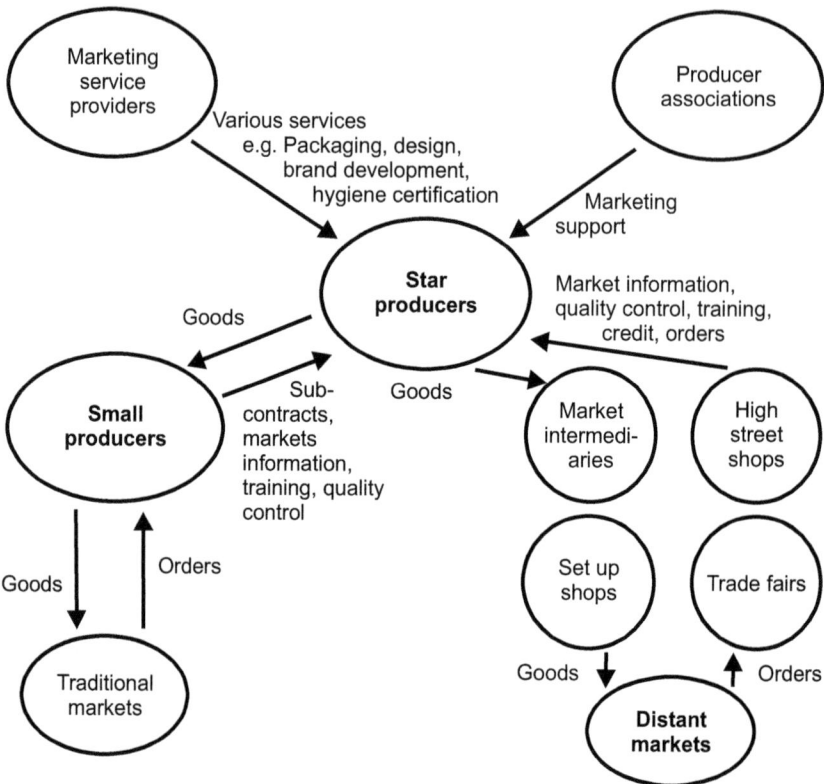

Figure 10.1 Creating linkages between small producers and 'distant' markets

markets opening up to them can be bridged. In fact, there was evidence in each case that, independent of the actions of development projects, private sector actors were already providing some market-linkage services – generally supplier–buyer and subcontracting arrangements – to easily accessible and well-placed small producers, services which the projects were able to build on in reaching less privileged small producers. This finding further confirms the view that there often exist networks of 'invisible' business development services provided by large businesses to small producers (see, for example, Anderson, 2000; Tanburn, 1999).

In each of the case studies, as a result of the services provided or facilitated by the projects, the quality of the products turned out by small enterprises or their packaging has improved substantially and consistently, to the point where they are attractive to customers purchasing from supermarkets and up-market shops. In addition, the 'transactional' practices of the small producers – to do with timeliness of delivery, transportation, invoicing, record-keeping and so on – have improved to the point that they satisfy the requirements of the various actors in the marketing chain: intermediary buyers, shop-keepers, traders, supermarkets and so on.

However, there continues to be a pivotal role for development organizations in facilitating these linkages. It is important not to lose sight of the limitations of the private sector in delivering the services required by small producers to penetrate higher-value markets. To begin with, the task of identifying market opportunities tends to fall to support organizations: as we have seen, small producers themselves, and even their associations, are generally too distant from such markets (especially where they are overseas) to be able to spot the opportunities.

Moreover, as a general rule, the capacity of small producers – both technically and organizationally – is often too weak for the private sector to gain much commercially in developing such linkages spontaneously. Each of the profiled projects invested heavily in upgrading clients' technical skills, while three of them (USSIA, SEEDS and SITE) also devoted much energy to strengthening group or association structures.

The point here is that while the private sector can be relied upon to provide training and other services that are specific to particular orders to relatively highly skilled and well-connected small producers, the job of upgrading producers' general skills and capacities to the point where they are able to meet these orders is likely to continue to require project interventions. This is especially true of relatively unsophisticated and poorly connected producers.

Co-operation among small producers

This is an important element of successful marketing strategies. The profiled projects include a number of different forms of co-operation among small producers in the production and marketing process. These include the establishment of central collection points and distribution systems; the appointment of 'link persons' at village level to liaise between producers and external buyers; the prominent role played by 'star' producers in winning orders and providing subcontracts, training and quality control services to peers and neighbours; the use of the brand identities developed by certain project clients to market the goods of many others; marketing services provided by producer associations; and the use of retail units established by some project clients to market the goods of others. The effectiveness of these mechanisms provides further proof of the importance of 'clustering' in enhancing the opportunities available to small producers and spreading the benefits to poorer and more disadvantaged segments within the sector (Clara et al., 2000; Nadvi et al., 1994).

These forms of co-operation have proved to be a key element of efforts to bridge the divide between small producers and non-traditional, higher value markets. Moreover, it is in such forms of co-operation that appear to lie the seeds of cost-effective service delivery. That is, the identification of key small enterprises capable of playing a catalytic role within the sector holds out the potential for support organizations to effect beneficial, sector-wide changes with limited and affordable interventions.

Poverty impact

The factors governing the likely poverty impact of market linkage projects are complex. There is controversy over the degree to which the market is able to deliver business development services that will bring benefits to relatively poor and marginalized people. That is, it has been clear for some time that the private sector can find it commercially attractive to deliver a range of services to more sophisticated enterprises (some of which are, in turn, better equipped to deliver goods and services to poor people). However, its ability to reach beyond this segment of the enterprise population and to have a significant poverty-related impact beyond the small enterprise sector has been called into question.

Each of the profiled projects has unquestionably had some beneficial impact on poor people. Most of the client enterprises that SEEDS works with, for example, are owned (often as one-person businesses) by poor, rural entrepreneurs: during 1999/2000, 2,416 poor, rural people (approximately 65 per cent of them women) enjoyed increased sales resulting from linkages to large-scale buyers brokered by SEEDS. USSIA too has achieved some success in terms of outreach: some 521 generally poor handicraft workers, 93 per cent of whom are women, derived some benefit from improved market access. Similarly, SITE's PMTS project has opened up new markets for poor people providing raw materials to the food-processing enterprises it assists, most of them women.

On the other hand, AKILI and USSIA in every sector other than handicrafts had a more limited impact in terms of poverty alleviation. In each of the other sectors in which USSIA was active – woodwork, metalwork and ceramics – impact was modest and tended to accrue primarily to a group of around 37 'star' producers and their employees. A similar picture emerges for AKILI, where it was unquestionably the 17 most sophisticated and wealthiest enterprises (out of a total of 330 that were trained) on which AKILI focused its efforts that enjoyed the lion's share of the benefits. It is important to recognize, however, that employment in enterprises owned by others is a preferable, and indeed often more secure, alternative to self-employment for many of the poorest people in the small enterprise sector, who lack financial resources, skills and contacts. In terms of understanding the poverty-related impact of small enterprise support interventions, two principal factors appear to be at work:
- *The technical difficulty of upgrading product quality or range required to access higher-value markets.* Small and unsophisticated enterprises are more likely to benefit from project interventions where the enhancement in product quality and range required is relatively minor. This is more likely to be true in, for example, food production, foodprocessing and handicrafts, where relatively small producers have much experience

(and in some cases, some natural advantages over larger competitors) than in, say, sophisticated furniture, clothing or metal items for middle-class markets. This explains why significantly more handicrafts than ceramics, woodwork and metalwork enterprises were able to adopt the new designs and products introduced by USSIA.
- *The potential for poverty-related ripple benefits.* Certain types of intervention enjoy significantly greater potential than others for leverage: that is, for delivering benefits to poor people beyond direct project clients, either upstream, downstream or among those benefiting from increased opportunities for subcontracting or for the imitation of goods introduced by the project.

   The potential for upstream and downstream benefits varies greatly between sectors and types of intervention. For example, enhanced market access for small-scale producers of ceramics, processed foods or handicrafts products is likely to create increased demand for clay, agricultural produce and the many materials used in handicrafts manufacture, which are often gathered by poor people. In other sectors, such as woodwork and metalwork, the likely poverty impact is much reduced, as poor people tend to have less involvement in the gathering and distribution of the raw materials used. Similarly, in terms of downstream benefits, interventions aimed at producing and distributing capital goods for microenterprises or at increasing the supply of foodstuffs at village level, for example, offer more scope for poverty impact than, say, those promoting the manufacture of consumer goods for middle-class markets or any product for export.

Figure 10.2 attempts to categorize the four projects according to these two variables. It can be seen that in the case of SEEDS, relative ease of technical upgrading (clients continue to be involved primarily in relatively simple agricultural, food-processing and handicraft activities) together with relatively strong potential for ripple benefits (backward linkages to the suppliers of agricultural products and raw materials for handicrafts) combine to create high potential for poverty-alleviation.

At the opposite end of the graph, USSIA, and to an even greater degree AKILI, can be seen to be battling with relatively difficult technical upgrading (high-quality wooden, metal and ceramics goods) and limited potential for upstream benefits (poor people have little involvement in the supply of metal and wood) or downstream benefits (products are primarily consumer goods for middle-class, tourist and export markets). Where potential did exist for poverty-related backward linkages (as in the case of the handicrafts and ceramics made by USSIA's clients, and hyacinth fibre products promoted by AKILI), a significantly greater increase in turnover than was achieved would have been required for these two projects to deliver substantial benefits to a large number of poor people.

SITE falls somewhere between these two poles, with relatively strong potential for upstream benefits (increased demand for agricultural produce)

108 VALUE CHAINS IN DEVELOPMENT

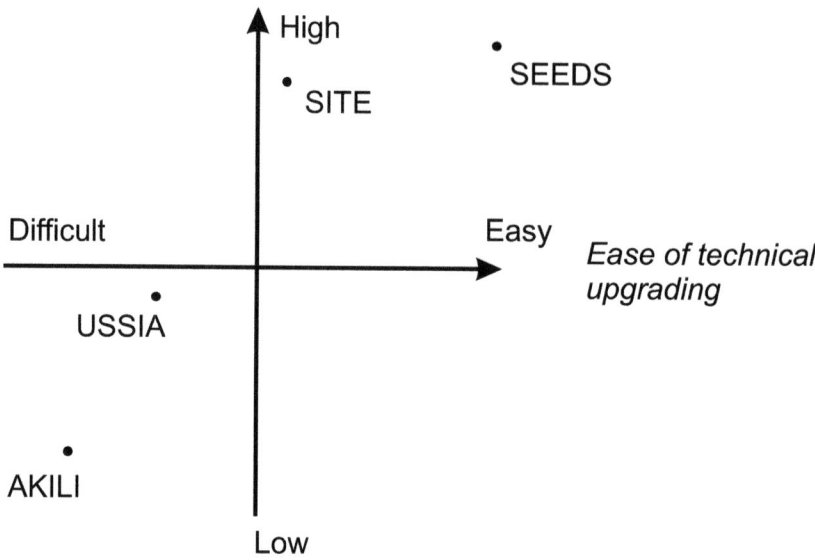

Figure 10.2. Categorization of projects according to potential ripple benefits and difficulty of technical upgrading.

but significant difficulties involved in the enhancement of many of the products involved, especially for the food products needing certification to be acceptable to supermarkets.

In sum, it is simplistic to argue in absolute terms either that market-driven approaches to small enterprise support are compatible with poverty alleviation or that they are not. A more accurate conclusion would be that while the market can deliver benefits to the poor, this is likely to be true only in certain specific circumstances.

Cost-recovery mechanisms

The most common mechanism for client payment for services was by way of mark-ups and commissions. That is, the costs of the various services provided were embedded in the mark-ups charged by the buyer, i.e. the difference between the price paid to the producer and that charged to the consumer. This form of payment for services has two merits from the point of view of the producer: it reduces risk and eases working capital constraints, in that there is no payment for services until sales are made. Moreover, it promotes sustainability in that it mimics mainstream private sector practice. In fact, in each of the profiled projects, these 'payments' are today made to the private sector operators who have taken over service provision from the projects.

Conclusion

There is much in the experience of the profiled projects to validate the emerging new paradigm for the support of small enterprise development, as described in the Donor Committee's *Guiding principles for donor interventions* (Committee of Donor Agencies for Small Enterprise Development, 2001). Each of the projects has enjoyed significant success in building markets for the provision of business development services; facilitating an increase in demand on the part of small producers for a range of services sourced from various, competing private sector providers. Each has also demonstrated that models and services pioneered by donor-funded initiatives can be transferred to private sector operators, illustrating the usefulness of the BDS facilitator/provider distinction.

Moreover, project experience confirms, to some degree at least, the assertion of the *Guiding principles* that, 'with appropriate product design, delivery and payment mechanisms, BDS can be provided on a commercial basis even for the lowest-income segment of the entrepreneurial small enterprise sector'.

Two caveats, however, are in order. First, as just noted, the circumstances under which the poor are likely to derive substantial benefit from BDS interventions are specific and limited: where only a relatively modest upgrading in technical quality is required or where there is significant potential for ripple benefits.

Second, while the *Guiding principles* acknowledge that there may be a difference between 'real needs' and 'perceived needs' and notes the problems associated with willingness-to-pay in the context of unknown services, a strong assumption runs through the document that the selection of BDS should be based on what 'small enterprises are aware of, currently want and are willing to pay for' rather than what external support agencies might suppose to be in their interests.

Laudable though this assertion appears to be, it sits uneasily with the experience of the four profiled projects. This is because, as noted above, many small producers tend to be both too distant from high-value, non-conventional markets to be able to spot new emerging opportunities; and lacking in the knowledge and the resources necessary to exploit such opportunities. This necessarily leaves small producer support agencies to play a leading role, both in identifying market opportunities and in designing and implementing project interventions.

The greater the distance between the market and the small producer, the greater the leading role that support agencies are likely to have to play. Yet, as we have seen, it is often in such 'distant' markets that many of the greatest opportunities are emerging as a result of the trends inherent in liberalization and globalization. Moreover, it is in just such markets that relatively small and unsophisticated enterprises (in which poor and marginalized people tend to be disproportionately represented) are also often most active.

This suggests that there may be a need to look beyond the 'growth enterprises', so central to the vision of the *Guiding principles*, that are seen to be freely making their own decisions about which BDS to purchase and at what price; and to give greater consideration to the different characteristics and needs of 'growth sectors', in which large numbers of enterprises – both stars and smaller, less sophisticated producers – are active and in which support agencies need to play a more interventionist role.

The challenge here is to look beyond minimalist interventions aimed at star producers able to pay for the services provided; and to take a more systems-oriented approach, seeking to identify more ambitious and comprehensive interventions that will deliver benefits more widely throughout the sector concerned. The 'sub-sector analysis' literature provides comprehensive theoretical and practical information on this (see, for example, Haggblade and Gamser, 1991; Buckley, 1999).

Substantial geographical, cultural and logistical gulfs need to be bridged for small producers to be able to exploit the numerous market opportunities emerging as a result of the processes inherent in liberalization and globalization. The four profiled projects have pioneered a number of interesting and innovative approaches, demonstrating in the process that the new, non-conventional, higher-value markets are potentially within the reach of small producers, given appropriate project design and implementation. Further work is now required to develop and refine these approaches.

References

Anderson, G. (2000) 'Business services for small enterprises in Asia: developing markets and measuring performance', Donor committee international conference on BDS in Hanoi.

Bagachwa, M.S.D. (1991) 'Choice of technology in industry: the economics of grain-milling in Tanzania', IDRC, Ottowa.

Buckley, G. (1999) 'Understanding the informal sector using sub-sector analysis', *Development in Practice,* Vol. 7, No. 4, Oxford.

Clara, M., F. Russo and M. Gulati (2000) 'Cluster development and BDS promotion: UNIDO's experience in India', Donor Committee International Conference on BDS in Hanoi.

Committee of donor agencies for small enterprise development (2001) 'Business development services for small enterprises: guiding principles for donor intervention', Washington DC.

de Crombrugghe, A. and J.C. Montes (2000) *UNIDO's experience on industrial subcontracting and partnership*, UNIDO.

Dawson, J. (1991) 'The development of small-scale industry in Ghana: a case study of Kumasi', in H. Thomas et al. (eds) *Small-scale strategies for industrial restructuring*, ITDG Publishing.

Grey-Johnson (1992) 'The African informal sector at the crossroads: emerging policy options', *Africa Development*, Vol. XVIII, No. 1.

Haggblade, S. and M. Gamser (1991) *A field manual for sub-sector practitioners*, GEMINI.

Heierli, U. (1999) 'Marketing and the development of an effective strategy for poverty alleviation with and through the private sector: a study of five SDC projects in Latin America', Donor committee international conference on BDS in Rio.

King, K. (1997) Growing up, but will the informal sector mature?, *Appropriate Technology*, Vol. 24, No. 1.

Lessard, G. (1992) *Le secteur industriel au Mali: reponses a l'ajustement*, CIDA, Ottawa.

McVay, M. (2000) 'SME marketing programs: trends, lessons learned and challenges identified from an analysis using the BDS performance measurement framework', Donor committee international conference on BDS in Hanoi.

Meagher, K. and M.B. Yunusa (1992) 'Limits to labour absorption: conceptual and historical background to adjustment in Nigeria's urban informal sector', UNRISD, Geneva.

Mikkelsen, L. (1999) 'Good practice in marketing MSE products: cases from Latin America', Donor committee international conference on BDS in Rio.

Nadvi, Khalid and H. Schmitz (1994) *Industrial clusters in less developed countries: review of experiences and research agenda*, IDS Discussion Paper 339, Institute of Development Studies, University of Sussex, England.

Onvango, M. (1998) 'The experience of ZIWA's designs in marketing MSE products in Kenya', Donor committee international conference on BDS in Harare.

Tanburn, J. (1999) 'A market-based approach to business development services: insights on sustainability gained in the FIT Project', ILO.

About the author

Jonathan Dawson is now a sustainability educator based at the Findhorn Foundation in Scotland, and President of the Global Ecovillage Network.

CHAPTER 11

Value chain programmes to integrate competitiveness, economic growth and poverty reduction

Olaf Kula, Jeanne Downing and Michael Field

This article was first published in June 2006.

Abstract

Identifying particular value chains that have the potential to compete globally should boost output and incomes. The challenge is to achieve this in value chains incorporating large numbers of small firms and microenterprises, and who are also in a position to benefit. This paper offers a step-by-step practical guide to intervention design for achieving competitiveness that benefits the poor. First industries are selected with potential for competitiveness, then a value chain analysis is carried out. A strategy is developed to improve competitiveness and achieve an equitable distribution of benefits, and an action plan is devised to achieve this strategy. Finally a system of performance monitoring and impact assessment is needed to evaluate the effectiveness of interventions.

In a globalized economy, industrial competitiveness is critical to growth in efficiency, output and incomes. The challenge for donors and development practitioners is to develop interventions that contribute to growth in industries with the potential to be competitive in global markets in which significant numbers of small firms and microenterprises participate. This approach to industrial competitiveness both fosters growth and reduces poverty.

Competitiveness is a process. No firm can remain competitive after only once increasing its efficiency, improving product quality and differentiation and exploiting new demand. Markets change, new entrants appear, margins decrease, new technologies are introduced, and consumer demand shifts. Programmes must create a process for industry participants to remain competitive as conditions evolve.

Successful development programmes often bear little resemblance to their original design. Responding to the local environment helps ensure the initial design's appropriateness and relevance, but flexible implementation is critical to success. Programme design is more art than science. The best approach is often to pursue a systematic design, while embracing the art by being flexible and modifying implementation based on lessons learned.

Approach and methodology

The overarching goal of programme intervention is to increase industry growth while assuring poverty reduction. Intervention strategy begins with a competitive analysis of targeted markets. The Value Chain Approach assesses the constraints to and opportunities for enhancing competitiveness using a diagnostic framework with six elements:

End markets. End market demands determine product or service characteristics and drive quality and standards. Analysis of end markets must demonstrate competitiveness potential.

Enabling environment. Trade agreements and standards affect constraints and opportunities for industries' growth. Both present opportunities for market expansion, but both can be expensive for MSEs and can easily preclude a developing country from being competitive.

Vertical linkages. These relate input supply and final market distribution, and are critical for moving a product from inception to market and for transferring learning and services up and down the value chain.

Horizontal linkages. Linkages among producers reduce the transaction costs of exporters or local buyers working with many small suppliers. By allowing for bulk transactions, horizontal linkages generate economies of scale, contributing to small firms' competitiveness and bargaining power.

Win–win relationships among firms can result in the vertical and horizontal co-operation needed to reduce transaction costs, achieve scale, and create incentives for adopting more value-added functions. Win–win relationships among vertically related firms can improve MSEs' access to new markets, new skills and better services.

Supporting markets. Supporting markets are key to firm-level upgrading and include sector-specific markets, financial services, business management services and information technology (particularly market information). Over the long run, these services must be provided by markets. Services can be provided by actors in the chain, or by stand-alone providers. Services provided by actors in the chain – such as input suppliers – tend to be embedded, with the cost of the service embedded in the product price. New technologies or technical services can have a substantial effect on industry competitiveness.

Firm-level upgrading. Individual enterprises improve competitiveness by producing more efficiently or improving product quality and differentiating it from competitors' products. Continual upgrading of product and process meets the market's demand for innovation. Within a value chain, learning and innovation are tied to incentives that encourage or discourage knowledge and skills transfer. For firms and value chains to innovate, learning mechanisms are needed to push new skills and know-how from where it is located within the chain to where it is needed. Value chains that institutionalize these learning mechanisms are the most competitive.

The value chain assessment approach to programme design has five steps:
1. Select industries with potential for competitiveness, employment growth, MSE participation and cross-cutting objectives.
2. Conduct a value chain analysis of the factors influencing competitiveness to identify interventions to create industry competitive advantage.
3. Develop a participatory competitiveness strategy in which stakeholders sustain competitiveness and equitable benefit distribution, while donor interventions minimize adverse market distortions.
4. Develop an implementation action plan that provides practical guidance on how to initiate a competitiveness strategy.
5. Establish a performance monitoring and impact assessment system to evaluate the effectiveness of interventions.

Step one: industry selection

Industry selection identifies industries with the potential to generate a return to donor investments as well as impact on employment, incomes and cross-cutting issues.

Competitiveness potential. The ability to sustain increases in efficiency, product differentiation and access to new demand or markets are the most important criteria in industry selection. Private sector leadership is critical: entrepreneurs must have the incentives, vision and commitment to address constraints and drive upgrading investments, while recognizing small firms' key role.

Impact. Growth in industries with high employment or levels of MSE participation are key to reducing poverty and optimizing growth with equity. Assessing impact and the multiplier effect requires data on employment, growth, regional and global competitors and changes in demand.

Cross-cutting issues. Governments and donors often have multiple objectives. For some donors economic growth is the end, for others it is a means to increased health, gender equity, poverty reduction, increasing bio-diversity or sustaining environmental resources. In many countries, economic growth and poverty reduction programmes must consider the impact of HIV/AIDS. Cross-cutting criteria should be applied after industries are screened for their growth with equity potential, without which investment gains will be unsustainable.

Table 11.1 summarizes frameworks used to assess industry competitiveness. Assessment can combine elements from multiple frameworks.

Given the critical link between competitiveness and sustainable growth, it is ill advised to cut costs during the assessment stage. Cost and accuracy trade-offs and the subjective nature of assessing competitiveness potential argue for considering multiple factors, including information from key informants, especially buyers who track global markets. Box 11.1 gives an example of selecting suitable industries in Zambia.

Table 11.1 Competitiveness assessment tools

Tool	Description	Strengths	Weaknesses
Labour-adjusted contribution to GNP	Contribution to GNP/percent of work force employed in sector	Quick measure of relative importance and potential employment effect	Does not measure competitiveness or directly consider global competitors; assesses past, not potential sector importance
Boston Matrix	Assesses local growth and market share against global market growth	Quick proxy for detailed tools; uses data from secondary sources	Does not directly address competitiveness; based on history, not potential
Porter's Five Forces and Porter's Diamond Framework	Based on five factors critical for an industry to become and remain competitive	Based on factors influencing industry competitiveness; assessment suggests location of driving constraints to industry competitiveness	Complicated, takes time; substantial analysis precedes industry selection
End market informants	Interviews with high-value end-market buyers regarding future trends and procurement strategies	End markets define opportunities; global buyers know competition, factors and trends that influence markets-information that is critical to assessing competitiveness	Requires knowledge of end market buyers; is not available in-country; subjective
Investor road	Maps opportunities, constraints and investment risks, emphasizing enabling environment and quality of infrastructure and services	Complementary to value chain analysis, high level of detail on identified opportunities and constraints	Costly; does not consider efficiency from vertical and horizontal co-ordination; does not consider global competition

There are a number of common mistakes in the process of selecting industries:
- selecting a donor's or policy maker's favourite can result in sub-optimal growth;
- selecting industries based on temporary trade policies can have unsustainable results;
- selecting an industry employing the poor but with no growth potential;
- selecting a high-growth industry but with little potential to generate broad growth and employment, for example, extractive industries;
- selecting an industry without comparing it to other industries that might have greater impact;

> **Box 11.1 Selecting industries in Zambia**
>
> In Zambia, USAID identified cotton, non-timber forest products (NTFPs), tourism, smallscale mining, high-value horticulture and livestock as having potential. Industry growth potential was based on market trends and Zambian capacity to organize an effective supply response to growing demand. Potential scale and impact were defined by the number of MSEs that could participate in and benefit from a growing industry, and by their potential income gains. Industry leadership was determined by lead firms' commitment to MSE upgrading and their commitment to growing the overall Zambian industry.
>
> Combining the three criteria, the potential of the six industries can be assessed to determine priority industries. Cotton and livestock provide the best potential for returns to investments, NTFPs and tourism also provide reasonable potential, and high-value horticulture and small-scale mining have less potential, primarily due to poor leadership and inability to achieve scale.
>
> | Criteria | Cotton | Tourism | Livestock | NTFPs | High-value horticulture | Small-scale mining |
> |---|---|---|---|---|---|---|
> | Growth | High | High | High | High | High | Medium |
> | Scale | High | Medium | High | Medium | Medium | Low |
> | Leadership | High | High | High | High | Medium | Medium |
> | Consolidated | High | Medium-high | High | Medium-high | Medium | Low-medium |

- overlooking external threats, i.e. not considering competitors from other countries;
- prioritizing cross-cutting criteria over competitiveness, which can result in investment in industries that are unable to sustain employment growth;
- selecting an industry where there is already significant investment regardless of its potential;
- adding complexity where it does not add value. Too detailed selection processes can defeat the purpose of the value chain analysis.

Step two: analyse value chains and identify interventions

Value chain analysis examines activities required to bring a product or service from conception to end markets, and helps design interventions to increase competitiveness. An ideal assessment team has a leader skilled in value chain analyses, an industry expert with private sector experience, and two to four members trained in information collection and value chain analysis. Value chain analysis has five steps:

Data collection. Collect secondary data about the value chain, including participants, factors affecting industry performance-enabling environment; end markets; supporting markets; inter-firm horizontal and vertical linkages; and firm-level product and process upgrading. The framework provides a structure for organizing data, analysing constraints, opportunities, and interventions. The team interviews value chain participants, including global

118 VALUE CHAINS IN DEVELOPMENT

> **Box 11.2 Value chain analysis from Mozambique**
>
> Mozambique's oilseeds sub-sector consists of input suppliers, smallholder producers, commercial producers, processors, wholesalers and retailers, with the feed industry becoming an important player. Four large input suppliers provide seed and chemicals to producers through rural stockists, farmer associations or directly. These farmers produce sunflower or sesame that they market through farmers' associations or sell directly to traders such as V&M Trading Company. V&M processes its own oil; Optima Industrial and smaller processors process oil from sunflower and sesame purchased from smallholder associations. The oil is then sold to wholesalers, and finally makes its way to the Chimoio area retail market. The byproduct of oil processing, called oilcake, is sold to millers in Beira for poultry (and potentially livestock) feed.

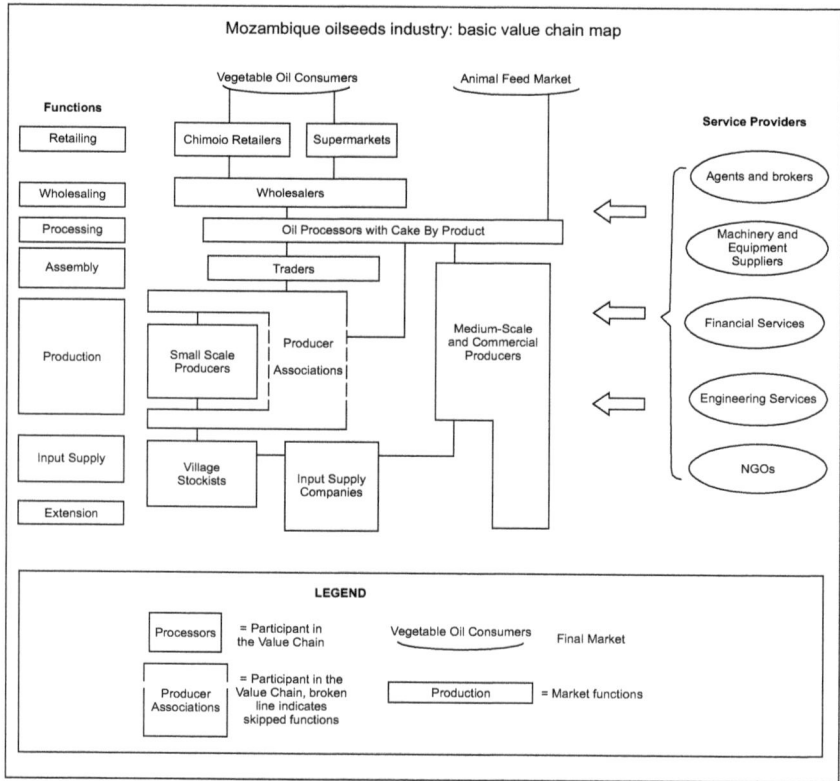

Figure 11.1 Value chain map of Mozambique oilseeds industry (Kula and Farmer, 2004)

buyers and industry experts to identify the value chain structure, participant perceptions of opportunities and constraints, and the extent of learning and benefit flows to participants.

Value chain mapping. The map depicts structure and functions and illustrates relationships between firms. The structure typically includes industry market segments, their relative importance and growth rates, the channels (supply chains) serving those markets, and the number of firms in each channel. The simplified map of the Mozambique oilseeds industry (Figure 11.1) illustrates these key functions. Creating the value chain map draws from sub-sector mapping techniques.

Analysis of constraints and opportunities. First, the dynamic factors and trends affecting performance and competitiveness are identified. The relationships between value chain participants are then examined, focusing on how these relationships affect access to information, learning and benefits. As opportunities for increased efficiency or improved product quality become apparent, it is then possible to identify who has the incentives to exploit these opportunities.

Vetting findings. Value chain analysis helps develop a private sector vision for greater competitiveness. A workshop is then held with stakeholders to vet the analysis and identify opportunities.

Identification of potential interventions. After vetting opportunities and constraints, a short list of those having the greatest impact on industry performance and competitiveness is developed. Stakeholders then identify competitive strategies and action plans. Activities should include only those that can be implemented by industry stakeholders, assumed by stakeholders after initial facilitation, or 'one-off' activities that will not require ongoing subsidy.

The mistakes to be avoided at this stage include:
- Failure to consider end-user requirements. Stakeholders will find detailed information on returns, costs, and prices of little value because they already know this. Policy makers will be frustrated by a focus on relationships among firms and areas where there are inefficiencies or failures in meeting market requirements, without price and cost information.
- Assuming a fixed industry structure and static stakeholder relationships, when these can all change in response to opportunities or external competition.
- Inattention to learning and information flows, and to relationship dynamics. Competitive industries require efficient, accurate and rapid information and learning flows from consumer to producer. Performance is based on relationships among firms, and power over terms of trade affects access to learning, the information needed to innovate and benefit flows.

- Missing factors. External end markets are often ignored. Analysis must capture the extent to which weak service markets constrain industry performance.
- Failure to verify data. Data should be checked for plausibility.
- Failure to filter constraints. Long unfiltered lists of constraints are data, not information. Constraints must be filtered by their impact on competitiveness, increased efficiency etc.
- Confusing what must be done to increase competitiveness with who has the incentives and capacity to do it. Donors may be tempted to figure out what to do and just do it. Analysis should identify constraints and opportunities without addressing who will fix the problem, which should evolve and be private sector driven.

Step three: develop an industry competitiveness strategy

Once interventions are identified, they should be filtered through a competitiveness lens. Designing a competitiveness strategy for industries with high MSE participation has three stages: identifying and establishing competitive advantage; developing a commercial upgrading strategy; and creating a process to sustain competitiveness.

Identifying and establishing competitive advantage. Consumer demand for a product or service and industry dynamics (leadership, organization, transparency, inter-firm co-operation) determine whether and how an MSE-dominated industry can create competitive advantage. Creating competitive advantage requires stakeholder investments in upgrading. The challenge is to identify stakeholders who have the incentives to create competitive advantage while ensuring the participation of micro and small firms.

Helping stakeholders identify a competitive advantage strategy must be participatory. Such a strategy is not proprietary, so broad participation builds buy-in by stakeholders and demonstrates that success depends on collaboration. The challenge is to convince value chain participants that they alone cannot create competitive advantage. This is best done by involving them in evaluating threats, substitutes, market share, market size and industry trends.

Developing a commercial upgrading strategy. Industries must resolve key constraints and take advantage of opportunities to make competitive advantage pay off. A commercial upgrading strategy – an action plan based on understanding the entire value chain – is a vision of achieving greater competitiveness by overcoming constraints in end markets, the enabling environment, horizontal and vertical inter-firm co-operation, and support services. Industry upgrading strategies can be developed with broad participation of stakeholders or with smaller numbers around a specific constraint.

Creating a process to sustain competitiveness. Achieving and sustaining growth requires participants to respond to changing market conditions, and requires strategic co-operation among industry leaders. An effective response requires transparency and improvements in industry relationships, rewards for learning and innovation and distributing benefits from upgrading. An efficient response requires inter-firm co-ordination and external economies from both vertical and horizontal relationships.

In globalized economies, firm and industry competitiveness are linked and require co-ordination among industry stakeholders. Facilitation techniques that emphasize short-term win–win activities and build on these to develop an industry vision for competitiveness can be effective. The following principles can be useful in facilitation.

- Build trust by rewarding collective action among stakeholders. Where there is little collective action, trust-building activities must focus on short-term results that benefit all.
- Move from activities to vision. As stakeholders recognize the value of co-ordination even while competing, facilitators should encourage longer-term activities including advocacy to improve the enabling environment. Once inter-firm co-ordination results in strong associations, facilitators can help generate a vision for change.
- Continue to address the business enabling environment. In the short-term, businesses can grow rapidly even in difficult business environments. However, industry competitiveness cannot be sustained without a strong, supportive, transparent business enabling environment that facilitates upgrading investments by innovative firms.

Developing and sustaining competitiveness is based on sound value chain analysis, participatory facilitation, and knowing where to start based on industry leadership and inter-firm co-ordination. Competitiveness assessment yields the information needed to develop industry competitive advantage and upgrading strategies.

Participatory strategies bring together individuals with common and competing interests to develop a shared vision. SWOT (strengths, weaknesses, opportunities, and threats) analysis and constraints analysis can help participants agree on opportunities and constraints to realizing this common goal.

Constraints-driven analysis may be less useful in developing a vision because it focuses on what is, not what could be. Vision-focused techniques such as Appreciative Inquiry are used to develop visions and action plans, based on the premise that effective vision is grounded in what works now. Where there is not enough co-operation to develop a shared vision, facilitation should focus on short-term results and win–win activities to reinforce co-operation.

At this stage a number of pitfalls should be avoided:

- Failure to ensure that the vision is private sector-driven. Donors or NGOs are often tempted to drive competitiveness strategy without buy-in from private-sector stakeholders.

- Lack of consensus about industry vision. Creating a vision for a competitive industry that is acceptable to stakeholders is essential, but this challenge requires strong facilitation.
- Overly ambitious action plans can leave participants discouraged. Because building incentives and rewarding co-operation are key to building competitive industries, it is essential that action plans be realistic with clear short-term gains.
- NGO/contractor provides services with inadequate exit strategy. Though NGOs and contractors should only facilitate service delivery, it makes sense to provide services where service markets are weak and the time needed to build local capacity would retard the industry. However, contractors should identify a clear exit strategy that ensures the services will continue after the project ends.
- Failure to tap end market catalysts. Many markets have buyers with the skills and incentives to drive investments in upgrading by participants further down the value chain. If the process of developing a vision does not include end market buyers, the power of market catalysts to drive change will be lost.
- Underutilization of market incentives. Competitive industries rely on incentives for all stakeholders to work towards and benefit from the factors contributing to increased competitiveness, such as efficiency, product differentiation and increased demand.

USAID's review of competitiveness reveals some important lessons for competitiveness initiatives (USAID, 2003). First, the most important determinant of success is the 'sweat-equity' investment of the cluster. Secondly, successful initiatives are private sector driven with links to the public sector – and not public-sector driven with links to the private sector. Finally, cluster-based competitiveness initiatives are not a 'quick fix' solution: they involve major shifts in thinking and hence take time (see Box 11.3).

Box 11.3 Building an industry competitiveness strategy in the Dominican Republic

The participatory planning process is uniquely strong in the Dominican Republic, where USAID's assistance has focused on strategy development at the national, regional and cluster level. A participatory planning process built consensus on a National Competitiveness Strategy, followed by the development of two pilot strategies, one for Santiago and one for fruits and vegetables. Next, the team facilitated participatory planning sessions for tourism in Romana-Bayhibe and Puerto Plata and eco-tourism and horticulture in La Vega. Cluster members have been deeply involved in strategic planning, wrestling first-hand with the research, writing and the wording of their strategies. The strategies developed by the clusters were not that different from what the implementing contractor would have recommended. The process took longer than if the contractor had prepared the strategies itself. The key difference was that these were now strategies that the Dominicans had grappled with, vetted, internalized and 'owned'.

Step four: develop an implementation action plan

The implementation action plan clarifies the actions and process to implement interventions identified in step three and to increase competitiveness. Several principles guide the development of an implementation action plan.

Keep industry stakeholders in the driver's seat. Establishing and sustaining industry competitiveness must be driven by industry stakeholders, principally from the private sector.

Start where the industry is, not where it needs to go. Successful development programmes consider stakeholder capacities and incentives and how they can drive the intervention strategy. For example, are there lead firms ready to upgrade and drive upgrading investments? Is firm behaviour atomistic, or does some inter-firm co-operation already exist?

Figure 11.2 illustrates how knowledge about market structure and interfirm conduct help put value chain competitiveness strategy into action. The top right quadrant illustrates a mature, competitive industry with lead firms where multiple firms value collective action, stakeholders strategize about sustaining competitiveness, and industry leaders take initiative and drive upgrading investments throughout the value chain. The top left quadrant suggests a less mature industry with no market leader, but with inter-firm co-operation, where interventions help identify threats and develop a competitiveness vision, and might include support for industry and trade associations, advocacy, or deepening service markets to reach smaller enterprises. The lower left quadrant reflects emerging industries, transitional economies and weak enabling environments with weak supply chains and high entry and exit rates,

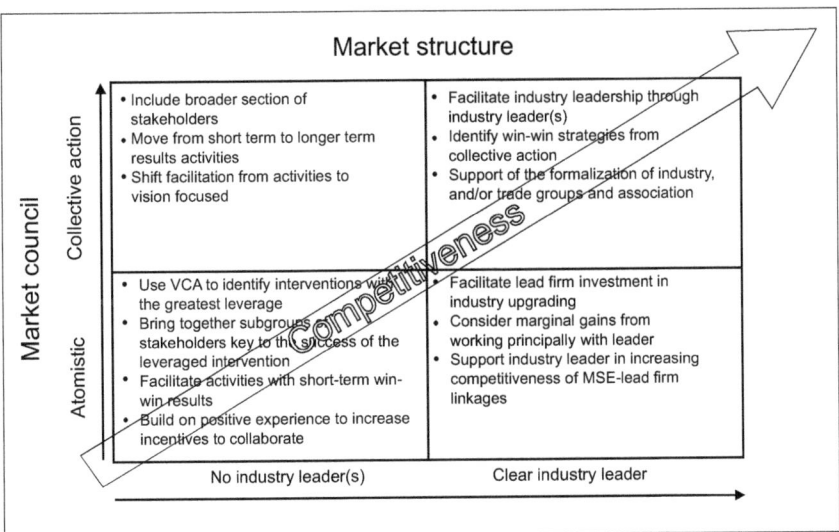

Figure 11.2 How market structure and co-operation affect competitiveness

entrepreneurs focusing on individual firms rather than the whole industry, weak linkages to higher value end markets, and few incentives for MSEs to upgrade. The bottom right quadrant describes industries where aggressive competition and innovation result in one or more firms emerging as industry leaders, either local firms or lead buyers in export markets. If a lead catalyst firm invests and drives upgrading investments by other firms, the immediate impact and demonstration effect may produce rapid change and innovation, leading to higher performance.

Relationships matter. An industry's ability to create value through increased efficiencies, product differentiation strategies and the exploitation of new demand depends on inter-firm relationships that are transparent and trust-based, where information flows facilitate rapid learning by essential participants and where the distribution of benefits is a win–win for all. Programme managers must work with stakeholders to achieve these goals.

Small firms can benefit from industry competitiveness strategies performing functions in which small firms have a comparative advantage, but projects should avoid encouraging MSEs to perform functions where they have no comparative advantage. Industries where small firms have a comparative advantage are characterized by: seasonal demand; low capital requirements; highly labour intensive; non-repetitive production processes that defy mechanization and small production volumes.

Successful implementation. Four activities are common in successful programmes where sustainability is a key goal.

- Develop a clear exit strategy and assess progress towards it. The importance of quick results when project life is short tempts donors to defer thinking about exit strategy and sustainability. Assessing progress towards the exit minimizes the risk that the industry cannot sustain services without subsidy.
- Remember the framework. The framework of factors that influence industry performance and the identification of constraints to competitiveness is a lens on the industry. Using this lens helps ensure that no critical factor is neglected.
- Develop a causal model linking proposed activities to expected outcomes and results. These links between project activities and expected impacts allow project managers to test proposed interventions in the context of expected impacts before implementation.
- Maintain flexibility within a systematic programme design process. Successful projects balance the advantages of flexibility in project management with a more systematic programme design approach. An example from Zambia illustrates this. For the cotton cluster in Zambia, commodity cotton may make sense for most firms, but the overall strategy may be strengthened if some firms develop niche lines such as organic or long-staple cotton. Industry-wide consensus is helpful when there are industry-wide threats or opportunities that require joint action, but this may not be the case for every market.

Regular discussions with stakeholders ensure ownership of the competitive strategy and assess project progress. Frequent site visits ensure that even small firms benefit from project interventions. Ensuring that implementation reflects the exit strategy and applies plausibility tests to project activities increases the likelihood of expected results. A monitoring and evaluation system to check project performance is essential (see step five).

Step five: monitor performance and assess impact

Figure 11.3 shows a causal chain for two smallholder tree fruit projects in Kenya. The far-left column has project activities, often involving facilitation of organizations that provide business services in market-friendly ways. The second column lists target outputs, which are often measures of service delivery by project-facilitated providers. The third column has immediate project consequences, known as outcomes or results. The furthest right column lists expected impacts. Typically, a project will try to increase the competitiveness of the entire value chain as well as MSE participation in sub-sector activities. It may also aim to expand employment or reduce the number of people living in poverty. In such projects, impacts are often sought at the value chain, enterprise and household levels.

Performance monitoring tracks the project as it is implemented so that interim results can be fed back to project managers and help them to make mid-course corrections. Performance monitoring plans should be developed near the start of implementation so the variables to be tracked can be defined and baseline values measured. Performance monitoring usually emphasizes activities and outputs links in the causal chain. It follows project activities and service delivery to determine whether they are going as planned.

Impact assessment develops information that will both prove that the project achieved its desired results and improve approaches to private sector development programming (see Box 11.4). Impact assessment emphasizes higher-level results than performance assessment – impacts and outcomes – and it is better done by an independent body to achieve objectivity.

The best way to estimate impact is to compare changes during project life for a sample of project participants with changes for non-project people who are similar to the participants. However, unless participants are chosen at random from an eligible population, which is usually not practical, participants often differ from non-participants in relevant ways. Data from baseline and follow-up surveys must be analysed to account for these differences, which are known as selection bias. Another difficulty in assessing impact is that benefits spill over from participants to non-participants, as good news about increasing productivity and profits spread by informal means, increasing the effectiveness of the project but making its impact harder to measure.

This approach is harder to apply at the value chain (sub-sector) level because there is no appropriate comparison group. One can measure value chain growth and competitiveness, but attributing change to the project is

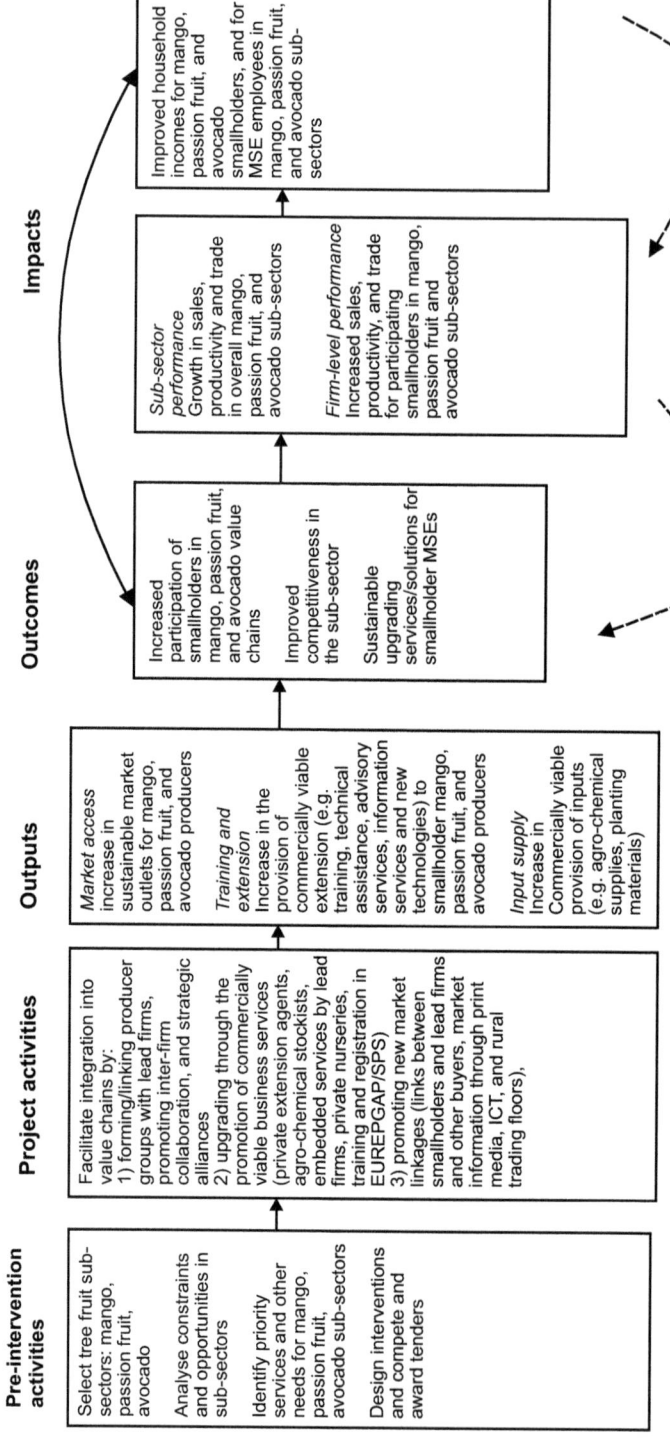

Figure 11.3. Casual model for Kenya BDS and FINTRAC HDC project

> **Box 11.4 Assessing the impact of USAID-Kenya's tree fruit projects**
>
> Impact assessments were conducted for Kenya Business Development Services (avocados, mangos and passion fruit) and the Horticulture Development Centre (HDC) project (passion fruit), evaluating the impact on value chain competitiveness, smallholder participation and benefits and rural household incomes. It included a baseline survey of nearly 2,000 smallholders in three provinces, and interviews and focus group discussions with more than 60 individuals.
>
> The business environment was characterized by the benign neglect of the Kenyan Government and a challenging international market. The tree fruit market data indicated that: all rural households have fruit trees, and most sell fruit, but few smallholders participate in export markets; Kenya is competitive in avocados, but not yet in mangos and passion fruit; smallholders rely on spot sales to brokers; and the East Africa Growers' Association (EAGA) is a model for linking smallholders to lead firms. For smallholders, contract sales are mainly in EAGA avocado and HDC passion fruit areas, and many farmers have recently improved cultivation and marketing methods. Among producer groups, there is nearly universal membership and high approval ratings among project participants, and membership is almost nil among non-participants. For households, where poverty was measured by asset scores and consumption levels, the K/BDS project reaches many poor and non-poor households, while HDC works with somewhat richer farmers; tree fruits are an important income source; and there is potential for raising household incomes among the poor and the non-poor.

challenging. Comparisons across regions, sub-sectors or countries may give some idea, but project impact at this level may be difficult to determine. Measuring impacts on markets poses similar difficulties.

Conclusions and challenges

Small firms can benefit from market globalization, they can upgrade and be important players in many value chains, and they can benefit from participating in these markets. Small firms in a wide range of product and service industries can both contribute to and benefit from overall industry competitiveness. In those industries, industry competitiveness and small firms' participation go hand-in-hand.

Projects can intervene in relationships just as they have intervened in more tangible factors that contribute to market failures. The challenge for implementing agencies is to create strategies for win–win relationships and incentives for small firm upgrading and risk-taking. Learning how to improve the competitiveness of industries made up of many small firms is an ongoing process. This paper is a basis for rethinking how best to move forward, and a rationale for a new direction for industry leaders, donors and practitioners as they test private sector market-based approaches to accelerate economic growth and poverty reduction. The challenge is to test these hypotheses and the limits of strategies to achieve both significant economic growth and poverty reduction.

References

Kula, Olaf and Elisabeth Farmer, (2004) 'Mozambique rural financial services study', Microcase Study No. 1, Accelerated Microenterprise Advancement Project.

USAID (2003) 'Promoting competitiveness in practice: an assessment of clusterbased approaches', prepared by The Mitchell Group, Inc., for the USAID.

About the authors

At the time of writing, Olaf Kula worked for ACDI/VOCA; Jeanne Downing worked for USAID and Michael Field worked for the Emerging Markets Group, and has since joined ACDI-VOCA in Liberia.

CHAPTER 12
From behind the veil: industry-level methodologies for disadvantaged communities in Pakistan

Linda M. Jones and Alexandra Snelgrove

This article was first published in June 2006.

Abstract

'Enterprise development' has evolved from the upgrading of individual businesses to the attempted advancement of entire industries using new approaches such as value chain development and making markets work for the poor. This change has resulted in an increased focus on macro-level issues such as enabling environments, trade agreements and national associations, and some policy makers question the relevance of programmes that target microenterprises. This paper presents the case of rural homebound women in Pakistan to illustrate that, although systemic analysis is essential to good programme design, projects that specifically target marginalized communities can produce significant results that would not be achievable through industry-level interventions alone. It provides an overview of MEDA's (Mennonite Economic Development Associates) work in Pakistan with sequestered women, a description of how the programme is attempting to integrate these homebound women into lucrative value chains, results of the programme to date, and conclusions relevant to the broader development industry.

In recent years, the field of 'enterprise development' has shifted from a focus on upgrading individual businesses – whether microenterprises themselves or the supporting firms that provide essential services – to the advancement of entire industries. Programmes have been designed to include hundreds and even thousands of producers who are being served by a wide range of competitive support services. Value chain development, making markets work for the poor and industry competitiveness are based on holistic views of economic systems that incorporate poor producers at the bottom of the supply chain. This approach is resulting in an increased focus on macro-level issues such as enabling environments, trade agreements, and national associations. Practitioners are wrestling with a host of critical challenges: for example, how can poor producers be integrated into global value chains and reach effective export markets if regulations and infrastructure are not supportive of this goal. As a result, some contributors to the development field are questioning the impact of activities that target producers at the microenterprise level. This position is manifested in strategies such as: strengthening of lead firms, streamlined export procedures, and improved standards at the processing level. Functioning as a kind of renewed trickle-down approach, higher level interventions are seen as having the potential to create wealth for all.

The authors do not question the need for interventions at various levels in market systems, particularly in environments that impede commerce and disrupt the flow of products to viable consumers. And, we fully endorse a comprehensive understanding of the industry and specific value chain in which one is intervening. However, we take a strong stand that direct engagement with marginalized communities must not be renounced for more glamorous interventions aimed at big business and government reform. Following a brief description of the evolution of the enterprise development field, this article presents the case of rural homebound women in Pakistan to illustrate that appropriate initiatives, focused at the producer level, can enable large numbers of disadvantaged people to become active partners in the development of a targeted industry.

Evolution of the enterprise development field

Since the inception of widespread microfinance initiatives in the late 1980s, microenterprises have had access to non-financial services such as business plan development and training. It was not until relatively recently, however, that these services became a distinct development field, established in response to the need for expanded support (McVay and Miehlbradt, 2002). In 1998, the Committee of Donor Agencies for Small Enterprise Development established a separate Business Development Services (BDS) working group, including agencies such as GTZ, ILO, SDC and DFID (Committee of Donor Agencies for Small Enterprise Development, 2001). Consistent with its roots, BDS was initially comprised of mainly training and technical assistance to address the internal business capacity of small enterprises. As firms began to demand additional products, the field evolved to encompass a wider array of services that helped entrepreneurs operate and grow their businesses, such as training on quality standards and control, product development and design, and market access and information (McVay and Miehlbradt, 2004). At this early stage, government agencies and NGOs were directly involved in the provision of BDS, either as providers or through subsidies for services delivered by other entities.

There was limited impact with this approach as outreach was restricted by the level of subsidies available, and underperforming commercial providers were crowded out of the market rather than upgraded as sustainable alternatives. The limitations of this model led to the emergence of the market development approach which focused on fostering vibrant BDS markets through the advancement of commercial providers. The role of government and NGOs in service delivery consequently evolved into that of facilitator, i.e. promoting the development of effective commercial and sustainable support markets (Committee of Donor Agencies for Small Enterprise Development, 2001). This shift also opened the BDS field to include an even richer range of services, such as infrastructure, product or technology development, market access, management and organization, policy, advocacy, and alternative finance for weak BDS markets. Initially, the facilitation approach was not as effective in reaching disadvantaged groups, causing further introspection by practitioners and, ultimately, greater progress in the field.

New methodologies, such as value chain analysis, have been developed to examine entire industries and identify leverage points to upgrade market players and improve their ability to participate in global markets. No longer stand-alone activities, BDS interventions are now part of larger market development programmes, viewed as one of many tools available for enterprise promotion (Miehlbradt and McVay, 2004). With this more holistic approach, greater emphasis is being placed on overall industry competitiveness with reduced attention to constraints and opportunities facing individual microenterprises. Agencies aim to address growth constraints by linking small enterprises to enhanced market opportunities, targeting entire sub-sectors or value chains, and focusing on higher level industry issues (USAID, 2005). Strategies, such as those that address supply chain efficiency or product differentiation, now centre on interventions that promote economic growth for entire industries based on a causal model that this expansion will improve opportunities for small enterprises.

MEDA's experience in Pakistan demonstrates that, while taking a systems perspective results in positive impact for disadvantaged populations, in certain circumstance, interventions must specifically target producers in order to achieve impact and realize the industry vision.

Rural women in Pakistan: extremes of marginalization

Poverty, illiteracy, remoteness and tradition combine to create some of the most marginalized communities in the world among rural women across Pakistan. For the past decade, 13.4 per cent of the population of Pakistan has survived on less than USD $1 per day, while almost two-thirds have lived on under $2 per day (United Nations, 2004). A significant percentage of the poor live in non-urban settings, with over 65 per cent of the total population residing in rural areas (United Nations, 2004). Contributing to rural poverty in Pakistan is an entrenched feudal system whereby large landowners benefit from agricultural production while tenant labourers live at a subsistence level. It is estimated that almost half of Pakistan's gross national product and the bulk of its export earnings are derived primarily from the agricultural sector, controlled by a few thousand feudal families (Shuja, 2000).

Women are effectively poorer than men, having little or no control over household income and, when engaged in paid employment, earn less than 35 per cent of the income of their male counterparts (United Nations, 2004). In fact, many rural women in Pakistan suffer from a triple burden of labour. We commonly hear of the double burden faced by women in poor agrarian societies: that is, while they have full responsibility for the home and children, they are a primary source of unpaid agricultural labour on the homestead or in the landowner's fields. In Pakistan, the FAO estimates that women engaged as unpaid family workers account for 25 per cent of all full-time and 75 per cent of all part-time agricultural labour (FAO website). Added to this, effectively creating a triple burden, women in rural Pakistan frequently supplement family income through handicraft piecework on commission for local middlemen.

Piecework is characterized by exceptionally low wages for long hours of work: for example, MEDA and its partner in Pakistan, ECDI (Entrepreneurship and Career Development Institute), have found that women earn as little as $1 for embroidering a complete woman's outfit that can take several days or even weeks to complete. Women around the world continue to produce piecework in their spare time, despite terribly low returns, as it is often the only way that they can augment poverty-level household income (Suich and Murphy, 2002).

Nationally, 65 per cent of women are illiterate (United Nations, 2004), with higher rates in rural areas: totalling 88 per cent across rural Pakistan, and climbing to over 93 per cent in Balochistan Province (ADB, 2000). Rural women are further isolated by remote living conditions in highly dispersed communities. Overall, the population is at approximately 166 people per square kilometre; while in Balochistan, the figure reaches a low of 19 people per square kilometre (Federal Bureau of Statistics website). Poor infrastructure heightens the geographic isolation of these communities. Only 56 per cent of the roads are paved in Pakistan, and there is a lack of access to communication technologies, with only 44.2 fixed line or mobile phones for every 1,000 people, and these are concentrated in urban centres (World Bank, 2004).

Conservative socio-cultural norms also contribute to the marginalization of women in Pakistan; this is particularly evident in impoverished rural areas such as interior Sindh. The UN Human Development Report rates Pakistan 107 out of 177 on the Gender-Related Development Index (United Nations, 2004). Despite their recent advancement to this mid-level ranking, the situation of poor women is dire. The condition of women's lives results in Pakistan having the lowest female sex ratio in the world with 105 men to every 100 women (CIA, 2004), and one of the highest maternal mortality rates (United Nations, 2004). But more significant in terms of economic development, communities of women are bound by traditional rules of purdah, confining them to the homestead and segregating them from the larger society. Home seclusion in rural areas ranges from approximately 50 to 95 per cent. (These estimates of home confinement rates are based on the experience of the MEDA and

ECDI, and other NGOs working in the region.) The economic impact of such isolation from the public arena is dramatic: with no knowledge of markets and consumer demand, and limited options for gainful employment, women are denied the opportunity to contribute their human capital to the economic development of their families, communities and nation.

Overview of MEDA's work in Pakistan

In 2000, the Aga Khan Foundation commissioned MEDA to carry out a study (Sauder and Shaikh, 2000) that would determine the feasibility of a marketing initiative for women entrepreneurs engaged in a range of handicraft production activities across Pakistan. MEDA partnered with Entrepreneurship and Career Development Institute (ECDI), a Pakistani NGO, to complete the research work. This collaboration allowed MEDA to leverage ECDI's extensive experience and network amongst women microentrepreneurs, NGOs and government agencies throughout the country. The study took economic, political, social and financial factors into consideration, and concluded with recommendations on the scope, size and institutional arrangements for the initiative.

Following on this feasibility study, MEDA and ECDI undertook a USAID-funded Small Enterprise and Education Promotion Network project under its Practitioner Learning Programme to analyse the availability of support services to women microentrepreneurs in Pakistan. The research focused on three sub-sectors in selected regions: urban and peri-urban garment manufacturers in Karachi, Lahore and Quetta; rural handicraft producers in Sindh, Balochistan and Punjab; and urban information technology entrepreneurs in Karachi and Islamabad (Jones and Shaikh, 2003). During the market assessment, MEDA and ECDI discovered a fourth industry with significant unrealized commercial potential that crossed both the garment and handicraft sub-sectors: embroidered garments. Findings revealed that there is a growing market amongst middle-class Pakistani women in urban centres who seek out quality hand-embroidered garments in contemporary styles, and are willing to pay a premium for these items. Although the quality of the embroidery of rural women is excellent, products are usually sold into low-value traditional markets by means of long-established monopolistic distribution channels. A primary reason for this disconnect in consumer demand and producer supply results from socio-economic norms; since traders are generally men, transactions must be mediated by a male member of the household. As a result, cloistered women have neither the knowledge nor opportunity to develop products for higher value markets such as those found in Karachi and Islamabad.

MEDA and ECDI consequently conducted a sub-sector analysis to understand the constraints and opportunities pertaining to market players and mechanisms involved in hand-embroidered garment production and sales. This led to the design of a market development programme for the integration of homebound rural embroiderers into more profitable value chains (Jones,

2006). Based on effective facilitation strategies, the project was launched in August 2004 with funding from USAID's Microenterprise Development (MD) Office's Implementation Grant Program.

Approach to integrate homebound women into lucrative value chains

Over the past year and a half, MEDA and ECDI have facilitated the development of commercial linkages and support services that are enabling marginalized homebound women to reach higher value markets with their products. There are two primary initiatives that specifically target rural embroiderers: the first focuses on the creation of a network of female intermediaries who link rural embroiderers to markets, providing product information, quality control and design advice as part of their service (Jones and Shaikh, 2005). The second key intervention affecting homebound embroiderers directly involves the introduction of commercial design services into the sub-sector, stimulating the flow of valuable product development information throughout the supply chain. These interventions place an emphasis on building the capacity of individual producers and intermediaries so that they are better able to contribute to the development of a dynamic and sustainable market system. Details of our original programme design regarding these initiatives are as follows.

Embedded package of market access, product development and quality control to rural embroiderers provided by women sales agents. The MEDA and ECDI programme planned to introduce mobile female sales agents directly to rural embroiderers, creating market linkages to urban buyers and developing an avenue for information flow from markets to producers. The project identified women who already acted or were willing to act as sales agents for rural embroiderers including: existing commercial intermediaries interested in expanding their reach or their services, town- and city-based sales agents and retailers who wanted to connect with rural women but lacked established contacts, and village-level female entrepreneurs with more mobility than the majority of the population. To develop the necessary links with buyers, sales agents would be assisted to foster relationships with retailers, wholesalers, exporters and exhibition organizers. New and existing sales agents would also be trained in areas such as community outreach, sales and marketing, and business development.

Product development and design services to mobile women sales agents, garment makers, retailers and exporters. MEDA and ECDI's research indicated that there are three types of product designers in Pakistan. The first are élite, well-trained designers that are out of reach of the target population in terms of cost and social status. The second are full-time employees of small- and medium-scale garment manufacturers. The third are independent contractors who design for small garment manufacturers, selected boutiques and their own outlets. Not surprisingly, the third group was identified as the most promising source of design services for the target clients. The project planned to raise the awareness of producers, intermediaries, retailers and other buyers regarding design services. At the same time, designers would be presented with an opportunity to expand their business, and the project would help them develop strategies for tapping into this new market: for example, affordable packages of services such as group consultations, workshops and training seminars, and off-the-shelf patterns and instruction kits.

Over the past year, adjustments have been made to the business models and strategies described above. These changes are reflective of both a holistic view of the value chain, and a focus on the integration and upgrading of microenterprises.

It was expected that homebound rural embroiderers would sell their products to mobile female sales agents who in turn would sell to male wholesalers and retailers. Yet, the level of segregation in project areas is so deep that even many female sales agents (seen as outsiders) are often unable to interact directly with the embroiderers. To overcome this constraint, a two-tiered model has been devised with embroiderers selling to lead women from their own villages – community sales agents (CSAs) – who in turn sell the products to town-based women intermediaries – local sales agents (LSAs). As this model has developed and as CSAs have gained greater skills, they sometimes compete with LSAs by selling directly to retailers and other buyers. This adds richness to the value chain and provides greater choice for women entrepreneurs, reducing the potential for the emergence of exploitative monopolies.

The threat of monopolies is an ongoing concern of the project. CSAs have been a positive response to this challenge since, as members of the village, they are less able to push inequitable business deals than outsiders who have no family or community connections. However, another step has been taken to improve the bargaining power of and increase benefit to producers: the programme has facilitated the establishment of informal joint ventures. In this model, the CSA is a part of the community producer group, but acts as a lead member. Order information is shared transparently with the group; CSAs receive a commission that recognizes their leadership role; and producers can choose to contribute to individual orders as time allows. The formation of these joint ventures therefore not only reduces the risks of monopolies, it also promotes the sharing of work that takes women's other commitments into consideration.

To enhance the ability of women to reach new markets, formal designers were identified for the introduction of contemporary designs into the value chain. However, although alternative pricing and delivery mechanisms were tested, neither CSAs nor most LSAs have been able or willing to purchase custom designs on an ongoing basis. At the same time, a cultural divide between the formal designers and the women operating in the informal market has emerged, and this schism makes the development of consistent win–win relationships problematic.

MEDA and ECDI conducted further market research to find a solution to this constraint and learned about the existence of another value chain actor who could offer the needed services: the tracer designer. These individuals, mostly men, design embroidery stencils and either sell the prints to input supply shops or provide an imprinting service directly to clients. The majority of these designers are located in local town markets where mobile SAs are not only able to interact with them but can also afford their services. The project has therefore invested resources to upgrade the capacity of tracer designers, which has proven to be a successful strategy for the introduction of contemporary designs into the value chain.

A final project innovation is the development of buying houses as a means to manage orders and ensure product quality. There are currently two in operation that have been facilitated by programme staff: one in Multan and the other in Karachi. The buying houses are owned by independent sales agents, although the latter was initially subsidized through non-project funds. The buying houses function as a link between urban buyers and SAs: they display samples, take orders, distribute orders to appropriate producer groups via a network of CSAs and LSAs, monitor timeliness, receive completed work, review quality, package, ship to buyers, manage accounts payable, and distribute payment to SAs and producers. SAs are not obliged to work through buying houses, and many still take orders directly from buyers.

These project modifications have led to increased quantities of higher-quality products moving up the value chain to more lucrative markets, while facilitating the flow of market information to producers. In this way, a more competitive value chain has been developed by focusing on the functioning and contribution of rural homebound producers.

Mid-term programme results

Rural homebound women, marginalized by geography, poverty and home confinement, are now active participants in the hand-embroidered garment sub-sector. Programme initiatives have enabled embroiderers to acquire information, respond to consumer demand, access higher value markets and raise revenues by two to three times, without an increase in actual labour.

Quantitative mid-term results. The goal of the market development programme is to reach 6,000 homebound embroiderers over three years, providing them with opportunities to participate in the embroidered garment sub-sector, and earn incomes of at least $30 per month by the end of the project. By December 2005, at the halfway point in the project, over 7,000 women had been reached and had some involvement in the initiative with at least occasional employment. Of this total, almost 2,000 are regular participants, already earning over $20 per month on average. At the same time, the programme is assisting over 160 urban garment makers and 185 women sales agents to participate in the value chain. The garment makers and sales agents have also seen increased revenues as a result of project-related sales, with profits of $14/month and $45/month respectively (average for both full- and part-time participants).

Qualitative mid-term results. The project offers women an opportunity for economic advancement, but for many it has also led to broader empowerment on a number of levels: participation in community groups, changing family relationships and engagement with the larger society. Some of these outcomes are briefly described below.

From the outset, MEDA and ECDI have been very clear in their offer to women, their families and communities, that the programme presents an economic opportunity. There is no pressure exerted on any woman or her household to participate in the initiative, or any aspect of programming with which they are not completely comfortable. And, the project does not preach social change: there is no discussion of gender or socio-cultural issues. As communities have become more involved in market development activities, they have developed trust for the MEDA and ECDI personnel and interventions, and this has led to increased participation by women in every facet of the programme.

Rural embroiderers are actively participating in group activities: workshops and seminars, meetings and joint ventures. Women have come together to act as an economic unit in order to fill larger orders and to negotiate with buyers. When a joint venture is formed, a community woman takes the role of lead producer, and the rest of the group negotiates both with and through her.

Group activities have also impacted family relationships. Initially, some producers would only participate in a group venue if a male family member accompanied them and observed the proceedings. As trust was built, this situation evolved through various stages: first, escorts waited outside the meeting room; next, women were dropped off and picked up; and finally, groups of producers travelled to meetings without a male escort. Families are often very supportive and proud of women as they become economically empowered and demonstrate their productive capacity outside the household sphere.

Finally, project activities have brought rural embroiderers more and more into the public arena. In particular, CSAs have left their village homes to participate in exhibitions and interact with LSAs and other buyers. Women who rarely left their rural communities prior to the programme have journeyed in pairs or groups on the train from Balochistan, Sindh and Punjab to participate in public exhibitions of their work in the teaming metropolis of Karachi.

Conclusions

The MEDA and ECDI programme is providing thousands of homebound women in Pakistan with the opportunity to increase incomes and contribute to the economic advancement of their households, communities and the selected industry. If MEDA and ECDI had chosen to focus on a higher level in the subsector – such as regulations concerning the formalization of microenterprises or trade agreements that surround the garment industry – the desired impact on poor rural producers would not have been achieved. Embroiderers' potential to organize, produce better outputs, and engage with the market would not have been realized and they therefore would not be able to meet market demand. Consequently, the entire industry would not have developed as it has, and a series of players in the chain – producers, community and local sales agents, urban buyers and exporters, tracer designers and retailers – would not have had the opportunity to participate in this lucrative sub-sector. Concentrating efforts at the producer level, in this situation, has not only enabled marginalized women to improve their livelihoods, but has also helped them to become active partners in the economic advancement of an industry.

A holistic approach that leads to an understanding of a market system in which practitioners plan to intervene is often an essential ingredient to programme success. Systemic analysis enables project facilitators to determine the specific interventions that will accomplish maximum growth for an industry and the stakeholders within it. In some cases, the greatest need may be at the industry level. However, under certain circumstances, significant impact can only be achieved by focusing on the capacity of individual producers at the bottom of the supply chain. The case in Pakistan illustrates how optimal results have been achieved through the design and implementation of producer-focused programming.

References

Asian Development Bank (2000) *Women in Pakistan: Country briefing paper*, Asian Development Bank, Manila.

Central Intelligence Agency (2004) *The World Factbook*, Central Intelligence Agency, Washington, DC, viewed March 3, 2006, <http://www.cia.gov/cia/publications/factbook/geos/pk.html>

Committee of Donor Agencies for Enterprise Development (2001) *Business Development Services for Small Enterprises: Guiding Principles for Donor Intervention*, Committee of Donor Agencies for Enterprise Development.

Federal Bureau of Statistics (2004) *Population Statistics*, Federal Bureau of Statistics, Islamabad, viewed 3 March 2006, <http://www.statpak.gov.pk/depts/pco/statistics/statistics.html>

Food and Agriculture Organization (2006) viewed 3 March 2006, Food and Agriculture Organization, Rome, <http://www.fao.org/sd/WPdirect/WPre0111.htm>

Jones, Linda (2006) 'Using market research to discern innovative solutions', Trickle Up 25th Anniversary Symposium Papers, New York.

Jones, Linda and Perveen Shaikh (2003) 'MEDA ECDI Market Assessment Report', for the Small Enterprise Education and Promotion Network Practitioner Learning Program, Washington DC.

Jones, Linda and Perveen Shaikh (2005) *Middlemen as Agents of Change: the case of MEDA and ECDI in Pakistan*, The Small Enterprise Education and Promotion Network Technical Paper, Washington DC.

McVay, Mary and A. Miehlbradt (2002) *Developing Commercial Markets for Business Development Services: Are 'How-to-do-it Recipes Possible?* International Training Centre of the International Labour Organization, Turin, Italy.

McVay, Mary and A. Miehlbradt (2004) *Developing Markets for Business Development Services: Pioneering Systemic Approaches*, International Training Centre of the International Labour Organization, Turin, Italy.

Sauder, Allan and Perveen Shaikh (2000) 'A marketing initiative for women entrepreneurs in Pakistan', The Aga Khan Foundation, Ottawa.

Shuja, Sharif (2000) 'Feudalism: root cause of Pakistan's malaise,' News Weekly Australia, viewed 3 March, 2006, <http://www.newsweekly.com.au/articles/2000mar25_pfrcopm.html>

Suich, Helen and Carol Murphy (2002) 'Crafty women: the livelihood impact of craft income in Caprivi', report for Directorate of Environmental Affairs, Ministry of Environment and Tourism, Namibia.

United Nations Development Program (2004), *UN Human Development Report*, viewed 3 March 2006 <http://hdr.undp.org/statistics/data/countries.cfm?c=PAK>

United States Agency for International Development (2005) *Value Chain Approach to Poverty Reduction: Equitable Growth in Today's Global Economy*, United States Agency for International Development Accelerated Microenterprise Advancement Project, Washington, D.C.

World Bank (2004) *World Development Indicators (WDI) database*, World Bank, Washington D.C., viewed March 3, 2006, <http://devdata.worldbank.org/external/CPProfile.asp?PTYPE=CP&CCODE=PAK>

About the authors

Linda Jones, an independent consultant, was at the time of writing Technical Director, International Operations, MEDA, and Alexandra Snelgrove was a MEDA Project Manager in the Production and Marketing Linkages department. Linda is now an independent consultant based in Canada.

CHAPTER 13
Value chain financing in agriculture

Calvin Miller and Carlos Da Silva

This article was first published in June/September 2007.

Abstract

This paper provides an overview of value chain financing concepts and applications. It highlights issues and directions in the commercialization of agriculture, value chain development, agricultural and agribusiness finance and discusses the potential benefits and cautionary pitfalls associated with value chain financing. It is argued that value chain development supported by appropriate policies, institutions and services that constitute an enabling business environment can be instrumental in leveraging access to financial services in agriculture in developing countries. In this regard, ideas for promoting value chain financing are proposed and questions on its future are offered for reflection.

Agrifood systems worldwide are being transformed in unprecedented ways. Farm production and distribution are rapidly evolving from the simple relationships and points of interaction of the past to the highly integrated linkages and closer alignments among business partners we witness today. Value chains are being promoted as the business development frameworks of choice in the agrifood sector. There is much more attention being paid to inter- and intra-organizational efficiency in production, processing and logistics. There is increased focus on marketing, product differentiation and product niche development. Furthermore, competition is now global: prices are less affected by local conditions, seasonality and markets. All these developments make a solid financing structure even more important than it has always been. Market competitiveness and market risks are becoming the drivers of financing decisions in the new agrifood systems.

While world agriculture, agribusiness and finance are evolving rapidly in many parts of the globe, in others the pace of change has been much slower. Entire countries and entire sectors, even in progressive economies, are losing competitiveness because they are not adaptable to the changing nature of agrifood systems. Without the development of efficient supply chains, there is little hope that agribusiness and agri-industrial market opportunities, domestically or internationally, can be competitively tapped. Developing countries that have most of their economies based on the agrifood sector are being particularly affected by this new competitive scenario. It is within this general context that value chain development and upgrading is receiving so much attention in the international development community.

Indeed, governments and donors have realized that a majority of rural households in the developing world effectively do not have access to finance, especially for agriculture and agribusiness-related activities. At the same time, business leaders in both finance and agriculture have come to realize that with the new innovations in communication technology, information management and business models, there is a wealth of new opportunities for them to work profitably directly and indirectly together. Traditional adversarial relations can be replaced by a win–win situation where transaction costs and mutual risks are reduced.

With the increased attention to value chains in the agrifood sector, the opportunities for utilizing the chain framework to promote and facilitate access to financial services has become apparent. Value chain financing has thus grown to be a subject of special interest among development planners, governments, international organizations, NGOs, donors, academics and financing practitioners internationally (Fries and Akin, 2004). Nonetheless, value chain finance is not entirely new. Especially in agriculture, much of what it offers is not any more novel than most any other form of finance. What is new are the numerous new ways of providing such financing, as well as the convergence and inter-linking of agribusiness and finance. What are also new are the innovations in supply chain financing modalities: the experiences are recent and there is much to be learned and shared. Yet, not only the strengths and opportunities of value chains to improve efficiency and access to markets and finance should be stressed; there is also a need to realize the limitations thereof and to offer alternatives for dealing with those left behind.

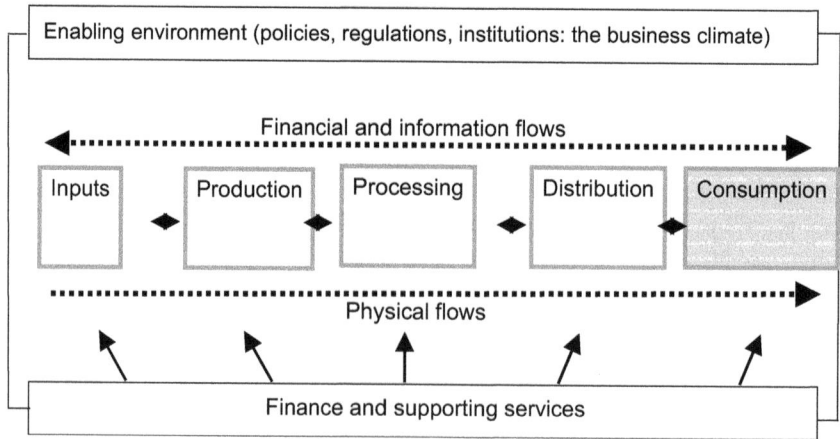

Adapted from da Silva and Batahla, 2000

Figure 13.1 A value chain at work

What is a value chain?

In order for a product to reach the consumer or user, there often are many processes or steps involved. Each step must have a direct link to the next in order for the processes to form a viable chain. At each stage, some additional transformation or enhancement is made to the product. Hence, a value chain is often defined as a sequence of value-adding activities, from production to consumption, through processing and commercialization. Value chains, or supply chains, in agriculture can be thought of as a 'farm to fork' set of processes and flows – from the inputs to production to processing, marketing and the consumer. Each segment of a chain has one or more backward and forward linkages. A chain is only as strong as its weakest link and hence the stronger the links, the more secure is the flow of products and services within the chain.

As shown in Figure 13.1, products typically flow from stage to stage along a chain in one direction, while financial resources mostly flow in another. Funds can also flow into the chain at any stage. Chains operate within a complex environment of policies, regulations, institutions and support services. Achieving chain competitiveness is thus no simple task: it requires operational efficiency in each of its segments, co-ordination of transactions among chain actors and insertion within a supportive business environment.

Why are value chains relevant for agricultural finance?

The inter-dependent linkages of a chain and the security of a market-driven demand for the chain's products provide producers, processors and other chain actors the access to the markets they all need. Being part of a chain reduces risk, thus making it easier for chain actors to obtain financing from banks and other lenders and to do so at a lower cost. For example, in case studies in Africa, Asia and Latin America (Röttger, 2004; Shepherd, 2004 and Gálvez, 2006) FAO found that agri-enterprise firms are turning to business alliances and related contracts in order to manage risks, gain access resources, improve logistical efficiency, reduce inventories and, in general, achieve increased control over competitiveness factors that are beyond their firm boundaries (Santacoloma et al., 2004). The linkages also allow financing to flow along the chain. For example, inputs can be provided to farmers by a processor or exporter and be repaid directly from the sale of the product, without having to go through traditional loan processes.

What is 'financing along the value chain'?

For centuries traders have provided finance to farmers for harvest, inputs or other needs such as emergencies. Many of the traders in turn receive finance from millers and processors who also may be financed from wholesalers or exporters who are farther 'up' the chain from production to marketing. These remain important today but there are often differences between regions. For example, as shown in Figure 13.2 for the rice chain, the case studies found that millers played the central financing role for rice in Asia and wholesalers were central in financing within the rice chain in Africa.

Even traditional forms of 'farming on shares' is a form of value chain finance since the farmer shareholder receives inputs and other required financing from business shareholders in a formal or informal contractual arrangement. Similarly, finance can flow up the chain such as from input suppliers who provide seeds and inputs on credit or farmers who deliver products to a warehouse or processor and wait for payment, as is often the case in industries such as dairy, sugarcane, rice and cotton. Even many products in supermarkets are sold on consignment through supermarkets or with delayed payments, thus reducing their costs of inventory.

Finance and agribusiness today often go far beyond simple linkages and have often moved into integrated systems. Large agribusinesses may integrate credit and other financial services directly or indirectly at many or all of the steps in the value chain. Directly they can provide funding upstream or downstream in the chain, at whatever level in the farm-to-fork continuum. Indirectly they do so in two manners. First, they can facilitate or intermediate funding from a third party to the client or company in the chain, such as when an export company helps arrange funding for the companies or producers it buys from or sells to. Alternatively, the mere fact of being within a value chain is often sufficient for the chain actor to obtain funding from financial organizations.

As found in Latin America, financial institutions can find security through the value chains of its partners. As part of its credit technology, nearly half of the sampled regulated institutions required clients to have a formal sales contract (compared to only 11 per cent of the non-regulated institutions

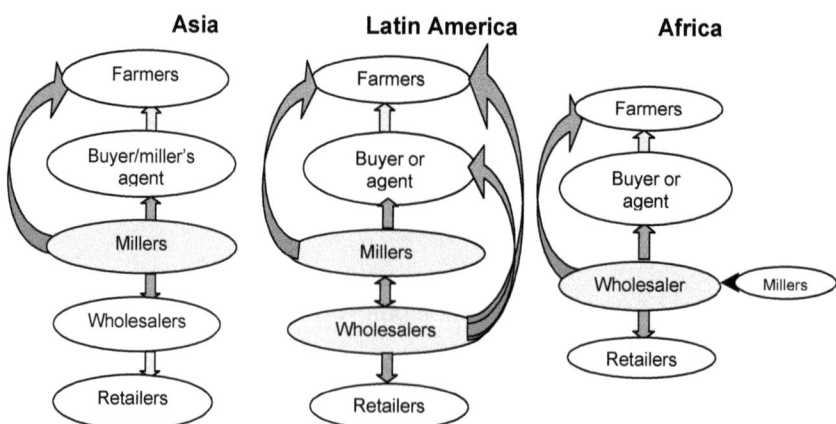

Figure 13.2 Financial flows within the rice chain

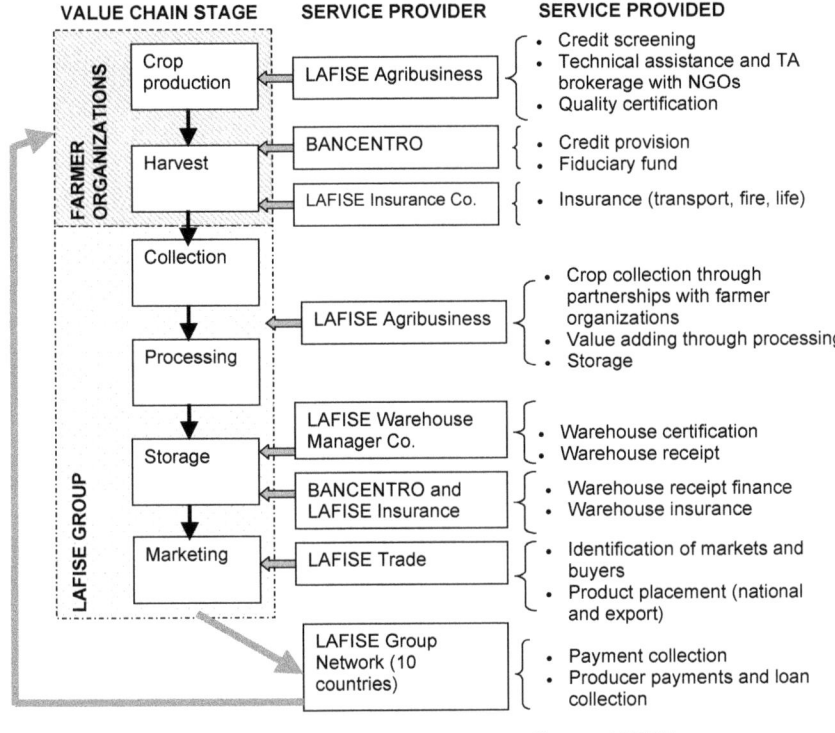

Figure 13.3 LAFISE group integrated service model

in the sample) and 39 per cent requested clients to be part of a value chain (Wenner, 2007).

Value chain finance is built not only upon physical linkages but also knowledge integration. A key to success in finance is to 'know the business'. Those who know the business the best are those persons and companies directly involved in the value chain. Having and using that knowledge of the chain, they can understand the risks and work to mitigate them much easier than a traditional banker who works with all types of businesses and clients.

For this reason, some business groups have formed conglomerates which provide both formal banking and a range of agribusiness services to serve the value chain. As shown in Figure 13.3, LAFISE in Central America provides an array of financial and non-financial services through both a business group structure and through strategic linkages with others (Zamora, 2007). The logic is to increase efficiency, ensure tighter control and accountability within the supply chains, and consequently increase profits. While this creates greater competition for other financial service providers, it can also create opportunities for collaboration and partnership.

On a smaller scale, El Comercio in Paraguay found that by studying and using the agricultural value chains, such as with soybeans and sesame, it has been able to improve their financial services to small farmers. By partnering with storage providers, the financial institution has benefited by reducing the costs of crop supervision, loan recovery and credit supervision and by sharing risk with the storage providers. It also uses its knowledge of value chain finance to develop new products such as insurance, savings, and current account facilities to meet the needs of 'unbanked' farmers (Wittinger and Mori Tuesta, 2006).

On the producer side, can access to finance increase when chains are organized? The answer is yes, primarily for four reasons:
- increased funding coming from suppliers and agribusinesses directly involved in the chain;
- increased creditworthiness, since participation in the chain can enhance the security of loan repayment;
- reduced transaction costs for obtaining loans in cash or kind; and
- decreased risk as a borrower due to secured markets and reduced income variability.

Value chain finance – approaches and products

Products and approaches which can be specifically applied to value chain financing are primarily either finance that is linked with the production or commodity or those which are used to reduce price and production risk. In addition other products such as secured transactions, factoring and joint venture equity finance can be additional sources of finance that take advantage of the relative security of the value chain system in order to provide additional alternatives for capital.

The typology presented in Table 13.1 provides a simple overview of the use and value of various approaches to the users and providers of finance and products. Interested readers can find additional information and examples in a series of papers and presentations of the Latin American and Asian Conferences in Agricultural Value Chain Financing promoted by FAO and partners in 2006 and 2007 respectively. The proceedings and presentations can be accessed through www.ruralfinance.org. It is important to note that each type of finance has its unique uses, advantages and disadvantages for each party in the agreement. Therefore the decision to use is dependent upon the relative options and opportunities in each given setting.

Product-linked finance uses the commodity as collateral and has a buyer-seller relationship. With trader finance, the trader is able to advance funds with the guarantee of the crop to be harvested. The price is normally fixed at the time of financing but in the many countries without functioning commodity exchanges, this price-setting is often done by the trader on speculation,

Table 13.1. Typology of value chain finance approaches

Value chain financing approaches	Financing purpose implement	Complexity to borrower	Advantage for producer/ borrower	Advantage for company/ lender	Disadvantage for producer	Disadvantage for company/ lender
Product-linked finance						
Trader finance	• Commodity procurement • Farmer finance for harvest/post-harvest	• Low	• Ease of transaction • Well known • May be competitive offers	• Secures commodities and price	• Often high discounts on market price	• Potential for side-selling • Unsecured quality and quantity
Marketing/ company credit	• Reduce transaction risk	• Low	• More secure product market • Technical sales assistance • Bulk input cost reduction	• Secures procurement • Contracts for finance, terms, and product specs	• May not be directly accessible to small farmers	• Increases financial outlay
Input supplier credit	• Sell/ purchase inputs	• Low	• Obtain inputs on credit	• Secures sales • Input costs may be excessive	• Lack of security in repayment	
Contract agriculture	• Overcome lack of access to credit	• Medium	• Secure market and price • Technical guidance for higher yields and quality	• Less options due to closer monitoring • Enforceable contracts	• Less access for small farmers • Restricts price rise gains	• Side-selling • Cost of management and enforcement of contracts
Warehouse receipts	• Overcome lack of collateral • Secure repayment	• Medium to high (depending on regulation)	• Cash advance and/or credit guarantee upon deposit of commodity	• Security of standards and inspection • Secured, deposited product	• Lack of available providers • Fees charged	• Often lack of regulatory structure • Costs • Uneven product flow
Producer risk-mitigation products						
Crop/ weather insurance	• Mitigate production income risk	• High	• Reduces production risk • Evens income	• Lowers procurement loss risk	• High perceived cost	• Added cost and added management
Forward contracts	• Secure price risk • Provide loan collateral	• High	• Reduces income risk • Can use contracts as loan collateral	• Lowers sale and purchase price risk • Secures procurement	• Not widely available nor understood	• Not widely available
Hedging	• Reduce price risk	• High	• Reduces production and income risk	• Lowers purchase risk • Evens farm income	• Not widely available nor understood	• Requires commodity exchanges

Other financing options for value chain agribusinesses

Secured transactions	• Reduce transaction fraud risk	• High	• Opens market opportunities	• Improves security	• High cost	• Time and paperwork • Cost
Factoring	• Obtain working capital	• High	• Buyers have more cash	• Source of capital for operations	• Not widely available	• Lack of knowledge and interest by financial markets
Equity finance and joint ventures	• Increase investment • Share company risk • Increase borrowing capacity	• High	• Provides additional capital to value chain	• Increases capital and borrowing capacity • Reduces risk to each investor • Adds expertise and/or markets	• Hard for small producers to participate	• Often a lack of investors • Dilutes investor returns

---

Box 13.1 Contract poultry production

A mid-sized poultry processing company in Minas Gerais State, Brazil engages about 300 small farmers in the production of broilers under contracts. The company provides farmers with all production inputs, including day-old chicks, feed mixes and veterinary products. Technical assistance is also provided throughout the growing cycle. Under this contracting scheme, most working capital needs of the broiler producers are pre-financed by the processing firm. Investment needs, on the other hand, have to be funded through alternative financial sources. In this regard, farmers have successfully used their contracts with the processing firm as a form of collateral to secure loans from private banks for investments in facility expansion. Their participation in a value chain that is known to operate competitively in the state increases their credit worthiness, thus facilitating access to finance (Silva and Batalha, 2000).

---

without knowing what the market price or the quality will be at the time of delivery. In order to reduce trader risk, the prices offered tend to be low and therefore a disadvantage to the farmer.

Marketing company finance works in a similar way, but whereas traders tend to be smaller and normally operate as intermediaries between producers and processors and marketing companies, the marketing financing is normally driven by the interest of the company to secure products to meet their marketing goals and commitments. They may or may not directly manage the funding since they may choose to involve a bank or other financial institution to directly manage disbursements, and collections are managed through receipt of the product. There is often an established relationship between

> **Box 13.2 DrumNet: facilitating finance, marketing and information management**
>
> In Kenya, DrumNet provides a supply management system for the flow of information and financial transactions among partners engaged in the production, financing, and marketing of agricultural produce. It links commercial banks, smallholder farmers, and retail providers of farm inputs through a cashless micro-credit programme using mobile phones and SMS and email that informs and enables the parties to do business together. Farmers, organized into co-guaranteed solidarity groups, access farm inputs at local participating stockists. At harvest time, DrumNet deducts principal and interest payments from farmer net returns, tracks credit history and enforces group guarantees. The participating bank is shielded from the complexity and costs of these many small transactions. Banks provide loans to farmers for the purchase of inputs and provide transactional banking services to all stakeholders to pay stockists for inputs, recover loans and interest from buyer payments and credit farmer accounts with the surpluses. Banks can also offer additional financial products and services to farmer group members (Campaigne, 2007).

the company and the producers or producer groups. Marketing companies may have more option to secure advance prices for their commodities and therefore have a more secure basis for setting prices of the products they procure through advancing funds to traders and producers.

Contract farming financing has some of the characteristics of marketing company finance but has strict contractual relationships that specify the type of production, quality, quantity and timeliness of the production to be delivered. Finance and technical assistance provision, if needed, is written into the binding contract. Contract farming can be defined as an agreement between farmers and processing and/or marketing firms for products under forward agreements and frequently at pre-determined prices (Eaton and Shepherd, 2001). The contractual commitments provide bankers with a signal of security and seriousness as well as a potential for ensuring repayment through discounting from sales income. This can be done with animal as well as crop farming, as shown in Box 13.1.

A key to success in this approach is the legal environment. If there is a weak enforcement of contracts, or if there are no agreed standards for product quality and control of the product, then the programme cannot work effectively.

Risk mitigation tools can help stabilize income and hence improve borrowing access and conditions. Crop or weather insurance provide an income stream to those insured in case of failure. Forward contracts provide an avenue to sell a product for future delivery at a specified price. This not only reduces price risk but also the futures contract can be used as collateral upon which one can borrow money. This is being used by small farmers in India and a few other countries but direct widespread use will be difficult in many developing countries. However, if millers and wholesalers use forward contracts, they can offer farmers prices with less risk and ostensibly with a higher price due to the reduction in uncertainty. Furthermore, they can access funding more easily due to the security of such contracts, thus providing more capital and potentially more competition and higher prices to producers.

Various hedging products are widely used in developed economies to allow farmers, millers, traders and others the option of reducing risk by purchasing options and derivatives which can limit future price drops. The concept of a hedge is to reduce or cancel an unwanted business risk such as a product's market price fluctuation, while still allowing the agribusiness to profit from the investment activity. These require stock market exchanges which are becoming more available at least for certain commodities and require careful understanding before using.

International trade finance makes use of secured transaction financing such as Letters of Credit which provide security of payment to the buyer upon delivery. These Letters are recognized collateral by financial institutions for obtaining financing. Another agribusiness financing option is factoring or accounts receivable. The financing business sells its accounts receivable at a discount in order to obtain additional working capital. A final form of value chain financing to note is that of equity finance. The strength of value chains is in the integrated alliances and linkages, which serve not only for the flow of product and funds, but also for building relationships and joint ventures.

Table 13.2 The opportunities and challenges in promoting value chain finance

Opportunities	Challenges
Value chain financing (VCF) linkages offer increased financial access: • Lower transaction costs to banks and producers • Reduces financial risks to lenders • Tailored to fit specific chain needs	Required bundle of services for investment in value chains is lacking: • Small, unorganized productive capacity of many producers • Missing physical and financial infrastructure
VCF concept provides increased understanding of agricultural and agri business finance: • Better understanding, coordination and control of the marketplace • Improved long-term horizon for financial entities • Adaptation to future market trends	Capacity, understanding and hence commitment are missing: • Small farmers lack capacity and often production competitiveness • Agribusiness and finance institutions lack experience and tools • Governments lack understanding and supporting policies
Increases opportunities for equity finance and capital market interventions: • Increased chain competitiveness • Improved understanding and risk mitigation for investors • Structured finance opportunities and new products	Required investment and support services are not available: • Risk reducing services not universally available • Enabling policies and conditions not in place in • Fear of unknown for long-term investment many countries
VCF is not socially exclusive (in principle, small farmers can benefit): • Leading NGOs in sector able to facilitate small farmer inclusion • New technologies open new frontiers	Livelihoods are at risk for those excluded: • Social exclusion of small producers • VCF benefits for actors integrated into chains; but many are not in chains

Opportunities and challenges

Value chain finance has shown it can provide many opportunities. Yet, in order for the financial industry to be able to take full advantage of its opportunities there are many challenges to address, especially in serving smallholders in less developed parts of the world. As shown in Table 13.2, most of the challenges are due to a lack of capacity, both human and physical. For example, for small producers to be able to integrate into value chains, they require organization to have the economies of scale required. They require technical and management training and they must have roads and communications systems that are adequate to compete in the marketplace. Similarly banks and MFIs need increased understanding on market assessment and need to gain experience in working with the various traders and agribusinesses in the value chains in order to structure their products and services to their precise needs in a way that can maximize the benefits of value chain finance.

Moving forward with value chain finance

As earlier indicated, FAO and a number of partners have organized two regional conferences on value chain financing, in Latin America and Asia. In these events, finance, agribusiness and international business development leaders concluded that the key issues and recommendations were the following.

Relating to value chain growth:
- The integration and intensification of agricultural value chains is expected to continue. Rapid growth is envisaged and can offer opportunities for chains to achieve competitiveness through lower costs and risks.
- Public investments in rural areas are needed in developing countries and should be used for creating and sustaining growth in agriculture and rural development. With growth and competitiveness, private financial and agribusiness services will develop.

Relating to knowledge:
- Knowledge is a key element of agricultural value chain finance in two critical aspects. The in-depth knowledge of a value chain is what gives agribusinesses a competitive edge in reducing financial risk.
- Knowledge of how value chains really work and on the role of each stakeholder, including government, is lacking. Highlighted knowledge gaps included: improved cultivation techniques, markets, prices, standards, quality and compliance, access to suitable financial services and information.
- Knowledge must be built on better practices, developed in collaboration with global and local experience and disseminated and applied widely to strengthen public understanding and provide conducive policies.

152 VALUE CHAINS IN DEVELOPMENT

Key areas of innovation are:

- Information and Communication Technologies (cashless banking; point-of-sale finance, cell-phone trading).
- Risk-management tools (crop and weather risk insurance, futures and options).
- Service providers (integration of facilitator companies into value chain).
- Group aggregation (farmers' associations, self-help group links).
- Financing models (contractual farming, warehouse receipts, collateral management, leasing, equity finance, supply and structured commodity finance).
- National spot and futures exchanges.

Innovation is both an equalizer and a threat to smallholders. The focus is practical options and modalities of mitigating risk and improving capacity.

Building scope and equity: the BASIX approach

India enjoys rapid overall growth of its GDP of 9 per cent per annum while growth in the agriculture sector is stagnant at less than 2 per cent. To maintain the overall growth it is critical for India to invest in the agriculture sector which is the livelihood of 60 per cent of the population. Such investments, which are critical for making growth inclusive, go well beyond finance as shown in Figure 13.4. Using a livelihood approach with a value chain business model, BASIX provides a comprehensive bundle of non-financial services with finance to build farmer competitiveness and address their livelihood needs.

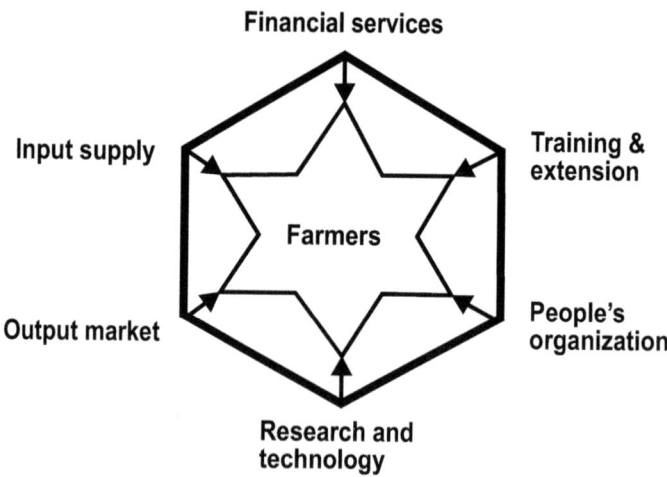

Figure 13.4 BASIX livelihood services model

This includes organizing and linking small farmers with markets, technology development for futures trading, training and financing (BASIX, 2007).

The future of value chain finance

Two principle points can be concluded for agricultural value chain finance. First, the growth of financial services embedded into or linked with the value chain can be expected to continue to grow as production and marketing system integration intensifies. Secondly, and perhaps most importantly, the concept and use of value chain systems is and should become even more important toward informing financial service providers in their lending decisions and product development for agriculture. Using the knowledge of a value chain, assessing its strengths, risks and trends and assessing a loan client's position and competency within that chain will inform the lending decision making at both the client level and that of their overall portfolio.

Additionally, the value chain knowledge allows for the structuring of finance to reduce repayment risk and lower transaction costs of service. As has been demonstrated by BASIX, DrumNet and others, such structuring will require new product development and innovation and will incorporate the advances of communication technology, management information systems and commodity exchanges in developing countries and will require work with policy makers to understand and adapt the regulatory frameworks to the changing environment. Policy and product development also include addressing the livelihood and financial service needs of those households whose production systems are not or soon will not be competitive within this changing environment.

References

BASIX (2007) 'Agri-revolution: financing the agricultural value chain', Mumbai, India, March.
Campaigne, J. (2007) 'DrumNet: financing the agricultural value chain' Agri Revolution: Financing the Agricultural Value Chain Conference, Mumbai, India.
Eaton, Charles and Shepherd, Andrew (2001) *Contract Farming*, FAO Bulletin No. 145, Rome, Italy.
Fries, R. and Akin, B. (2004) 'Value chains and their significance for addressing the rural finance challenge', *Microreport* 20, USAID, Washington.
Gálvez, E. (2006) Financiación de la Comercialización en América Latina, AGSF Occasional Paper 10, FAO, Rome.
Miller, C. (2007) 'Managing credit risk in rural financial institutions in Latin America', presentation based on unpublished research by M. Wenner, et. al. Rural Finance Research Conference, FAO, Rome.
Röttger, A. (ed.) (2004) *Strengthening Farm-Agribusiness Linkages in Africa*, AGSF Occasional Paper 6, FAO, Rome.

Santacoloma, P., Suárez, R. and Riveros, H. (2004) *Strengthening Agribusiness Linkages with Small-Scale Farmers: Case Studies in Latin America and the Caribbean*, AGSF Occasional Paper 4. FAO, Rome.

Shepherd, A. (2004) *Financing Agricultural Marketing: The Asian Experience*, AGSF Occasional Paper 2. FAO, Rome.

Silva, C. and Batalha, M. (2000) 'Competitiveness in agroindustrial systems: methodology and case study', Anais do II Workshop Brasileiro sobre Gestão de Sistemas Agroalimentares; USP, Ribeirão Preto (in Portuguese).

Wenner, Mark, Navajas, Sergio, Trivelli, Carolina and Tarazona, Alvaro (2007) *Managing Credit Risk in Rural Financial Institutions in Latin America*. Sustainable Development Department Best Practices Paper Series. No. MSM 139. Inter-American Development Bank, Washington, D.C.

Wittinger, Bettina and Mori Tuesta, Tiodita (2006) *Providing Cost-Effective Credit to Small-Scale Single-Crop Farmers: The Case of Financiera El Comercio*, InSight, No. 19, ACCION, August.

Zamora, E. (2007) in: Quirós, R. (ed.) *Finanziamento de las Cadenas Agrícolas de Valor*, Academia de Centro América, FAO, RUTA and Serfirual, San Jose.

About the authors

Calvin Miller and Carlos Da Silva are within the Rural Finance department of the Food and Agriculture Organization of the UN (FAO), Viale delle Terme di Caracalla, 00159 Rome, Italy.

The views expressed in this article are those of the author(s) and do not necessarily reflect the views of the Food and Agriculture Organization of the United Nations.

© Food and Agriculture Organization of the United Nations & Practical Action Publishing, www.practicalactionpublishing.org

CHAPTER 14

How to assess if markets work better for the poor: experiences from the Katalyst Project in Bangladesh

Harald Bekkers, Alexandra Miehlbradt and Peter Roggekamp

This article was first published in June 2008.

Abstract

> There is increasing demand for reports on the results and poverty impacts of private-sector development projects. This article suggests that projects can respond to this demand through internal monitoring systems that provide both useful information for project management and estimated impacts on enterprises and poverty reduction. The article discusses the case of Katalyst, an M4P project in Bangladesh that has installed an internal monitoring system that uses a mid-range approach to impact assessment. Katalyst's impact assessment in the pond fish sector is presented, giving the details of what was measured, how it was measured, the conclusions drawn and follow up decisions made. Katalyst's overall impact monitoring system is then presented with an emphasis on how Katalyst balances accuracy with simplicity. The article concludes with Katalyst's perspective on how this system has been useful both for internal management and external reporting.

There is growing demand from donors, governments and other stakeholders for reports on the results of private sector development (PSD) projects. Some PSD projects are making a greater effort to estimate their impacts on poverty reduction and other social goals. But the number of projects providing information on their overall results is still too few (Tanburn, 2008). This article aims to demonstrate how more PSD projects, particularly M4P projects and other projects that take a systemic approach to poverty reduction, can credibly estimate their poverty reducing results. It discusses the system that Katalyst, a multi-donor funded project in Bangladesh, has installed to provide both timely and useful information for internal decision making as well as regularly assess and report on its quantitative and qualitative impacts on poor people.

All types of projects struggle to reasonably and credibly assess impact. So, what are the particular challenges in M4P projects and other projects that reduce poverty through market development and stimulating systemic change?

- Interventions address systems that surround and affect the poor. They do not directly choose or interact with each beneficiary. Instead, poor people choose whether to 'participate' or not by choosing whether to react to new incentives, information and opportunities in the systems around them. Therefore, M4P projects cannot identify beneficiaries in advance.
- M4P projects tend to start out with minimal interventions to see if they address identified constraints and adjust as required during implementation. Thus, practitioners often do not know upfront exactly what actions will be taken.
- When systems around the poor change, it is not always easy to identify who has benefited and who has not. Some people may have benefited directly. Others may have benefited indirectly, for example by copying behaviours of those that benefited directly.
- M4P interventions aim to address the root causes of the failure of particular systems to serve and benefit the poor. This often means that the causal chains linking interventions to poverty impact are long and there are many other factors that also influence the links in the chain (Springfield Centre, forthcoming).

These characteristics of M4P and other systemic projects make it difficult to pinpoint beneficiaries, design quasi-experimental surveys and isolate impact resulting from projects as opposed to other factors in the economy.

This article outlines how Katalyst has dealt with these complexities by describing one example of an impact assessment in Katalyst and then discussing Katalyst's overall system for monitoring and assessing results. This system takes a mid-range approach to impact assessment, aiming to be useful and credible as well as manageable (see Hulme, 2000). The system provides information on the extent of, and reasons for, changes that may result from Katalyst's activities. The system is designed to document Katalyst interventions and generate information on resulting changes in service markets, service providers and enterprises using the services. The specific indicators of change tracked by the system are based on a causal model that is developed for each market and intervention. Based on this information, reasoned estimates are made of Katalyst's contribution to overall changes at the sector level, and to changes in poverty indicators related to employment, income and well being.

The system is unconventional in that it aims to provide useful information both for internal management and for regular reporting of estimated impacts on service markets, enterprises, sectors and poverty reduction to donors and other stakeholders (see Kirkpatrick and Hulme, 2001). However, there are some similarities between Katalyst's system and social performance assessment, which has contributed both to accountability and improved management in microfinance institutions (Copestake, 2004).

Katalyst

Katalyst, funded by DFID, SDC and Sida, and implemented by Swisscontact and GTZ, aims to increase incomes and employment for the poor by improving the competitiveness of selected sectors. The project works with the public and private sector to improve support markets that are important for these sectors. Katalyst began operations in 2003 and is now beginning its second, five-year phase. Currently, Katalyst works in 16 sectors including agricultural sectors such as maize and vegetables, industries such as plastics and furniture and business service sectors such as advertising.

Impact assessment in the pond fish sector

In 2004, Katalyst began working in the pond fish sector in Faridpur, one of the poorest regions of Bangladesh. At that time, there were around 42,000 farmers, retailers, hawkers, traders and nurseries involved in pond fish cultivation in Faridpur. The majority of people involved in the sector live below the poverty line. Demand for fish is strong in Bangladesh and the returns for pond fish farmers are generally good (see de Ruyter de Wildt, 2007).

Katalyst's interventions in pond fish

The quality of inputs and poor cultivation practices were preventing pond fish farmers from fully realizing the market potential. Mortality rates for fingerlings were high because of incorrect breeding, feeding, handling and transportation techniques. In Faridpur, the vast majority of farmers were using inappropriate and out-of-date cultivation practices. Together with three local fishery associations in Faridpur, Katalyst developed a range of interventions to address these issues. By the end of 2006 one intervention, a fingerling nursery training programme, was 'ready' for impact assessment.

Nurseries sell fingerlings to farmers directly, or to hawkers who transport and sell them to farmers. As part of their interaction with farmers and hawkers, nurseries may also provide information on how to transport and grow fish, for example, how to prepare and clean a pond, how to release fingerlings, how to feed the fish and how to prevent and control diseases. Providing useful information to farmers and hawkers makes good business sense for nurseries. Farmers are in search of such information and reliable sources are highly valued. Nurseries and hawkers that are able to provide good information improve their reputations among fish farmers, leading to an increase in clients and sales. Katalyst found that nurseries are the main source of information for fish farmers, but that the information provided is often limited and inaccurate.

The logic of the intervention is captured in Figure 14.1. Katalyst expected that training nursery staff would improve the quality of their fingerlings and increase their capacity and motivation to provide appropriate and useful information to farmers and hawkers on fish cultivation practices. This

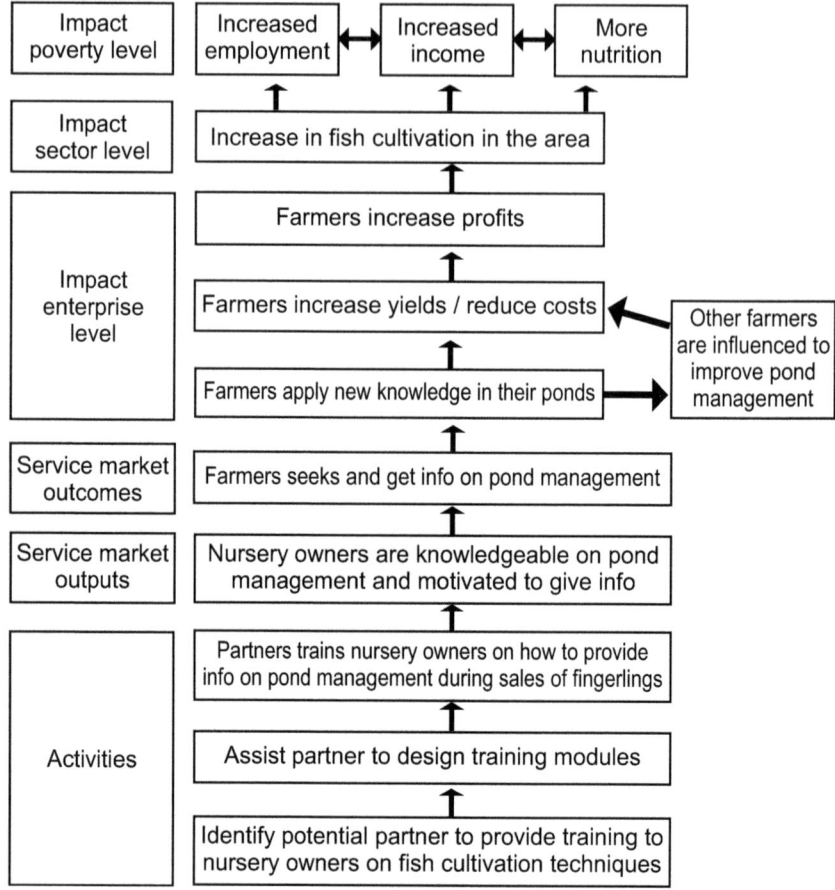

Figure 14.1 Fish fingerling nursery training logic

information would help farmers to improve the productivity and profitability of their fish ponds. Raising farmers' productivity would not only raise the incomes of those farmers but also encourage more farmers to enter pond fish farming in the many unused ponds in Faridpur. The increase in pond fishing would generate additional income and employment; pond fishing is labour intensive and relies primarily on unskilled, seasonal rural labour. The additional income and employment would translate into better standards of living for affected poor people. Katalyst also expected that increasing farmers' fish output would improve nutrition among poor families.

The nursery training programme was implemented from April to August 2005. With help from Katalyst, the local fishery associations, together with an NGO knowledgeable about fish cultivation, organized a fee-based programme for 400 nurseries, about half the nurseries in Faridpur.

Impact assessment design

In December 2006, at the end of the first fish season that could show impact, Katalyst commissioned an impact assessment to test key links in their intervention logic. The assessment measured if trained nurseries provided more and better information to hawkers and farmers and if hawkers passed on information to farmers. It measured to what extent more and better information resulting from the training made farmers more productive and profitable. The assessment also examined to what extent and how these changes were affecting poor people's incomes, employment opportunities and nutrition.

Katalyst's intervention was not the only factor affecting the pond fish sector in Faridpur. Nationally, domestic output in the pond fish sector continued to grow by 10–15 per cent per year (de Ruyter de Wildt, 2007; Bangladesh DOF, 2006). The Bangladeshi Department of Fisheries and other donors were also conducting programmes in the pond fish sector, although with very limited reach in Faridpur. In the assessment, Katalyst wanted to isolate its contribution to the pond fish sector in Faridpur from these and other factors. A quasi-experimental survey design was chosen using treatment and control groups among nurseries, hawkers and pond fish farmers. The survey was complemented by in-depth interviews with the fishing associations, selected nurseries, selected fish farmers and selected fish labourers.

The survey included: 55 trained and 60 non-trained nurseries; 165 farmers buying (directly or indirectly) from trained nurseries and 165 farmers buying from untrained nurseries; 55 hawkers buying from trained nurseries and 60 hawkers buying from untrained nurseries. The farmers were divided into micro (farming a pond less than 0.3 acres), small (0.3–0.6 acres) and medium (0.6–1.0 acres) sized fish farms. The trained and untrained nurseries were chosen randomly in two districts in which nursery training took place. Each nursery was asked to cite four different clients – a micro farmer, a small farmer, a medium farmer and a hawker who were subsequently interviewed. Three questionnaires were administered (for nurseries, farmers and hawkers) that captured changes in business size, volume, practices, investments, relationships and information flows over a period of three years. The survey sampling strategy and size were chosen to yield statistically significant results for each type of market player and each farmer size category.

The measurement of impact was based on the difference between changes over three years in the treatment group and in the control group. The comparison of changes in the treatment and control groups allowed Katalyst to isolate the impact of interventions from natural growth in the sector, the influence of other programmes and the existing differences between the treatment and control groups. It is possible that some businesses in the control groups benefited from seeing and learning from the improved practices of the treatment groups. It is also possible that nurseries tended to cite their 'best' clients. These effects were not controlled for in the assessment.

Survey findings

The survey indicates that information exchange between trained nurseries, farmers and hawkers has improved over the past three years, and to a significantly larger extent than seen in the control group. For example, 64 per cent of farmers that bought from trained nurseries had learned from them how to recognize and remove unwanted fish, compared to 48 per cent in the control group. Hawkers also confirmed that information exchange had improved. For example, 78 per cent had learned about fingerling release from trained nurseries, as compared to 32 per cent in the control group. Hawkers also had learned from the trained nurseries about the importance of giving more information to farmers: 95 per cent stated that providing cultivation-related information to farmers was important, as compared to 19 per cent in the control group. These findings are statistically significant.

Trained nurseries and the farmers they serve have increased investments in spawns, feed and medicines as well as improved their cultivation techniques more than those in the control groups. Consequently, fish mortality rates decreased for all treatment groups, for example a 15 per cent drop in fish mortality for farmers compared to a 3 per cent rise for the control group. Better fingerlings and more advice paid off for trained nurseries. Their client bases grew on average from 60 to 104 farmers as compared to 45 to 50 in the control group.

Productivity increased more for farmers in the treatment group as compared to the control group. The effect was greatest for micro farmers. While yield per pond acre was less in the treatment group as compared to the control group in 2004 and 2005, the treatment group surpassed the control group in 2006 (see Figure 14.2). For small farmers the results are similar but for medium farmers impact on productivity is less clear. The findings on both farmers' cultivation practices and productivity are statistically significant.

For micro and small farmers, profits also increased more for those buying from trained nurseries as compared to those in the control groups. While profits for micro farmers were almost identical in the treatment and control groups in 2004, the treatment group had 6 per cent higher profits than the control group in 2006 (see Figure 14.3). However, differences in profits are not statistically significant.

Qualitative research findings

Katalyst's qualitative research supported the expected changes laid out in the intervention logic. For example, cases showed that trained nurseries had begun to help farmers much more actively and were often helping new farmers begin pond fish cultivation. Cases also showed the different ways in which the changes brought about by the nursery training programme were affecting poor people. Rural labourers were gaining more work from the intensification of pond fish farming in trained nurseries and their fish

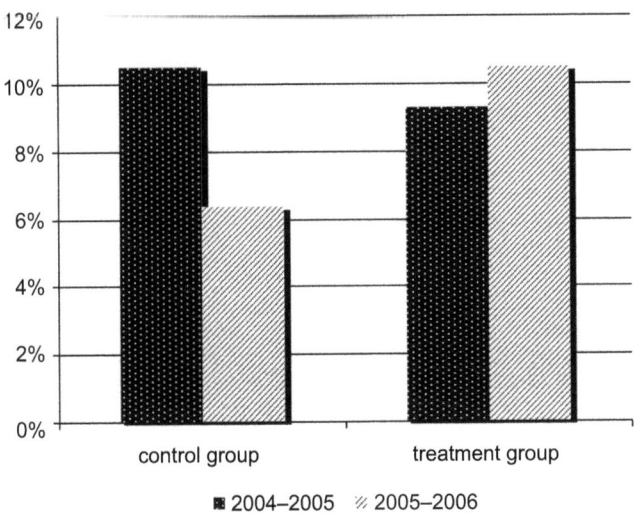

Figure 14.2 Average growth in productivity for micro farmers

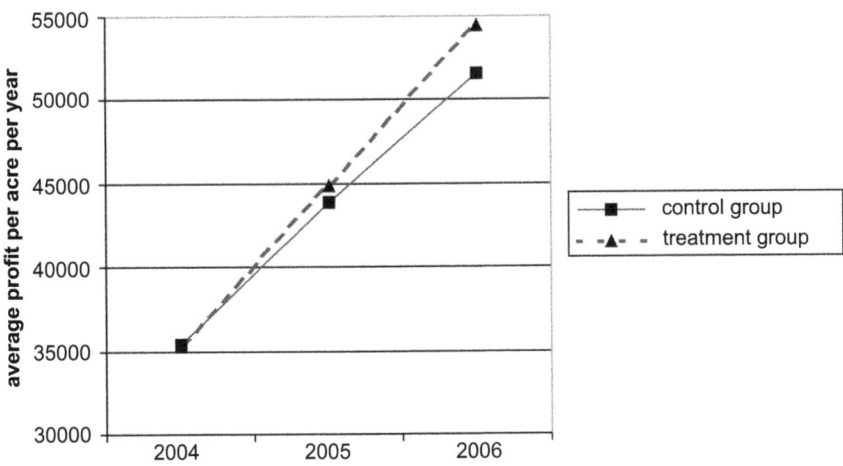

Figure 14.3 Average profits for micro farmers

farming customers. Some farmers were experiencing significantly greater profits while others chose for their extended families to consume the majority of their increased outputs. One example of the cases collected is detailed in Box 14.1.

> **Box 14.1 Mr Hossain's fish pond, Faridpur, Bangladesh**
>
> Sohrab Hossain Sardar started rearing fish in 2006 encouraged by the high returns the previous year of a local pond fish farmer and trained nursery owner, Mr Zahid. Mr Hossain, 70 years of age, is a retired police officer with four sons who are all in service living away from home. He owns 1.65 acres of land that he leased out as he is too old to work on it himself. He claims that what he receives from the lease is just enough to feed him and his wife for six months. For the rest of the year he depends on his sons for support, but this is a sensitive issue. His daughters-in-law weren't too keen on supporting him and for that reason he was looking for additional income.
>
> In April 2006, Mr Hossain started fish cultivation in his idle 0.10 ha pond next to the house after having spent a few informal 'learning sessions' with Mr Zahid. Fingerlings worth Tk3,500 (US$51) were released in the pond according to Mr Zahid's instructions but the fish didn't grow very fast. Mr Hossain confessed that he hadn't followed Mr Zahid's advice on feed. Mr Hossain lacked the energy and perhaps also the funds to feed the fish every few days. To get the best size with the least investment, he kept the fish in his pond as long as possible. If he had leased out the pond, he would have earned Tk2,500 ($36), but with Mr Zahid's support and without following all his 'best practices', he still managed to sell his fish for Tk20,000 ($289). With around Tk5,000 ($72) invested in labour to 'net' the pond regularly to increase the level of oxygen in the water, this still makes a nice supplement to a meagre pension.
>
> *Source:* de Ruyter de Wildt (2007)

Estimating outreach and impact on poverty

Based on the assessment, Katalyst estimated the intervention is increasing the incomes of 6,750 pond fish farmers who learn directly from trained nurseries and 12,000 pond fish farmers who learn from hawkers or other farmers who interact with trained nurseries. This estimate assumes that only half of the nurseries were able to successfully use the training to help their customers and that only regular customers were able to apply new information in their fish ponds. The cost of the intervention was approximately USD $25,000 including direct costs, staff time and overheads.

The assessment confirmed that large numbers of poor families earn their main incomes from hawking or farming fish. Katalyst estimated that over three years, the intervention will have increased farmers' incomes by over $140,000. This increased income, which is most significant among the smallest and therefore poorest farmers has a significant impact on reducing the poverty of these farmers. However, it is not possible to estimate from the assessment data what percentage of people were raised out of poverty due to the intervention.

The assessment showed that the nursery training programme has accelerated sector growth. Partly as a result of more active and more knowledgeable nurseries and the resulting increases in pond fish productivity and profits, farmers are bringing additional ponds under cultivation and more families are beginning to cultivate fish in previously unused ponds. This growth is creating additional demand for seasonal labour. In 2008, Katalyst aims to assess the extent of employment created as a result of sector growth resulting from the intervention.

The survey indicated that fish farming families increase their consumption of fish as output increases. The highest increases were among the smallest farmers: micro farmers increased consumption by 18 per cent and small farmers by 16 per cent. In-depth interviews with farmers supported this finding, although the differences between the treatment and control groups were not significant. In addition, the increase in the supply of fish in local markets may be beneficial to poor families, although this was not captured by the study.

It is likely that additional income and jobs are also being created through the backwards and forwards linkages in the pond fish sector and related sectors. For example, it is likely that the increased demand for fish feed resulted in more profits and jobs in the fish feed sector. However, to keep the assessment manageable, Katalyst chose not to investigate these benefits. It may also be that some fish farmers in Faridpur or nearby districts who were not benefited by the intervention were actually negatively affected by the increased supply of fish from affected farmers. While staff observations did not indicate evidence of negative impacts, Katalyst chose not to investigate this possibility formally, again to keep the assessment manageable. They reasoned that this effect was likely to be limited given the fast growing demand for fish both nationally and in Faridpur (Bangladesh DOF, 2006).

Analysing sustainability

Beyond the immediate impact on businesses in the pond fish sector and on incomes, jobs and nutrition, Katalyst wanted to know to what extent the effects of the intervention would continue. Would nurseries continue to gather new information and pass it on to farmers? The quantitative research indicated that providing more useful information to farmers had paid off for nurseries and hawkers, so they would be likely to continue this practice. The qualitative research also yielded some positive signs. As a result not only of the nursery training but also of Katalyst's efforts to build the capacity of the local fishery associations, the associations strengthened their relationships with members and with external bodies such as the Department of Fisheries. Trained nurseries consistently named associations as their key source of information on a broad range of business issues. The associations are organizing events and training courses more frequently than before and around more varied issues in the pond fish sector.

Using information

In response to the assessment findings, Katalyst has continued to invest in its fish programme and to intensify the focus on nurseries. Because nurseries are such important sources for continuous local learning, the project, together with the associations, has introduced a number of cultivation techniques and fish species that are new to the area through a training and demonstration programme centred around nurseries. Because the research showed that hawkers are a more important source of information for farmers than was expected, the project has started an intervention in which nurseries can nominate hawkers for a training programme on basic fish cultivation techniques.

Katalyst's overall monitoring and impact assessment system

In November 2005, Katalyst's donors accepted the recommendation of a review mission that the project should monitor and assess impact up to the poverty level. Since then, Katalyst has worked to install a system that not only provides its donors with reasonable estimates of the project's impact on poverty reduction but also provides managers and field staff with more information to steer project interventions towards maximizing poverty reduction. While the system is now operational, Katalyst continues to address problems in it.

Impact logics – the foundation of the system

For each intervention and for each sector as a whole, managers and field staff design an impact logic (see Figure 14.1 for the pond fish example). An impact logic starts with the project's activities and ends with poverty reduction through increases in incomes, jobs and other social benefits. The logic unravels each expected change between the project activities and increases in income and employment. The impact logics are similar to logical frameworks but tend to have more levels to allow for a more thorough exploration of the many links between activities and poverty reduction typical of market development programmes (see AusAid, 2005). While each logic is tailored to the specific intervention or sector, they generally cover:

- immediate outputs in the business service markets Katalyst is targeting, such as service providers trained;
- outcomes in the service market such as service providers offering better services and increasing their number of SME customers;
- changes in SME behaviour in the sector, such as farmers adopting new practices;
- changes in SME performance in the sector, such as increased productivity and profits;
- additional businesses entering the sector as a result of seeing improved performance of directly affected businesses;
- increased incomes and employment as a result of better business performance and additional businesses in the sector as well as any other poverty reducing impacts.

By September 2007, Katalyst had impact logics covering most of its interventions and sectors.

Managers and staff then choose one or two key indicators for each level in the logic to assess if and to what extent expected changes actually happen. At the start of interventions, expected changes in the indicators due to interventions are put in the logics, based on experience, previous studies, expert opinions and/or bench mark data. These projections give staff targets to aim for and provide the staff with feedback on the extent to which an intervention is on track. The projections also allow managers to predict expected impact per sector and overall, and to assess progress towards these projections as information is gathered and analysed.

Assessing changes and estimating impact

Katalyst gathers data on the key indicators at various levels of the impact logics over time using surveys, interviews and simple observations. A mix of quantitative and qualitative methods for assessment is always used (see EES, 2007).

However, managers not only need to know what changes have taken place, but also what changes are a result of the project interventions as opposed to the many other factors affecting the markets in which Katalyst works (see Figure 14.4). Assessments must gather information on the situation before the project interventions, how it has changed after the interventions and how the situation would have changed anyway without interventions. Katalyst uses a range of methodologies to isolate the changes produced by project activities (see EES, 2007).

Information on each level of the logic is always gathered to see if the expected intermediate changes are happening that would lead to later changes and finally poverty reduction. The project also always uses qualitative research to investigate the change processes happening in a sector. Field staff keep a diary on everything they observe during field visits. These observations are an important part of the system and help to understand what changes are really happening. In-depth interviews are often used to explore changes from activities through the various levels in the impact logic.

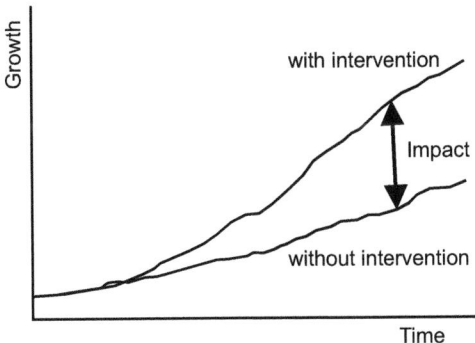

Figure 14.4 Isolating project impact

In addition, quasi-experimental surveys with treatment and control groups are preferred when practical and when the investment in the intervention justifies the assessment costs. Quasi-experimental designs are not practical when the target group is quite unique, as is often the case with large urban clusters, or when interventions can influence the control group as well, as in enabling environment interventions. Control groups also work better for specific interventions than for whole sectors. In these cases, the project uses other methodologies to isolate changes resulting from the project including asking service providers, SMEs and others why changes happened, comparing areas where Katalyst works with other areas, against national trends and/or against historical trends and tracking other significant factors that might induce change such as new infrastructure or other projects. For most sectors, Katalyst commissions larger surveys (sample size of a few hundred) every two years to get statistically significant data on changes in sector businesses including business practices, business performance and poverty-related information, such as profits and employment.

Staff develop a monitoring and evaluation plan for each impact logic that specifies the types of assessment methods that will be used. Information gathering is planned for different levels of the impact logic depending on when changes can reasonably be expected. Currently, Katalyst collects data by gender only when outreach to women is expected to be significant. The project is working on a simple system to disaggregate all data by gender.

Katalyst complements its basic system for monitoring and assessing impact with special studies on areas of interest such as gender, working conditions and common types of interventions such as training. The project also uses studies to validate common assumptions that cut across many sectors. For example, staff observations and secondary source data show that for each farmer that experiences significant benefits by changing business practices, two other farmers, on average, will copy those practices to some extent. Katalyst is planning a study to validate this assumption across a number of agricultural sectors; this data will then not be gathered for each agricultural sector in which the project works. These special studies are led by outside consultants.

Aggregating findings

Katalyst aims to aggregate impact assessment findings across all its activities in order to be able to regularly report its overall estimated contribution to poverty reduction. While the project reduces poverty in a number of ways, the most significant and common ways are through increases in incomes and employment for poor people. Katalyst calculates consolidated figures on income for small entrepreneurs, farmers and workers as well as the number of full-time equivalent, sustainable jobs created. To do this, managers add up the additional incomes and jobs resulting from project activities in each sector. Katalyst also reports its overall outreach to SMEs and farmers by adding up outreach in each sector. Where necessary, the figures are reduced to account for overlap among the sectors.

Using this system, Katalyst came up with its first consolidated figures in 2007. The consolidated figures estimated impact from the first five years of the project based on data already gathered and impact projections for on-going activities. The projections take into account that some activities in 2007 will not show poverty level impact until 2009.

By 2009, the first five years of the project will have benefited approximately 730,000 farmers and entrepreneurs directly and an additional 950,000 indirectly. Katalyst estimates that the first five years of the project will have led to at least 183,000 additional jobs (full-time equivalent). The jobs are almost all for daily labourers, people without land or productive assets who largely fall within the 50 per cent of Bangladeshis living below the poverty line.

Keeping the system manageable

Katalyst has found that assessing changes and impact across all its sectors and interventions can take up a lot of time and money. Therefore, managers have tried to balance accuracy and simplicity in a number of critical decisions that help keep the system manageable.

Assumptions. Sometimes staff make assumptions about the extent of changes resulting from the previous step in a logic. These assumptions may be based on information in secondary sources, expert opinions or staff estimates from observations and experience. For example, the amount paid for advertising services is used as a proxy for the amount of sales businesses will generate from those advertising services.

Crowding in. If Katalyst helps some business service providers to thrive, it expects other service providers to follow the successes. Similarly, SMEs will copy other successful SMEs. More profits in a certain value chain or sector will stimulate farmers or entrepreneurs to enter the sector. This crowding in is one of the reasons to develop markets instead of giving direct support to enterprises. Where it can be expected, Katalyst *does include* crowding in at the service market and enterprise levels in its impact logics. The extent of crowding in is then assessed both for interventions and for whole sectors. Aggregated figures separate direct impact from the indirect impact created by crowding in.

Forward and backward linkages. More growth in a targeted sector often stimulates growth somewhere else in the economy. For example, more maize production results in the availability of more and better poultry feed, which increases the profitability of poultry production, leading to growth and increased employment in this sector. Katalyst has decided *not to include* these types of indirect impacts in their impact assessments and aggregated figures.

Sharing credit. Katalyst implements all its activities in partnership with private-sector companies, associations and/or organizations. Given this way of working, managers do not feel that the project can take sole credit for changes resulting from interventions, even if they would not have happened without the project's involvement. Therefore, Katalyst *only takes credit for part of the changes* resulting from interventions. How big that part is depends on the relative investments of ideas, time, funds and risk by Katalyst and its primary private-sector partners for each intervention.

Displacement. Katalyst interventions benefit some enterprises but did others suffer as a result? For example, if furniture makers benefited by project interventions sell more furniture, maybe other furniture makers sell less. Usually, Katalyst chooses to work in fast growing sectors and therefore expects displacement to be minimal. However, displacement may become a bigger issue if sectors become saturated or growth slows. Katalyst is developing internal guidelines on how to account for displacement.

Unintended impacts. Impact logics lay out what managers and staff expect to happen as a result of their interventions. However, market players and markets may react differently than expected. Katalyst does not have a formal system for investigating unintended impact. Instead, staff look for unintended impacts, either positive or negative, during field visits and while interacting with market players. Questions about unintended impacts are also integrated into qualitative tools such as in-depth interviews.

Timing of assessments. Katalyst aims to create a lasting basis for growth. Impact does not happen only at one moment but continues over time. It also takes time before substantial impact on enterprises and poverty is visible. Managers think that in most cases, enterprise and poverty-level impacts become visible between one and three years after an intervention. Impact will continue to increase after this, but the longer the timeframe, the more difficult it is to isolate the impact of the project. For simplicity, Katalyst calculates its poverty impact figures assuming that only impact within three years of starting an intervention can be attributed to project activities. Only in very exceptional cases does Katalyst assess or claim impact beyond three years after an intervention.

Challenges

Katalyst's key challenge is ensuring that the information from the monitoring and impact assessment system is systematically fed into ongoing decision making at all levels of the project. The project is installing a regular review of each market every six months. During the review, project staff and managers analyse the overall market strategy as well as the progress of interventions in the market. All findings from the monitoring and impact assessment system over the last six months, based both on formal and informal information gathering, are reviewed to identify successes, problems and lessons learned in the interventions and overall market strategy. These are then used to plan for the next six months. For example, data showed that an awareness-raising campaign for rural ICT centres did not create the expected results. New approaches to awareness creation were then developed.

Katalyst is also working on improving its monitoring and impact assessment system in the following areas:
- Analysing and interpreting data, particularly from larger market surveys, so that the information can inform decision making.
- Simplifying the system and strengthening oversight so that there is greater uniformity in the application of the system across all sectors.
- Estimating the number of people exiting poverty as a result of interventions.
- Estimating cost per sector and conducting cost/benefit analysis.

Conclusion

Katalyst initiated this new monitoring and impact assessment system because their donors required it. But has it been useful to Katalyst beyond satisfying their donors?

Managers have found the system to be an excellent management tool. Katalyst has been able to increase all staff's focus on maximizing poverty reduction both during the design and during the steering of interventions. By writing impact logics, staff are compelled to think through the potential poverty impacts before the intervention starts. Projections allow staff to compare the potential of interventions and choose those with the greatest potential for poverty reduction. Regular data collection helps show if interventions and sectors are on track or if remedial action is required. Assessing each level in the impact logics helps staff understand the processes of change and adjust interventions accordingly. Once the system has been in place longer, it will also help to guide relative investments in sectors. Estimating Katalyst's contribution to poverty reduction for Phase I gave both staff and managers a motivational boost.

Managers have also found that the system helps with reporting. Katalyst is better able to project future impact and better able to report on estimated impacts. Katalyst is also able to more systematically show qualitative examples of how its interventions reduce poverty.

Installing the new system did take time, resources and involvement from all staff. However, Katalyst managers feel that the investment was worth it, not only for generating figures, but more importantly, for the gains in project effectiveness.

References

AusAid (Australian Agency for International Development) (2005) 'AusGuideline 3.3 The Logical Framework Approach', Commonwealth of Australia.
Bangladesh DOF (Department of Fisheries) (2005) *Annual Statistics*, Department of Fisheries, Dhaka.
Bangladesh DOF (2006) *Annual Statistics*, Department of Fisheries, Dhaka.
Bangladesh DOF (2007) *Annual Statistics*, Department of Fisheries, Dhaka.

Copestake, J. (2004) 'Social performance assessment of microfinance – cost-effective or costly indulgence?', *Small Enterprise Development* 15 (3): 11–17.

de Ruyter de Wildt, M. (2007) 'Accelerating Growth in the Pond Fish Sector', Springfield Centre for Business in Development for Katalyst, Katalyst, Dhaka.

EES (European Evaluation Society) (2007) 'EES statement: The importance of a methodologically diverse approach to impact evaluation – specifically with respect to development aid and development intervention', EES Secretariat, Nijkerk.

Hulme, D. (2000) 'Impact assessment methodologies for microfinance: Theory, experience and better practice', *World Development* 28 (1): 79–98.

Kirkpatrick, C. and Hulme, D. (2001) 'Basic Impact Assessment at Project Level', Department for International Development, London.

Springfield Centre (forthcoming) 'The Making Markets Work for the Poor (M4P) Approach', for Swiss Agency for Development and Cooperation (SDC) and UK Department for International Development (DFID), Springfield Centre for Business in Development Ltd,.

Tanburn, J. (2008) *The 2008 Reader on Private Sector Development: Measuring and Reporting on Results*, International Training Centre of the International Labour Organization, Turin.

About the authors

Peter Roggekamp is the General Manager of Katalyst; Harald Bekkers was the Division Manager – Industry and Rural Sectors Division but has since become a consultant associated with the Springfield Centre. Alexandra Miehlbradt is an independent consultant specializing in pro-poor enterprise and market development. This article draws on the case study of Katalyst's work in the pond fish sector written by Marieke de Ruyter de Wildt of the Springfield Centre. The authors would like to acknowledge the significant contributions of Katalyst's pond fish market team and monitoring and evaluation team to the study and the article.

CHAPTER 15

Managing the process of change: useful frameworks for implementers of making markets work for the poor programmes

Marshall Bear and Michael Field

This article was first published in June 2008.

Abstract

This article presents project management frameworks developed and used by PROFIT Zambia – a five-year USAID-funded programme supporting agriculture/natural resources development – to guide its interventions in facilitating inclusive and sustained industry competitiveness. The frameworks showcased in the article are two: an industry pathway and related knowledge management process. The article describes the frameworks and illustrates their use as tools by PROFIT in guiding its interventions in Zambia's domestic beef industry and supportive veterinarian services market. The article concludes by drawing lessons on the use of these frameworks for agencies taking or planning to take a facilitation approach to implementing pro-poor agriculture development projects.

A systemic approach to promoting pro-poor agriculture competitiveness considers a broad range of market functions (core transactions, support functions and rules), market players (private, public, civil society) and the incentives and relationships that drive and sustain an industry upgrading strategy. Facilitators of change within these market systems set themselves the challenging task of stimulating change without becoming a part of it. PROFIT Zambia, which is a five-year programme supported by USAID, is attempting this task, catalysing a process of constant upgrading among local industry actors.

The economic incentives and cultural norms that drive behaviour and constantly changing market dynamics make the environment fluid, often resulting in conflicting economic and social incentives. It is the job of the market facilitator, in the face of these conflicting incentives, to foster new and shifting relationships, on-going innovation and shifting benefit flows such that the direct value chain and associated actors behave in a way that, in the collective, makes the industry more competitive.

172 VALUE CHAINS IN DEVELOPMENT

Two frameworks have proven useful for the PROFIT programme to facilitate an industry upgrading strategy – an industry pathway tool and knowledge management process.

An industry pathway

This shows the interaction between a sequenced set of interventions and the anticipated systemic changes – in shared benefits, in win/win relationships and in continuous learning/innovation – required to drive and sustain an industry upgrading strategy. Figure 15.1 depicts the pathway tool. The top arrows show the sequencing of PROFIT's interventions from demonstration to scale up leading to exit. In the *demonstration stage*, the programme designs an initial set of interventions to 'buy-down' (reduce) the costs (search, information, enforcement, bargaining) of early adopters (both vets and farmers) to properly assess risk of entering a transaction in a setting with very little information. This initiates an ongoing process of comparing how and why value chain and associated actors react (or not) to opportunities and perceived threats catalysed by project interventions. The scale up and exit stage in the intervention process aims to institutionalize and broaden the incentives that have been proven to drive behaviours consistent with a competitive industry. In practice, this means both replicating successful activities to more regions and 'crowding-in' more system functions and players with incentives and capacity to drive/respond to change.

The programme observes over time anticipated changes in three systemic characteristics – benefits, relationships and learning/innovation – that are interrelated and crucial to an industry's ability to compete over time (the arrow at the base of the diagram):

- Benefits accrue in terms of incomes, social status and reduced risks. Benefits must be great enough to provide incentives to change behaviours so that actors take on new risks, take on new types of relationships, change the nature of their commercial relationships, and embrace learning and innovation as the basis for competition.

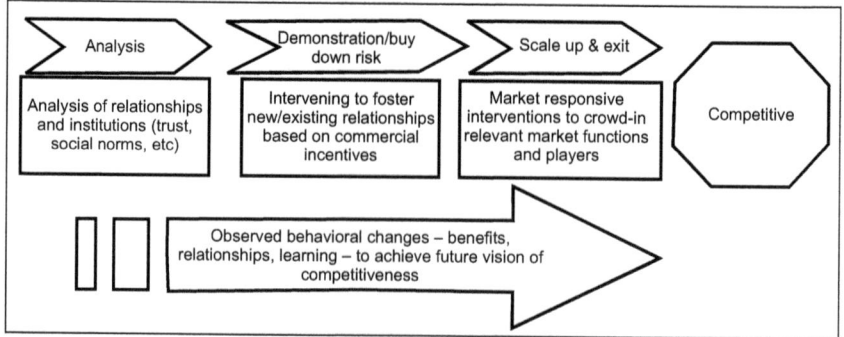

Figure 15.1 An industry pathway (adapted from The Springfield Centre, 2007)

- Relationships that are more transparent, longer term and focused on industry level goals are critical to an industry's ability to respond and adapt to changing demand. Incentives that foster win/win relationships enable industries to push knowledge and skills from where they are located to where they need to be within the broader industry.
- Learning and innovation happen only when incentives are in place to encourage firms to invest in learning and/or risk adapting innovations. When learning and innovation are an integral part of an industry's norms that industry's competitive position is more likely to be sustained over time.

Knowledge management process

Because market change is a complex process, PROFIT needed a way to constantly compare actual versus expected behavioural changes along the pathway to competitiveness and determine if/when shifts in its interventions should be considered. The programme put in place a knowledge management process, as depicted in Figure 15.2, to capture tacit (held internal to an individual) and explicit (defined through a report or presentation) knowledge and to engage staff/partners in a process of collectively assessing and learning from this knowledge to guide intervention decisions. It would be only through a knowledge management foundation that PROFIT could determine if a project was headed in the right direction at an acceptable pace within the timeframe necessary to modify project activities assuring the best possibility of success. You will see in the case of the veterinarian services market how the programme uses both the industry pathway and knowledge management system to facilitate advancing an industry along the pathway to greater competitiveness.

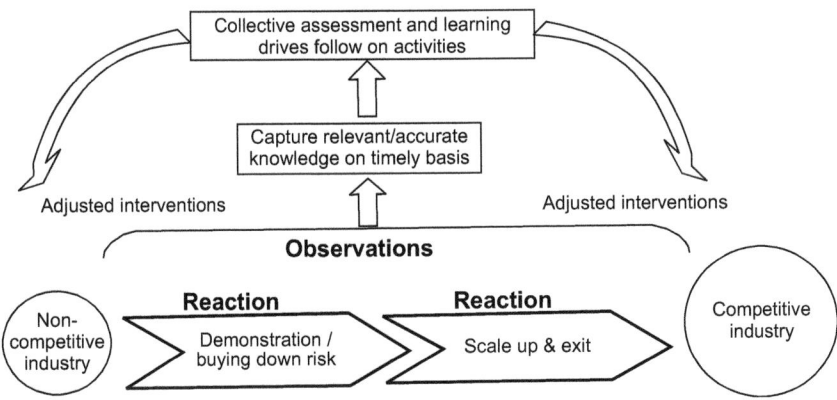

Figure 15.2 Knowledge management process

The tools in use: the case of beef/vet services

Why beef? Today, Zambia's beef industry is uncompetitive due primarily to weak and ineffective linkages between market actors that plagues the industry's ability to respond to critical threats such as low productivity, competition from imports, drought and disease outbreak (estimates range from 40 to 60 per cent of the national herd – almost all held by smallholders – has been lost in the last 10 years). Still, PROFIT chose to work in Zambia's beef industry because the growing demand/supply gap (depressing historical demand due to high beef prices) presented an opportunity to significantly increase supply by improving the stock quality of the large numbers of smallholders nationwide who own 70 per cent of herd total (up to 1 million head of cattle) and represent 230,000 households.

To act on this opportunity, the industry would have to address three major weaknesses – low productivity, poor animal health, and high transaction costs. The programme discovered through its industry analysis that a key underlying cause – or systemic constraint (the bold circle in Figure 15.3) – of these problems related to social rules and behavioural norms of smallholders that limit commercial risk taking, define cattle in terms of social capital and limit the development of mutually beneficial commercial relationships.

Why vets first? The combination of these constraints/behaviour norms led PROFIT to determine that controlling disease and shifting smallholder

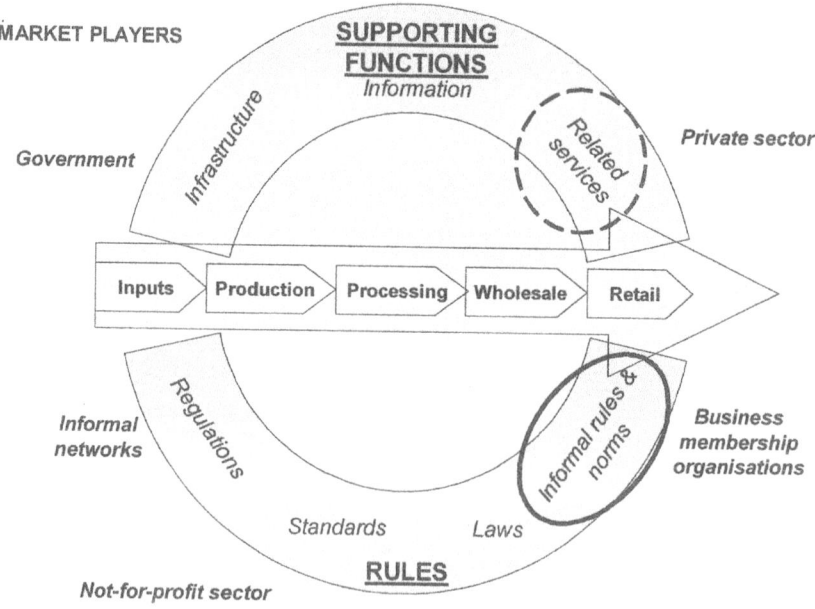

Figure 15.3 Beef market system

management practices had to provide the foundation on which the beef industry could improve its competitive position and become an engine for growth and poverty reduction. Private veterinary services were identified as a weak supporting function (the dashed circle in Figure 15.3) that when addressed could foster disease control, establish a platform for ongoing behaviour shifts in smallholder management and resonate with smallholder consumers. In Zambia where government vet services had collapsed and the shift from government to private vet services was very slow this presented an enormous challenge.

The veterinarian business service model

Based on its initial industry analysis, PROFIT knew that commercially viable yet affordable veterinarian services targeting smallholders would have to address three major issues to be appropriate under Zambian conditions: the delivery of services in dispersed communities with few people separated by large distances with poor and limited roads would be costly; the lack of vets in the market place to serve distant communities would stretch the capacity of any individual vet to deliver services; and the regulatory requirements set by government to protect animal and public health would still have to be satisfied by a registered vet business. To meet these conditions the programme facilitated a prepaid preventative health maintenance service plan where interested private vets would bundle together multiple services (for example,

---

Box 15.1 Market understanding of vet services

PROFIT's approach to privatize vet services did consider past efforts in Zambia and elsewhere (Mercy Corps in Azerbaijan – see Alimardanov et al, 2006). Two relatively recent donor-supported programmes in Zambia took a direct versus market approach to increase service access. One programme provided start-up capital and training to vets to encourage them to start a business. Another programme trained a network of community-based para-vets to provide preventative and referral services. When PROFIT started its work in beef and related vet services it found very little evidence of private vet services to smallholders (see Table 15.2 on baseline data below).

PROFIT determined that these previous efforts to privatize vets services did not take into account key Zambia smallholder market requirements – high transaction costs, the social context of why smallholders own cattle, the need for regulatory oversight and the need to shift from diagnosis and treatment to prevention.

Lessons from a vet service market programme by Mercy Corps in Azerbaijan showed the importance of understanding how markets work as the basis for intervention design (Mercy Corps addressed the high transaction costs of serving remote areas by organizing farm clusters and vet networks). But the comparison with Zambia basically stops there: the incentives were different (Azeri farmers started with a commercial mind set) as were the market entry barriers/costs (dairy high turnover versus cattle low turnover). Lessons on private-sector solutions elsewhere can be instructive provided programmes understand the underlying systemic constraints of the local context any model/approach intends to address.

diagnostics, dipping, medications, etc.) with a predefined timetable for service delivery and offer the plan to interested farmers. Most services would be delivered by a community member under contract from a formal vet business. The preventative nature of the services would allow for non-vets to administer the specific services since there would be less stringent controls on the substances used (for example, dipping chemicals) than if the services were disease treatment based. Community-based delivery would enhance viability and scalability of the vet service product by reducing transaction costs (for example, less vet travel to and time in the community) while at the same time enabling the formal vet business to satisfy regulatory requirements through trained and supervised community livestock workers (CLWs). The presence in the community of a livestock worker would also foster trust between the vet and the community.

Advancing along the pathway to vet services market competitiveness

Demonstration stage

Change strategy. The objective of this stage was to demonstrate the viability and scalability of the business service model (for example, prepaid health services) with a small number of willing and interested communities and vets. PROFIT used a mix of self-selection methods to identify vets and communities who saw the value of the service, were ready to enter into agreements with vets and willing to innovate with the CLW delivery model. The programme served as match maker between two parties that had not previously seen the value of working together. Agreements were negotiated and reached (although not always) by vets and communities with PROFIT mediating when the parties talked at cross purposes. With agreements in place, it was expected that the sales and profits for vets and improved herd productivity for small farmers would yield sufficiently strong incentives to encourage scale up as farmers reduced their per animal cost by adding more animals and signed up their neighbours, and as vets invested in their business capacity so that they could renew existing contracts and expand to new areas.

Advancing along the pathway. Five important divergences happened between expected and actual responses by users and providers of vet services to PROFIT interventions. Each divergence was triggered by knowledge gathered by the programme through tacit (staff meetings) and/or explicit means (tracking reports) and so they are introduced using headline statements that most certainly were uttered when programme managers and staff gathered to review progress:

- *Many more farmers sign the contract than pay* – in the early stages of product launch by vets, there was a disconnect between the initial signal of demand (contract signing) and the actual payment by farmers. Had PROFIT and the vets misread farmer demand? Though willing to sign contracts were farmers unwilling and/or lacked the capacity to pay for the service (about USD $18 per animal per year)? Programme staff learned that there was a divergence between the vet promotional message of selling productivity and income generation and the farmers' desire for relief from their problems of cattle sickness and death. Vets reworked their promotional message with PROFIT advice and repromoted the service as reactive to the problem of cattle disease and death. Farmers were willing and had the capacity to pay for the service; sales increased sharply. Programme staff learned early on the importance of understanding the social incentives (wealth preservation is why most smallholders own cattle) as the basis for promoting future relationships between vets, small farmers and other business partners that would be driven by increased productivity and wealth creation in the domestic beef market.

- *Vets find it difficult organizing payment* – in some communities, farmers didn't pay the scheduled instalment even though the vet delivered the services as agreed. It became time consuming and very expensive for vets to collect payment, limiting or eliminating their profit margin. Initially, it was looked at superficially as a limitation in farmer capacity to manage cash during rich and lean periods, but closer analysis by field staff showed that much of the hesitancy in paying was tied to trust issues related to forming a relationship with someone outside their friends and family network. What emerged was the need for an upfront 'trust' investment by vets in relationship building. The vets needed to spend quality time in the communities to gain their trust. (Correspondingly, farmers needed to make an upfront 'cash' investment for services to overcome the vets' concerns about non-payment.) Vets who made this investment had minimal payment problems while vets who did not make this investment continued to have payment problems.

- *Vets 'cry' loss despite payment by farmers* – PROFIT learned that vets complained to communities under contract they were losing money even though the farmers had paid upfront for six months and only two months had elapsed in the six-month service period. About 50 per cent of the early adopting vets were public vets already stationed in rural areas and who had established private firms to provide a few vet products. PROFIT certainly expected public vets in private business to have limited business skills and a lack of openness to learn effectively until they were forced to learn by business pressure. What was not expected was that a substantial percentage would ignore their business capacity limitations – primarily poor cash and inventory management – resulting in serious threats to their businesses. Programme staff reacted to the identified capacity gap by organizing a firm-specific participatory assessment and planning process to ensure that vets internalized the information. The response from most vets was solid with improvements in cash management and profitability.

- *Herd health plan (HHP) sales are necessary but not sufficient for vet business viability* – in many cases, sales of prepaid health services tended to level off which pointed to the limitations of the number of farmers that could/would buy the service in the near to medium term. Table 15.1 depicts the levelling off of prepaid services. The one spike in August of 2007, the direct result of promotional efforts conducted by vets and facilitated by PROFIT, could not be sustained in subsequent months. While the herd health service was the cornerstone of kick-starting the market, the scaling up of vet sales/small farmer services based primarily on the health service was proving to be incorrect. The divergence led programme staff to help vets shift to using the herd health service as a platform and then adding one-off services (for example, dipping, injections, supplements) and product sales to non-members in the community priced at a premium to maintain the value of the herd health plan. This three-revenue-stream strategy integrated into the CLW business model has moved vet businesses to solid profitability.
- *Some vets are slow to embrace the CLW-based delivery model* – the CLW-based service delivery exposed a tension between risk and cost for a vet business. Could they trust their hand-picked CLW to represent them and protect their reputation? Was there any other way to reduce high transaction costs without a community-based worker? PROFIT expected vets to learn the value of the CLW distribution structure and therefore push skills and responsibility down so that they could take on a more supervisory role allowing for greater expansion. It turned out that some vets were slow in understanding the business rationale for CLWs, often limiting the types of activities the CLW were allowed to perform. The result was that the vet tried to conduct all services, essentially eliminating the ability to grow the business. PROFIT responded with ongoing facilitation and advice pushing vets to train CLWs up to the agreed upon standards, shifting CLW pay structures to incentivize promotional activities and broadening the vet business model to include the three-revenue strategy as mentioned in Box 15.2.

Table 15.1 Sales from HHP (herd health plan) contracts (ZMK 1 mn = USD 270)

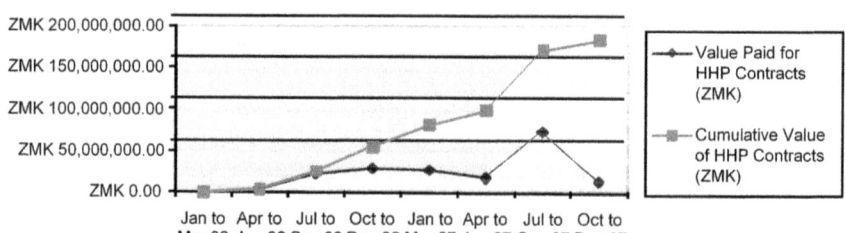

> **Box 15.2 Multiple information sources trigger adjustments in intervention**
>
> PROFIT's decision to foster a change from a single (herd health plan sales) to a three-revenue stream business model came from different information sources: (i) strong demand from non-HHP members for services whenever the vet performed regularly scheduled services to HHP members (suggesting a market segment of single service users); (ii) the levelling of HHP sales (as shown in Table 15.1) set against a high rate of contract renewals (suggesting cash constraints for a large upfront payment versus service demand or satisfaction); and (iii) lumpy cash inputs set against a vet's limited capacity to better manage working capital resulting in inventory shortages at times of scheduled service delivery (suggesting adjustments in the revenue model and strengthening vet business management capacity).
>
> Though self-evident, it is important to note that no single indicator or source of information is sufficient to guide decisions in complex and evolving markets.

Scale up and exit stage

Change strategy. Table 15.2 summarizes key changes in the vet services market set against a baseline established early on in the project (Abdul-Rahaman and Zulu, 2007). The table shows that more small farmers had purchased services from private vets to prevent animal disease and death and they had realized the benefit from these purchases. PROFIT had succeeded in demonstrating a business service model – the right promotional messages, upfront time investments by vets and cash investments by farmers to overcome trust issues, cost-reducing CLW-based delivery, and a diversified revenue stream – that was working. But, it was working with a limited number of vets and at a limited scale.

Table 15.2 Vet services market changes

	Project start (2005/2006)	*Current status (December 2007)*
Use of preventative services*	Most: agricultural input dealers Some: government vets Least: private vets Did nothing: 10%	Most: private vets Some: agricultural input dealers Least: government vets Did nothing: 2%
Farmers under HHP contract	—	850 (cumulative)
Animals under HHP contract	—	10,000 (cumulative)
Farmer spend/animal	—	$18/per animal/year
Vets in programme	—	10 in 5 regions
Sales (HHP plus)	NA (as above)	$66,000
Animal Health*		
Deaths reported	48% of farmers surveyed	15% (69% reduction)
Disease reported	93% of farmers surveyed	48% (48% reduction)

Note: * denotes variable reported in baseline of 50 farmers in 32 villages.

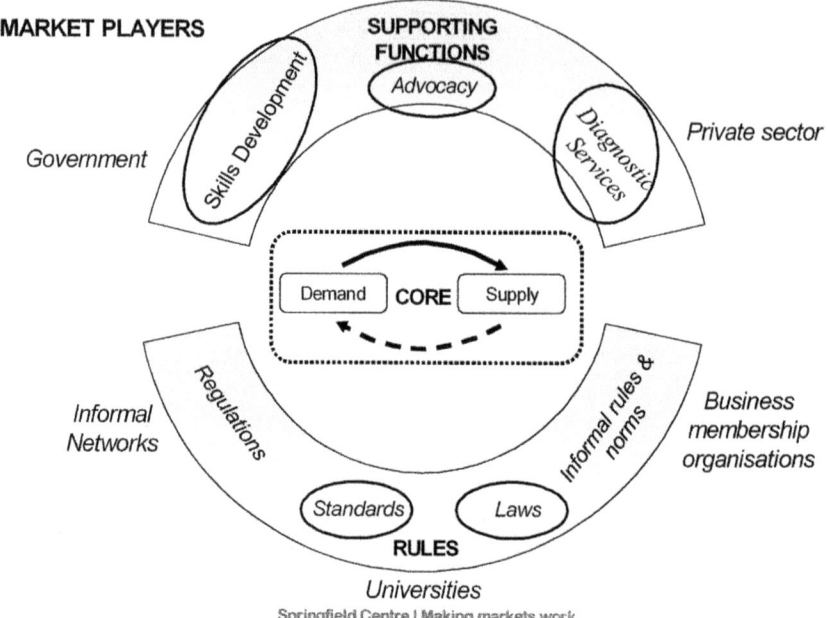

Figure 15.4 The vet services market

After 18 months of implementation, there was a slower than acceptable pace in the adoption by farmers of changed cattle management practices required to improve stock quality in sufficient numbers to foster changes in beef markets.

In the scale-up stage, PROFIT moved to address systemic constraints in the vet services market – better standards, pharmaceutical laws, diagnostic services, skills development, advocacy – that if effectively addressed would stimulate a stronger supply response to underserved small farmer demand for preventative services and accelerate the rate of herd quality improvements. Figure 15.4 shows the systemic constraints being currently addressed by PROFIT in this stage of project implementation.

Advancing along the pathway

Early adopters but probably not market drivers

PROFIT observed that some of the early adopters – public vets with a private business add-on – lacked the capacity (business acumen) and the willingness (investment in business growth) to drive longer-term vet services industry growth. With a proven business service model, PROFIT redirected its efforts to push just private vets to take a look at the business potential of the rural smallholder market for vet services. The private firms that have entered the vet services market with the programme's encouragement – 4 of the 10 vets supported by the programme – have demonstrated more business skills and a better grasp of the CLW delivery model. Though unwilling to enter an untested market, they are likely to be the drivers of longer-term growth and vet market competitiveness. In this scale-up stage, it is critically important to foster competition between firms. The public vets with a private business add-on will need to be pushed to improve or will fail to ensure consumer choice and continued movement along the pathway.

Who is responsible for setting standards anyway?

Vet services are and should be a regulated service market. CLW-based service delivery is a key feature of a viable/scaleable service yet there were no standards recognized or endorsed by the government. The process of fostering standards was initiated with a smaller group of private vets to ensure commitment and understanding of the role standards play in building a market while also satisfying government regulations. The private vets agreed to and established standards for CLW training/testing and on the basic level of quality and care for herd health services as a means to protect the fledgling industry. As the private vets established standards on CLW and service quality, PROFIT fostered a link with the government to review and discuss the privately adopted standards. Through this process another divergence was noticed in that central government officials were supportive while regional government vet officials were at times hostile to private vets. The extent of this inter-government conflict came as a surprise. This conflict led programme staff to offer the Vet Office within the Ministry of Agriculture assistance in fine tuning and communicating policy guidelines in regards to private vets delivering services in rural areas.

New market entrants with new services respond to incentives

When vet services to commercial farmers (i.e. cattle and poultry) and smallholders reached the point in terms of turnover to warrant localized diagnostic services, PROFIT began facilitating local interests in such a start up. The programme fostered links between the vet, poultry and beef industries to form a joint venture veterinary laboratory services firm as a means to lower the cost and increase the speed of disease diagnosis. What followed was not expected: the veterinary lab chose to position itself in the market as a centre of excellence and foster a more localized (i.e. not pushed by PROFIT) vet-to-vet network for shared learning and dealing with joint issues affecting their market (for example, pharmaceutical laws, standards, disease outbreaks/response mechanisms, etc.). New players with a new and critical service crowded-into the vet services market in response to the opportunity; now the lab is having a substantial catalytic affect on advancing the vet service market towards greater competitiveness. The lab achieved breakeven within the first year and has been operating profitably since mid-2007.

Few professional vets exist to answer the call

As vet sales grow in response to growing smallholder demand, PROFIT could foresee a mismatch between growing demand and supply. Would the educational system create future vets with the willingness and capacity to answer the demand signals? It was clear that for students there was no clear career path for a private vet targeting rural smallholders. Of a typical graduating class of 12, only half would enter the vet profession. Of these, only one or two would enter private practice and more likely than not focus on the urban dog and cat market. The others who remained in the vet profession would work for the government. In response to this serious structural problem, PROFIT initiated an internship programme for young vet graduates. The internship would last one year with PROFIT covering a portion of the student's stipend on a declining scale over the year, with the private vet picking up the remaining balance and all other costs. After an initial intensive mentoring period, the young vets are charged with overseeing the smallholder services for the vet firm. Three young vets entered the internship in the first year.

New arrangements/new channels for disease prevention services

The ideal preventative regime – dipping/spraying, deworming, access to vet services – requires capital investments (cattle dips) and more trained vets and this will take time to evolve and develop, as is evident from the programme's experience. Spraying for parasites offers another option to improve animal health (80 per cent of disease and death of cattle is from parasites). The programme is now also advancing this option by leveraging its prior work in fostering a network of private spraying service providers for row crops (such as cotton) and retooling the network to add tick prevention to their service mix. Two different commercial arrangements are about to be launched: one where the agriculture input supply company hires a vet and another where the company and the vet share revenues and costs. In both models, sprayers will be trained and certified by vets so that they can offer a skilled and credible service to farmers. Vets will be able to extend the message of prevention for better animal health and build future clients while agriculture input supply companies will be able to diversify the range of products and services it offers to small farmers.

Case summary

Figure 15.5 summarizes the advances that have been made by the PROFIT project along the pathway to a more inclusive (smallholder-focused) and competitive vet services industry. The vet services market is working better for small farmers and private service providers. Transactions for preventative animal health services are growing and are more likely to continue to grow because of the role PROFIT has played in facilitating (not directing) changes in the incentives and commercial relationships required for a competitive and growing services industry.

So, where's the beef? This article started by noting that a key systemic constraint to more small farmer participation in growing beef markets had a lot to do with social rules and behavioural norms of smallholders that limit commercial risk taking, define cattle in terms of social capital and limit the development of mutually beneficial commercial relationships. The proof of PROFIT's decision to address a problem in the beef market by facilitating changes in the vet services market should be indicated by more and better priced cattle sales by small farmers. To date, however, few cattle sales by small farmers have been recorded. Is this an appropriate indicator? Yes. Is it the appropriate indicator at this stage of the project? No. If it were, key market changes – in realigning incentives towards shared benefits on productivity/income generation (to see cattle as a wealth generator) and in fostering trust and confidence in commercial relationships – would be missed. PROFIT has begun leveraging progress made in input service markets into establishing relationships in output markets by fostering relationships between smallholders and two commercial feedlots and one processor/retailer that have demonstrated interest in establishing transparent and commercially grounded links with smallholders on vet contracts for more than one year.

A small group of farmers will set up a sales point in the community where all cattle will be sold to commercial buyers. The idea is to use this as a starting point for organizing farmers – driven by economic incentives (for example, wealth creation versus preservation) – into an outgrower model producing young cattle that will go directly into a feedlot. PROFIT expects to shift more

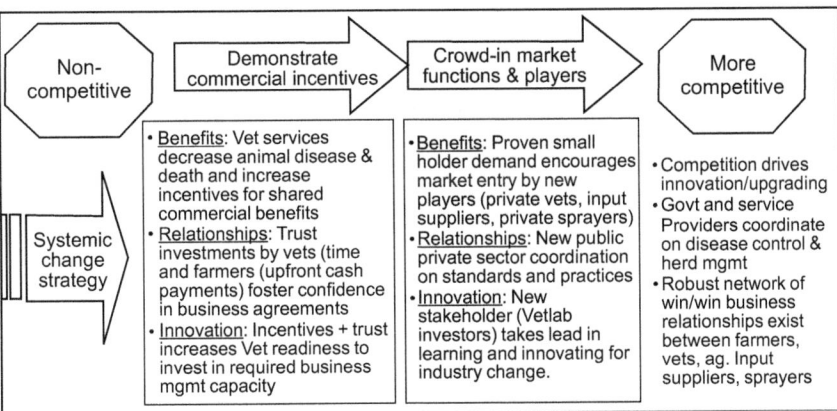

Figure 15.5. Advancing along the pathway

of its resources towards these output relationships as a means to both deepen the incentives for ongoing growth in the vet industry and to advance along the pathway to a more inclusive and competitive domestic beef industry.

Lessons for market facilitation and facilitators

Facilitating what? Systemic change for sustainable impact

Market facilitation is about fostering the evolution of the market system in a direction and at a pace that generates wealth in an inclusive manner. A static focus on short-term income gains, sales or capacity building efforts can lead projects to make counter productive investments. The pathway framework asks facilitators to think through how change in underlying systemic constraints – benefit flows, relationships, innovation – is likely to be influenced by project interventions. Knowledge management puts in place a system to guide and track this systemic change process.

Replication versus wider system change as the means to achieve scale

Achieving scale is a prerequisite for market system change: scale offers the commercial incentives for competition and competition stimulates the process of learning and innovation. Scale – in this case more vets services transacted – has been achieved partly by replicating what works in one location with either the same or different vets in new locations. The potential to achieve greater scale came when PROFIT expanded its interventions from a sole reliance on replicating the vet business service model and to address related but different system problems: new services (for example, diagnostics), standards, advocacy, laws, and skills development (for example, for tick sprayers). Too much reliance on replication as a scale up strategy can be counterproductive as it may send the wrong signals to prospective market actors and dilute resources better used elsewhere.

Sequencing does not mean linear!

Sequencing interventions by a third-party catalyst is important; at the very least it builds presence and credibility with market players. Sequencing, however, is not a step-by-step linear process where one intervention and related benchmark must be completed before moving sequentially to the next. Facilitators have to be guided by a future vision of industry competitiveness. At any slice in time, PROFIT has been in multiple places along the pathway to a competitive vet services market (entry, re-entry, scale up and exit) depending on how each region, vet and community took up responsibilities and changed behaviours.

Failure is required in a market system

For market systems to function properly failure of individual businesses is a norm. Understanding the power of churning (for example, the cycle of failure, reorganization of components and new start-ups) is central to fostering market system growth.

Effective market facilitation requires effective knowledge management

To effectively facilitate a change process, the facilitator must understand and adjust to the adoption and crowding in processes of local actors. The triggers that result in a social shift that then pushes a behaviour towards being the norm are dynamic and often defined by starts and stops. This has profound implications for managing projects both inside the market with market actors and outside the market with project donors. The typical two-year work plan with accompanied command and control hierarchy and rigid unidirectional reporting processes are outdated and ineffective for managing a facilitated change process.

References

Abdul-Rahaman, Hamdiya and Zulu, Joseph (2007) 'An assessment of household income/production and accessibility to social services in Choma and Mkushi Districts', PROFIT Zambia.

Alimardanov, E., Abdullayev, K., Rothenberger, C. and Young, A. (2006) 'Livestock services for small-scale cattle holders in rural Azerbaijan', *EDM* 17 (4).

Springfield Centre (2007) Making Markets Work, Training Programme, Springfield Centre, Glasgow.

About the authors

Marshall A. Bear, a US-based enterprise consultant, has advised the PROFIT project over the past few years on staff and management systems development; he is also a core faculty member of the Springfield Centre's 'Making Markets Work' training programmes. Michael Field worked as the Private Sector Development Advisor for USAID's PROFIT Project in Zambia, and has since joined ACDI-VOCA in Liberia.

CHAPTER 16
Business environment reforms: Why it is necessary to rethink priorities and strategies

Tilman Altenburg and Christian von Drachenfels

This article was first published in September 2008.

Abstract

> Reforming the business environment is high on the agenda of the international donor community. The Doing Business reports suggest that excessive regulation is a key obstacle to private sector development. Simplification of the regulatory business environment is thus recommended as the most important reform for private sector development. Countries achieve the highest score on seven out of ten Doing Business Indicators if they do not regulate at all. Furthermore, it is alleged that reforms can be achieved with the stroke of a minister's pen. This ignores important benefits of regulation and underestimates the difficulties of institutional change. This article argues that the real challenge is to define appropriate levels of regulation, which differ across countries, regions and sectors, and to make governments accountable for services – rather than abolishing them altogether.

Reforming the regulatory business environment is high on the agenda of the international donor community. Mainstream reforms are strongly influenced by the World Bank/International Finance Corporation's (IFC) Doing Business Indicators, which provide a simple and popular tool to benchmark the performance of countries.

This article sets out to explain why reforming the regulatory business environment has become so popular. It continues by showing that, while there is no doubt about the need to adopt regulatory reforms, some of the key assumptions of reform proponents do not hold. Parts of the reform agenda are misguided and may in fact do more harm than good, and they grossly overstate the relevance of regulatory reforms on private sector development (PSD) and growth. Furthermore, several reasons are provided why implementation of reforms is a highly complex process of searching for and negotiating appropriate sets of regulation that are country-, region- and sector-specific.

Why reforming the regulatory business environment has become so popular

As Tanburn (2006) shows in a previous issue of this journal the good news in recent years is that the fundamental role of PSD for sustainable poverty reduction is now almost universally acknowledged by governments and donor agencies. But the debate about what the most binding constraints are, and what the right mix of proactive support, regulation and deregulation should be, remains unsettled. Some private sector development experts and practitioners advocate comprehensive programmes to foster the development of national industries in general and SMEs in particular, whereas others reject a strong public involvement and instead prioritize deregulation and simplification of procedures that hamper business activity. In general terms, developing countries' private sector polices and donor strategies seem to shift away from sector- or cluster-specific support and towards reforms to get the regulatory business environment right.

There are two main reasons for this. First, there is growing consensus that 'institutions matter'. Research on institutions and institutional change confirms the fundamental role of the 'rules of the game' for economic development (North, 1994). An institutional framework that guarantees property rights and enables actors to enforce contracts is thus generally acknowledged as being important for development in general, and for the dynamics of the private sector especially.

Second, targeted interventions for PSD have often had little positive impact on the performance of the target group, for example SMEs. Service provision is often not very efficient and only benefits a small fraction of the target group. In some cases it introduced incentives for enterprises to stay small, in other cases public funds benefited those who were not exactly in need (Committee of Donor Agencies, 2001; Tanburn, 2006). Moreover, causal relationships between support programmes and alleged programme achievements can hardly be proven due to the great number of external factors that influence PSD.

Against this background, the *Doing Business* series of the World Bank/IFC and related research papers (for example Djankov et al, 2006; Klapper et al, 2006) have been very successful in creating a new private sector development paradigm that builds on simple messages: first, that deregulation of the regulatory business environment will immediately stimulate entrepreneurship and unleash economic growth, benefiting especially the informal poor who suffer most from unfair regulation; and second, that reforms to achieve this can easily be implemented and are less costly than traditional targeted support policies.

Regarding the first proposition, the Doing Business series argues that burdensome and unnecessary regulations are causing considerable costs for firms, which reduces the scope for productive investments. Furthermore, it is argued that complex regulations are frequently abused by bureaucrats who extract bribes from companies that either cannot afford the time and costs to clarify the legal situation or who are just willing to pay bribes to speed up registration processes. It is also claimed that red tape is the main cause of the widespread informality in developing countries. Informality in turn limits the growth potential of firms. Firms that cannot afford the cost of formalization are excluded from formal business transactions, and their access to public services and to formal sources of finance is restricted. Proponents of Doing Business reforms therefore claim that deregulation would immediately benefit the poor more than proportionally because 'heavy regulation and weak property rights exclude the poor from doing business' (World Bank/IFC, 2005: 3; Djankov et al, 2002; Klein and Hadjimichael, 2003).

Concerning the second proposition, the Doing Business series points out that 'the cost of reform to ease business entry is minor. Often it is done by the stroke of a minister's pen' (World Bank/IFC 2006: 9). The reports are also suggesting a number of policy measures taken by good performing countries that seem to be easy to implement, such as one-stop-shops.

Why the reform agenda is partly misguided

The *Doing Business Report* and other (mainly World Bank) publications rightly stress the need to improve the regulatory business environment in many developing countries. The key message, that investments are held back by unreliable market institutions (such as property rights and contract enforcement mechanisms) and cumbersome regulations, are probably true for most developing countries. Highlighting this message to governments and donors is a great merit of these publications. However, the reform agenda is misguided in five important aspects:
- The main challenge for societies is to search for an optimal, rather than a minimal, degree of institutional and normative regulation.
- Burdensome regulations are not among the most binding constraints for private sector development in developing countries – especially not in the informal economy.
- Empirical evidence does not show a clear link between level of regulation and micro- or macro-economic performance.
- Empirical evidence also shows that property titles have no significant positive effect on access to credit.
- Property titling may have undesired effects, crowding out poor producers and leading to a more unequal distribution of assets.

Let us now discuss each of these points.

Optimal vs. minimal regulation

In the Doing Business rankings, countries achieve the highest score on seven out of ten Doing Business Indicators if they do not regulate at all. This is why in an earlier paper we called the Doing Business reform agenda the

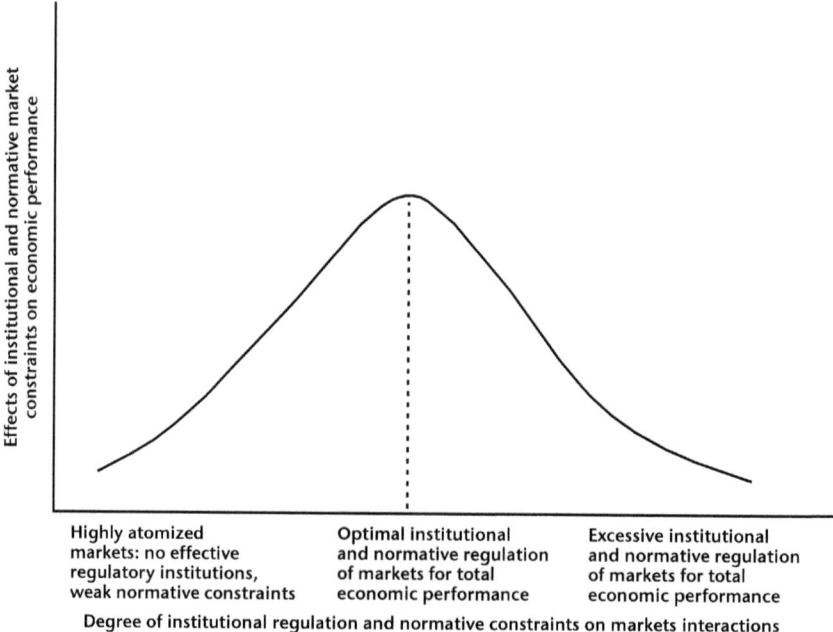

Figure 16.1. Effects of socially embedded institutional and normative market constraints on economic performance

'new minimalist approach' to PSD (Altenburg and von Drachenfels, 2006). Figure 16.1 shows that while excessive regulation is problematic, less regulation is not necessarily better. Instead, Wright (2004) argues that there are instances of highly atomized markets where regulation improves economic performance and only beyond a certain optimum regulation becomes counterproductive. As a result some countries may be over-regulated while others may be under-regulated. Te Velde (2006: 1) is therefore correct when he states that the 'key dilemma facing business regulation is to ensure an optimal level of regulation, not just a minimum level of regulation'. With regard to the informal economy Arruñada (2008) argues that simply lowering the initial costs of formalization is a wrong priority as the key challenge for developing countries is to increase the value of formalization. In his words (2008: 2): 'Reforms should aim for efficiency, which means that not only the costs but also the value of the services being provided must be considered. And this is especially so for institutions such as business registers, whose services act as catalysts in the economy'. He further elaborates that the costs associated with the introduction of new systems and in general with the improvement of the provision of public goods (which will be an essential incentive for firms to formalize) may as well justify a recovering of these costs via higher fees.

Burdensome regulations as constraints

Proponents of lowering the costs of registration assume a dynamic response by firms, in particular the informal ones that suffer from administrative entry barriers. This is based on two assumptions: first, that a majority of the people in the informal economy are vibrant entrepreneurs who only wait for their chance to expand their businesses significantly once they are formalized; and second, that cumbersome registration procedures are the major barrier to growth.

The assumption about the entrepreneurial potential represents a major deviation from the traditional view according to which the majority of own-account workers and microentrepreneurs are 'necessity entrepreneurs', who mainly seek to sustain their livelihoods in the absence of better job opportunities. Informal firms according to this traditional view are trapped in a vicious circle in which low skills, low capital formation, low productivity and low returns on investment reinforce each other. A recent attempt to better understand the extent of entrepreneurial potential in the informal economy was undertaken for Sri Lanka by de Mel et al (2008). They find for their sample that about two-thirds of own-account workers can be classified as wage workers rather than entrepreneurs.

These findings suggest that ease of entry does not solve structural problems for the majority of informal firms. 'Necessity entrepreneurs' are unlikely to turn into highly dynamic businesses just as a result of lower registration costs. Any approach to tackle informality and increase economic opportunities for the poor in a sustainable way therefore needs to consider additional barriers to growth. Developing informal enterprises requires specific support measures including entrepreneurial capacity building, technical training, financial services, market information, and linkage building with formal enterprises. Lowering the costs of registration makes sense as one element of an integrated strategy to develop the informal economy.

There are also doubts about the second part of the assumption. Van Stel et al (2007) find no evidence that number of procedures, time and cost to start a business have a significant impact on start-up rates and therefore conclude that countries that are heavily regulating entry are not becoming more enterprising and wealthy by lowering these barriers.

Link between regulation and performance

The *Doing Business* series builds on the assumption that there is a strong causal relation between the level of regulation and micro- or macro-economic performance. This is not the case. Eifert (2007: 42) analyses four Doing Business Indicators (starting a business, closing a business, employing workers and enforcing contracts) and concludes that 'de jure regulatory reform over the period 2003–06 has not significantly boosted either aggregate investment or employment in the short run... The results contrast with recent research that uses the cross-sectional dimension of the Doing Business data and finds strong cross-country correlations between regulatory burdens and economic outcomes'. Likewise, Gørgens et al (2005: 16) draw the following conclusion based on their econometric analysis using the Fraser Institute Economic Freedom Index: 'there is no simple, linear relationship between growth, income and regulation. A low level of regulation is optimal for rich countries, and highly regulated middle-income countries can benefit from deregulation. However, regulation does not matter much for poor countries, nor for middle-income countries with low levels of regulation'.

This applies not only to the macro but also to the micro level. Using data from the Business Environment and Enterprise Performance Survey for 26 transition countries, Commander and Svejnar (2007) do not find much of a relationship between constraints and performance. Their findings indicate 'that country fixed effects, reflecting time-invariant differences in the business environment but also other factors, matter for firm performance, but that differences in the business environment observed within countries across firms do not. Moreover, the limited firm and country-level variations in the business environment over time do not appear to affect performance either. This suggests that the effect of business environment on performance and the analysts' ability to identify this effect are more limited than has been widely assumed to date' (2007: 8).

For many companies it is in fact perfectly rational to stay informal because the disadvantages of formalization exceed its advantages. This is because formal companies have to pay more taxes and have higher compliance costs; in addition, they become more visible to authorities, which may subject them to more, rather than less, bureaucratic harassment, and they may still have as little access to credit as their informal counterparts (Krause et al, 2008). Kenyon (2007: 9) draws the conclusion that 'measures to reduce the costs of entry are unlikely to be sufficient in the absence of positive incentives or carrots. Common sense suggests that linking these changes to access to other resources, such as training, finance and the provision of physical infrastructure may be even more effective'.

Property titles and access to credit

The provision of property titles is supposed to enable even the poor to use land as collateral to obtain formal bank credit. As lack of access to credit is usually reported in enterprise surveys of developing countries to be the top constraint for enterprise development, this title-to-credit link is potentially very relevant. Furthermore, security of ownership provided by formal titles is believed to stimulate land markets and increase incentives for long-term investments. Reviews of case studies on Asia and Sub-Saharan Africa, however, show that evidence of increased access to credit and higher levels of investment as a consequence of obtaining a property title is patchy (Altenburg and von Drachenfels, 2007; 2008).

One prominent example is the large-scale property titling programme that has taken place in Peru since 1996. Around 400 laws were amended and over a five-year period more than 1.2 million urban households obtained legal property titles. While some studies find that this resulted in higher investments various authors cannot find a link to better access to credit due to a property title. Calderón for instance concludes that, even after the property rights reform, 'the poor are as scared of borrowing from the banks as the banks are reluctant to lend to the poor' (2004: 300).

Property titles are usually only one among many preconditions for obtaining bank loans. Even if they hold titles, micro and small enterprises face enormous difficulties when applying for bank loans – mainly because the size of loans is unattractive for larger commercial banks and/or because SMEs lack convincing business plans.

Property titling and asset distribution

According to Doing Business, land titling benefits the poor because it increases the value of their assets. This is partly true, but land titling is a sensitive issue that has often caused conflict and sometimes anti-poor concentration processes. Programmes that promote land titling and formal land markets frequently collide with long established customary land management systems. Customary land management systems often have a security and equity function as they ensure certain access to land even for the very poor, thereby reducing the risk of falling below the subsistence level. Individualization of these traditional land rights may undermine this function by encouraging exclusionary land usage. It is also reported that women may find themselves in a worse position after land registration if their rights are not set down in the newly set up registry (see Hampel-Milagrosa and Frickenstein, 2008). Outcomes of titling programmes may also be anti-poor if increasing land market activity leads to speculation and increasing costs of land and housing. While there are also good reasons for strengthening property rights – both for efficiency and equity reasons – property rights regimes need to be improved in a way that takes existing local customary land rights into account and develops socially acceptable solutions.

For Côte d'Ivoire, Stamm (2006) reports on how badly implemented land reform may be worse than no reform at all. Starting at the beginning of the 1990s, the Ivorian government prepared a new land act. It planned to provide certificates to anyone who held any form of usufruct right, but this was never done. Consequently, for instance, the rights of herders were not taken into consideration and pressure to speed up the overall process made it nearly impossible to resolve ownership disputes. According to the author, this caused disregard for the customary land management. Even though the proposed new land law has not been enacted to date, the tensions caused by the preparatory work for it have contributed considerably to destabilizing the country.

Why reforms of the regulatory business environment are tricky

As been shown earlier, the *Doing Business Report*s allege that regulatory reforms are not only necessary and highly relevant for growth, but also that they are easy to achieve. Both theoretical considerations and practical experiences, however, show that the difficulties of implementing reforms are underestimated. Quick wins may occur, but they are exceptional. The nature of regulatory reforms is often highly complex, and it is thus not easy to inform the design of reforms on the basis of international benchmarks.

Four aspects need to be highlighted that make reforms of the regulatory business environment rather tricky:
- *Specificity*: Appropriate regulatory systems need to be country-, region- and sector-specific.
- *Overlap with informal institutions*: Formal institutions always co-exist with informal institutions. Especially in developing countries where the outreach of formal institutions is limited, these informal institutions will stay and interfere with reforms of formal institutions.
- *Implementing capacity*: Simplifying *de jure* regulations is not sufficient. What matters are *de facto* administrative burdens, which depend on the capacities and incentives of the public administration.
- *Opposition*: Reforms always create losers who are likely to oppose reforms.

Specificity

The previous section has shown that the challenge is to establish appropriate regulation rather than just to abolish any kind of regulation. What is 'appropriate' is highly context-specific and depends on the preferences of societies. First, regulatory requirements vary across countries, regions and sectors. In the food industry, phytosanitary standards are a major issue, whereas abuse of labour standards may call for stricter regulation in the garment industry, and anti-trust regulation is key in the telecom industry. Second, socio-cultural values matter. Some societies attach a high value to the economic freedom of individuals whereas others have a preference for egalitarian development and confine economic freedom where it may jeopardize the livelihood of some of its members. Careful context- and country-specific analysis is therefore needed to identify reform needs. What is more, stakeholder dialogue is needed not only to identify constraints but also to negotiate solutions in the light of tradeoffs and to build consensus on the reform agenda. Consequently reforms are – and need to be – contested, incremental and time-consuming social search processes.

In this incremental search process transferring 'one size fits all' regulations as they are at least implicitly suggested by *Doing Business* is in most cases ineffective. Already North (1994: 366), who is so frequently cited in recent documents focusing on reforming the regulatory business environment, has argued: 'economies that adopt the formal rules of another economy will have very different performance characteristics than the first economy because of different informal norms and enforcement. The implication is that transferring the formal political and economic rules of successful Western market economies to third-world and Eastern European economies is not a sufficient condition for good economic performance'.

Overlap with informal institutions

Societies always have formal as well as informal rules. In developing countries, decisions tend to be less based on formal rules than they are in most industrial countries. Informal land markets or informal substitutes for formal contracts for example are widespread phenomena. Formal rules are usually more effective for modern business transactions, and they may be less exclusive than informal rules, as the latter are often only made for insiders from a certain group of society. However, even in the process of institutional modernization, informal rules will usually not fully disappear. Hence there will be overlaps of formal and informal institutions. Informal institutions can either complement formal ones, or they can compete with them, especially if the latter are not effectively enforced (Helmke and Levitsky, 2004). Policy-makers need to take this into consideration. Formal rules need to create value for the public, build on consensus and be enforceable. Otherwise substitutive informal rules will come up that may render the formal institutions ineffective.

Implementing capacity

Administrative costs depend not only on the number of procedures but also on the effectiveness of the administration. If public officials lack administrative skills or have little incentive to serve customers, business licensing for example may be very burdensome, even if the number of procedures is low. Reformers should therefore look beyond 'cutting red tape' and address a broader public sector reform agenda. Public sector reform and the fight against corruption is also about changing mindsets and setting better incentives. Public officials may need to be trained and given incentives to act in a business-like and customer-oriented manner, while the private sector may need better information about public services.

Opposition

Proponents of administrative deregulation stress the fact that a considerable part of existing unnecessary regulation was created to serve vested interests – either those of incumbents who want to create entry barriers for potential competitors, or by bureaucrats who want to increase their influence (and possibly even extract bribes). If this is correct, then a simplification of the regulatory business environment takes away rents from privileged and politically well-connected groups. It is quite unrealistic to expect that these groups would not oppose reform – which makes reforms 'by the stroke of a minister's pen' arguably rather exceptional.

Conclusions: How targets and strategies need to be adapted

It is absolutely reasonable to assume that unnecessary regulations and insecure property rights are harmful for economic development. It is therefore important to adopt reforms that cut red tape and improve the basic institutions that make market economies work.

The Doing Business Indicators have triggered a public debate about bureaucratic over-regulation that was long overdue. Some of its implicit policy messages, however, are misleading. They reflect a truncated understanding of determinants of competitiveness and the role of public services in supporting the private sector and broad-based economic development. Policy-makers should therefore not overestimate the explanatory power of the Doing Business Indicators, and donors should definitely not use them for imposing conditions on debtors, as has happened in some cases (Arruñada, 2007: 731).

The private sector in developing countries is constrained by manifold factors that are not part of the regulatory business environment – lack of entrepreneurial, managerial and technical skills, deficient infrastructure, weak financial systems, low levels of innovation and specialization and lack of international exposure, among others (Altenburg and von Drachenfels, 2007; 2008). Country and sector specific strategies are therefore needed that focus not only on deregulation, but also on better services to enhance information, technological learning, linkage building and other measures that increase competitiveness and make economic development socially inclusive.

References

Altenburg, T. and von Drachenfels, C. (2006) 'The "New Minimalist Approach" to private-sector development: A critical assessment', *Development Policy Review* 24: 387–411.

Altenburg, T. and von Drachenfels, C. (2007) *Creating an Enabling Business Environment in Asia: To what Extent is Public Support Warranted*', Discussion Paper 2/2007, German Development Institute, Bonn.

Altenburg, T. and von Drachenfels, C. (2008) *Creating an Enabling Environment for Private Sector Development in Sub-Saharan Africa*, United Nations Industrial Development Organization and Deutsche Gesellschaft für Technische Zusammenarbeit, Vienna.

Arruñada, B. (2008) 'Will Doing Business keep damaging business?' *Journal of Comparative Economics* 36 (forthcoming)

Calderón, J. (2004) 'The formalisation of property in Peru 2001–2002: The case of Lima', *Habitat International* 28: 289–300.

Commander, S. and Svejnar, J. (2007) 'Do institutions, ownership, exporting and competition explain firm performance?: Evidence from 26 transition countries', Institute for the Study of Labor – IZA (Discussion Paper Series No. 2637), Bonn.

Committee of Donor Agencies for Small Enterprise Development (2001) *Business Development Services for Small Enterprises: Guiding Principles for Donor Intervention*, Committee of Donor Agencies for Small Enterprise Development, Washington DC.

de Mel, S., McKenzie, D. and Woodruff, C. (2008) 'Who are the microenterprise owners?: Evidence from Sri Lanka on Tokman v. de Soto', paper presented at the 'International Differences in Entrepreneurship Conference' of the National Bureau of Economic Research (NBER), 1 and 2 February 2008, Savannah, Georgia.

Djankov, S., La Porta, R., Lopez-De-Silanes, F. and Shleifer, A. (2002) 'The regulation of entry', *Quarterly Journal of Economics* 117: 1–37.

Djankov, S., McLiesh, C. and Ramalho, R.M. (2006) 'Regulation and growth', *Economics Letters* 92: 395–401.

Eifert, B. P. (2007) 'The economic response to regulatory reform: 2003–06', Draft, 21 September 2007, Berkeley.

Gørgens, T., Paldam, M. and Würtz, A. (2005) *Growth, Income and Regulation: A Non-Linear Approach*, Working Paper 2005-12, Centre for Applied Microeconometrics (CAM) Department of Economics, University of Copenhagen, Copenhagen.

Hampel-Milagrosa, A. and Frickenstein, J. (2008) 'Taking the woman's perspective: Gender risks of regulatory reforms in Sub-Saharan Africa', *EDM* Vol. 19 No. 3, pp. 204–219.

Helmke, G. and Levitsky, S. (2004) 'Informal institutions and comparative politics: A research agenda', *Perspectives on Politics* 2: 725–740.

Kenyon, T. (2007) *A Framework for Thinking about Enterprise Formalization Policies in Developing Countries*, Policy Research Working Paper 4235, World Bank, Washington DC.

Klapper, L., Laeven, L. and Rajan, R. (2006) 'Entry regulation as a barrier to entrepreneurship', *Journal of Financial Economics* 82: 591–629.

Klein, M. U. and Hadjimichael, B. (2003) *The Private-sector in Development: Entrepreneurship, Regulation and Competitive Disciplines*, World Bank, Washington DC.

Krause, M., Ackermann, M., Hirtbach, C., Koppa, M., Siciliano Brêtas, L. and Traub, L. (2008) *Business Development in Mozambique: What is the Role of the Regulatory Business Environment in Supporting Formalisation and Development of Micro, Small and Medium Enterprises?*', forthcoming in the Studies series, German Development Institute, Bonn.

North, D. C. (1994) 'Economic performance through time', *The American Economic Review* 84, 359–368.

Stamm, V. (2006) 'Côte d'Ivoire: Fatale Land reform', *E+Z Entwicklung und Zusammenarbeit* 47: 428–429.

Tanburn, J. (2006) 'Private sector development and the poor – current thinking and future directions', *Small Enterprise Development* 17: 11–20.

Te Velde, D. W. (2006) *Whither Business Regulation? Institutions and Private Sector Development*, Briefing Paper 5, Research Programme Consortium on Improving Institutions for Pro-Poor Growth, Manchester.

van Stel, A. J., Storey, D. J. and Thurik, A. R. (2007) 'The effect of business regulations on nascent and young business entrepreneurship', *Small Business Economics* 28: 171–186.

World Bank/IFC (2005) *Doing Business in 2005: Removing Obstacles to Growth*, World Bank, Washington DC.

World Bank/IFC (2006) *Doing Business 2006: Creating Jobs*, World Bank, Washington DC.

Wright, E. O. (2004) 'Beneficial constraints: Beneficial for whom?', *Socio-Economic Review* 2: 407–414.

About the authors

Tilman Altenburg and Christian von Drachenfels are both with the Competitiveness and Social Development Department of the German Development Institute (DIE), Bonn, Germany.

CHAPTER 17
Integrated approaches to enabling the most vulnerable to participate in markets

Alex Daniels and Andy Jeans

This article was first published in June 2009.

Abstract

Even when markets become more accessible to poor people in general, wealth differentials occur and the most vulnerable are the ones excluded. The reasons for their exclusion are complex and inextricably linked with many aspects of their lives; an integrated approach takes these multiple dimensions of poverty into account, whilst addressing their deep levels of poverty through employment and enterprise. This article focuses on reaching those who are excluded from markets due to pervasive social discrimination and other challenges specific to their disability and health context.

Two case studies of people with disabilities and those affected by HIV/AIDS describe entry points and key services required to facilitate and sustain their participation as employees and enterprise owners. They demonstrate how successful models use participation in economic activities to achieve sustainable impact through stimulating attitude change, and create a more level playing field for their access to markets and wider development processes.

Market development approaches, or making markets work for the poor (M4P), are generic approaches to developing market systems that benefit poor people. M4P allows facilitating agencies to address identified systemic constraints and bring about large-scale and sustainable change, and has resulted in many positive large-scale results (Elliot et al., 2008). It aims to make market systems work more effectively, but also more inclusively. However, such approaches tend to operate in isolation, have a narrow focus and be very specialized to achieve the high quality and scale in specific service areas or markets (SEEP, 2008). The opportunity to include severe discrimination in the process of analysis in M4P approaches is often not taken up. As a result inadequate attention has been given to reaching some of the most marginalized – and poorest – groups, and few market development programmes consider including them amongst their beneficiaries. There is a risk that the systemic marginalization and consequent severe poverty that is the experience of the most vulnerable is perpetuated, rather than reduced.

Yet traditional approaches to people with disabilities and those affected by HIV/AIDS focus on medical, welfare or charitable interventions; promoting the general perception that working with these groups is costly, specialist and unsustainable. The view that such groups of people can only participate in markets as consumers or recipients of welfare is not only disempowering to those who can participate as employees and employers but has significant consequences for tackling poverty. The case studies in this article indicate a requirement for integrated interventions at a different level, preceding market development approaches, in order to overcome the depth and multi-dimensional nature of challenges faced by severely discriminated groups in their integration. The interventions address these challenges and at the same time enable market-led economic empowerment so that these discriminated groups have the potential to participate in M4P or wider development approaches.

Like many of those particularly vulnerable and marginalized in society, both these groups of people are in vicious cycles of poverty that can be passed down through generations with consequent long-term impact. Disabled people face a range of complex societal issues in many developing countries, which include: discrimination (negative social and familial assumptions), internalized oppression (stunted ambition and negative self-image), isolation (social and physical marginalization) and asset poverty (lack of social or other forms of collateral) (Albu, 2004). Their absence in productive employment helps to lock them in a vicious cycle of poverty. By becoming economically active they not only release their families from the 'burden of care' but they also begin contributing to the local economy. Likewise, low-income people affected by HIV and AIDS are often caught in a downward spiral of sickness and poverty. Poverty fuels the epidemic: through factors such as limited access to health care and education, minimal economic options and lack of sexual rights for women; and the epidemic exacerbates poverty, as income and assets are depleted with the cost of health care, caring for the sick, orphans and funeral expenses (Sumartojo, 2000; Parker et al, 2000; Pronyk et al, 2007). There are many critical factors influencing discrimination within these groups, not least gender and the form of impairment, but in-depth analysis of this is beyond the scope of this article.

HIV and AIDS are reversing years of forward progress in social and economic development. Nearly 22.5 million people are living with HIV and AIDS in sub-Saharan Africa (UNAIDS/WHO, 2007) and there are (debated) estimates of 20 per cent of the world's poorest being people with some form of disability (Elwan, 1999; Braithwaite and Mont 2008). With both disability and HIV/AIDS being inextricably linked with poverty, projects that focus on the economic empowerment of such groups should be a high priority.

This article centres on models that demonstrate how participation in economic activities and integrated support can transform the negative beliefs that underpin the exclusion of discriminated groups, creating a better foundation and a more level playing field for their participation in wider development processes. Despite the limitations of scale in these two case studies, which were also not established as research projects, it is hoped that the experience and analysis provide some helpful pointers on the factors affecting the levels of participation of some particularly vulnerable groups and the techniques that enhance their inclusion in markets and the wider society, and contribute to wider systemic change.

Background to the case studies

The two case studies were both developed and implemented in partnership with APT Enterprise Development (UK) from 2004 to 2008. The examples given cover different forms of marginalization and exclusion. With disability, many people have been discriminated against from birth, excluded from participating in education and many other life experiences. With those affected by HIV an AIDS, many are affected much later in life; their rapidly altering health has consequences for the support needed to sustain their participation as employers and employees.

LIFE project in Kenya

Kenya has approximately 1 million people (5.1 per cent of the population) living with HIV/AIDS (UNAIDS/WHO, 2008), with one of the worst-affected areas in Western Kenya being the Butula Division, an isolated rural area, with HIV prevalence at 33.5 per cent in 2001 and 21.8 per cent in 2007 (NACC, 2007). The LIFE project in Butula Division, Kenya, aimed to improve the livelihoods of people living with HIV/AIDS (PLWHA) and their dependents through microenterprise development; and to raise awareness and reduce the stigmatization that PLWHA encounter. It was an attempt to break the vicious cycle of HIV/AIDS by assisting PLWHA to pursue self-supporting and positive lives, making a productive contribution to the socio-economic well-being of their local community and helping to reduce the stigmatization.

The project was implemented by Rural Education and Economic Enhancement Programme (REEP) in collaboration with SITE Enterprise Promotion (Kenya), which provided technical and capacity building inputs on enterprise promotion, supported by the Big Lottery Fund. REEP aims to ameliorate the suffering of PLWHA through actions that help them access better care and support, including medication, post-testing care and support, peer education, publicity campaigns and advocacy for changes in, for example, wife and land inheritance – practices that perpetuate the spread of HIV/AIDS. Its outreach programmes emphasize the message that people can live positively with AIDS. REEP works with approximately 1,000 unpaid volunteers – community change agents including community health workers, peer educators and paralegals who have been strengthened with knowledge and experience in their field of expertise. The livelihood development work was implemented at two levels – at supplementary levels and earning incomes through enterprise, working largely through volunteer enterprise development animators (EDAs). These were selected beneficiaries (PLWHA) who were trained by a small team of enterprise development staff.

Disabled people project in Uganda

Approximately 2.4 million disabled people (DP) live below the poverty line in Uganda (Lwanga-Ntale, 2003) and make up 50 per cent of those who are chronically poor. The project was based in six districts of Northern Uganda (Lira, Apac, Arua, Gulu, Soroti and Nebbi), an area suffering from the consequences of a devastating 20-year conflict. It aimed to build the capacity of DP in Northern Uganda to access livelihoods, enabling DP to participate in enterprise as employers and employees, gain access to appropriate enterprise services and change attitudes both towards and of DP.

The project primarily used an enterprise-based training model (EBT) – including apprenticeships, work experience placements and exchanges – to promote the acquisition of marketable skills. EBT was selected because it enables DP to participate in work (and life) experience from which they have previously been excluded (such as contacts/negotiation with suppliers and consumers, working with colleagues), whilst accessing relevant enterprise skills. It also enables community members, employers, customers and others to see DP engaged in productive activity, rather than 'hidden' in a specialist institution that highlights their impairment,.

Key lessons learned from an initial project were built into this project, most notably to increase the visibility of DP as economically active through the promotion of disabled role models. This phase of the project therefore added an awareness and communications element to the activities with the aim of directly challenging and changing attitudes. It also supported the district disability unions and advocacy campaigns. The project (funded by the UK Government's Department for International Development) was implemented by National Union of Disabled Persons of Uganda (NUDIPU), the national umbrella organization of disabled people's organizations in Uganda. Table 17.1 details the population reached by the two projects.

Entry points

Many of the reasons for the exclusion of these groups relate to non-enterprise factors and apply to many of the markets that they would like to enter. To enable their entry into markets as enterprise owners and employees requires a holistic analysis of the barriers hindering them. In addressing objectives beyond that of entry into the market, both these projects enabled greater attention to be paid to the fact that markets are embedded in social systems and social constraints – and non-enterprise factors can have an overwhelming influence

Table 17.1. A brief summary of the population reached

LIFE Project in Kenya	DP Project in Uganda
• 2,415 people (71% women) with increased income levels either by expanding or by starting a livelihood; having received direct intervention in enterprise; 75% in agriculture based ventures. Profits were made by 80% but ranged widely, with about one third attaining over KES1,000/week* (Approx. \$13). • 16,305 (59% women) with improved care and support from services provided (e.g. counselling, testing, legal advice, support to groups), including 5,843 in 44 support groups, many of which indirectly benefited from enterprise interventions. Some changes to service provision. • An estimated 17,735 sensitized on HIV/AIDS; 30,000 children participated in awareness-raising campaigns. • Clear impact on attitude and behavioural change – particularly in PLWHA confidence – and reduction in community stigma.	• 400 (36% women) obtained marketable skills leading 312 to operate their own enterprises and 56 to obtain positions as employees, with most increasing incomes to at least USH6,000–12,000 (\$3–\$6) per day; 1 secured a USH1.2 million (\$600) contract*; 32 dropped out**. • Number of organizations, NGOs and private sector, made changes to service provision and practice to become more inclusive. • Number of beneficiaries reached as a consequence not quantified. • 13,770 directly participated in awareness-raising activities; 20,000 reached by awareness-raising campaigns. • Qualitative evidence of behavioural change outside direct beneficiaries, including an increase in enterprise activity by DP.

Notes: * These profits enabled people to be self-reliant and independent, removing the need for welfare/food aid. ** Much of the 'drop out' data refers to the fact the project team had been unable to trace the beneficiary due to displaced people returning to home villages).

on participation in markets. Analysis (including that from earlier stages of the projects) indicated that these groups were not participating because there is widespread discrimination among customers, service providers, family members and other community members in the market environment, as well as the negative self-image of people with disability and those affected by HIV/AIDS themselves. PLWHA are additionally excluded through challenges related to their health.

The models considered have entry points for these marginalized groups through EBT, which is placed within and sustained by the private sector; and community-based animators with understanding of enterprise, health and other social issues, sustained within local communities. Both are assisted by the fostering of support networks, particularly needed because the traditional family networks are not working for them.

Findings: Techniques to stimulate participation in enterprise

The projects were involved in facilitating a number of services that are often included in MED microenterprise promotion – such as enabling access to skills, finance, agricultural extension, markets, linking with intermediaries and group work. In summary, business development interventions were:

- Technical inputs/skill development – including a range of sources of technical learning from institutions and businesses (including apprenticeships in the DP project) and skilled community volunteers (LIFE project).
- Business counselling services and market linkages – assistance with identification of profitable market niches appropriate to the individual and means of accessing them, problem solving and follow up. These were developed according to beneficiaries' requirements (for example, working together to access market information through mobile phones).
- Business management training – including standard courses required to access credit, tailored individual or group assistance with business planning.
- Credit – support groups enabled the establishment of savings systems. Linkages with microfinance organizations to access start-up and working capital were increasingly accessed as the projects progressed.

However, the following describes key services and areas that are particular to enabling excluded groups to participate in microenterprise. There are insufficient data to prove which services are most critical but there is a clear indication that a package is required. A brief illustration of known elements is provided.

Initial advocacy/sensitization

The first key step to overcoming ingrained discrimination was to build confidence and awareness of rights and obligations and of the potential of people themselves to generate incomes through employment and enterprise. Families, as well as target beneficiaries, were included in this step due to their high level of influence.

In the LIFE project psychological counselling was offered to those who were initially uncertain of their capacity to take on a new venture. Many people, following an HIV positive diagnosis, lose their self-respect and self-confidence. REEP's volunteer community health workers (CHWs) gave reassurance and advice on managing their HIV treatment with a work routine, even during periods of ill health. The twin strategies of providing individual counselling by health workers and enterprise workers (who met together regularly) and group support systems helped to nurture the self-confidence of PLWHA as their businesses grew, and living and working with HIV/AIDS became a practical proposition rather than a daunting prospect.

In the DP project, initial sensitization, including of the families of DP, was undertaken through the connection with the district disability unions, who raised awareness of rights as part of their remit. The project also integrated this sensitization into business skills training helping disabled people to overcome their own and their families' reservations to becoming independent, and provided counselling and advice as businesses progressed.

Market-led enterprise selection and access to skills

Knowledge of market and understanding of enterprise needed to be integrated with knowledge of health status (for example, the different stages of HIV/AIDS), forms of impairment and understanding the depth of discrimination and other challenges faced at home and from institutions. This integrated approach was relevant to enterprise selection and access to skills, with benefits apparent in the impact on different facets of beneficiaries' lives and different project objectives.

In the LIFE project, the volunteer EDAs, together with star entrepreneurs and farmers, trained other PLWHA within the vicinity of their homes in agriculture-related enterprises, and in commerce, taking up the responsibility of mobilizing other PLWHA in their community, visiting and helping to organize them, and using their fields/home gardens as demonstration plots. The roles of these animators and specialized extension workers are different, but in an environment where the majority of extension services are not reaching the community, animators were invaluable in filling the gap.

The first function of the EDAs was to ensure that PLWHA learned to engage in livelihoods at a supplementary level (see the middle box in Figure 17.1) and

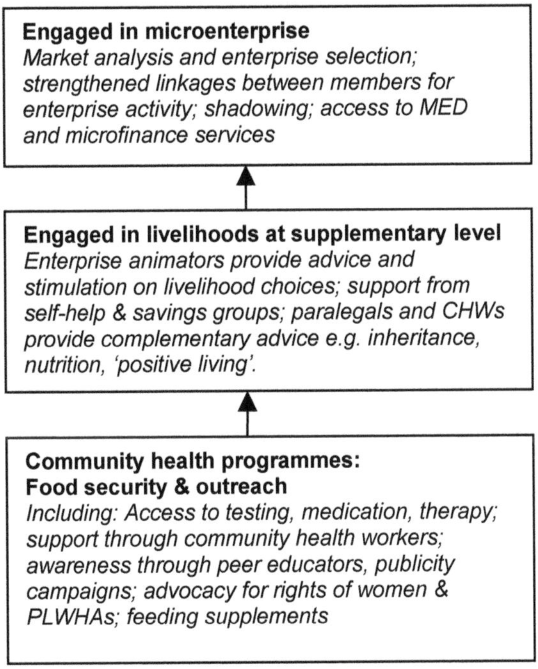

Engaged in microenterprise
Market analysis and enterprise selection; strengthened linkages between members for enterprise activity; shadowing; access to MED and microfinance services

Engaged in livelihoods at supplementary level
Enterprise animators provide advice and stimulation on livelihood choices; support from self-help & savings groups; paralegals and CHWs provide complementary advice e.g. inheritance, nutrition, 'positive living'.

Community health programmes:
Food security & outreach
Including: Access to testing, medication, therapy; support through community health workers; awareness through peer educators, publicity campaigns; advocacy for rights of women & PLWHAs; feeding supplements

Figure 17.1. LIFE Model

learned how to cultivate kitchen or pot gardens, where land space was restricted, in order to meet their dietary requirements. The majority of participants engaged in farming, although other activities included horticulture and fish trading, garment and other retail, pre-school work, hotel keeping, tailoring, basket weaving, rope making and carpentry. Each individual was trained in one or more complementary enterprise activities in order to safeguard against the risk of failure in one area of production (for example, a poor horticultural harvest would be supplemented from honey production). This shift in livelihood practices from traditional labour and resource intensive ventures to appropriate small-scale income generation options helped PLWHA to engage in livelihoods and made an essential contribution to their survival with dignity in the community.

At the next stage, market niches were identified depending on both market analysis and the needs of the clients. For example, because PLWHA do not possess the stamina required to produce some of the traditionally grown crops in the area, such as maize and sorghum, the EDAs, by being trained in market analysis, helped their clients to select produce, such as tomatoes and water melon, that generally involved lighter workloads, shorter maturation periods and fetched higher prices at local markets. Because the EDAs were themselves PLWHA, this enabled them to understand both the physical and mental constraints that faced their livelihood trainees. Trainees could choose to form a group enterprise or to start their own businesses. Another APT project that had involved an analysis of the honey sector in the country facilitated the selection of beekeeping as an enterprise sector. Skills of the staff of the organization (SITE Enterprise Promotion) involved were shared with the LIFE project; knowledge and skills of working with PLWHAS were taken back to their enterprise projects.

In the DP project, DP identified the skills they were keen to learn, and local opportunities were researched, depending on what was viable in the market and according to the needs of the beneficiary. Clearly different forms of impairment had an impact on this and although there was a bias towards physically disabled people among the direct beneficiaries of this project, a wide range of economic activities were engaged in by the disabled beneficiaries. The project made a deliberate attempt to try to break away from the more traditional skills associated with disabled people – deaf people as carpenters/welders and blind people as cane chair makers for example. There were at least 22 different business activities ranging from tailoring, electronic repairs, baking, motor vehicle repair to beekeeping, ploughing, fishmongers, a variety of petty trading and small arts and crafts work. This gave disabled people a greater voice in what they chose to do, in response to the market.

The Uganda project also followed a step-wise approach (Munasinghe, 2008). The EBT model, summarized in Figure 17.2, was implemented alongside a complementary model for advocacy and sensitization (working with DP, community self-help groups and disabled people's organizations at national,

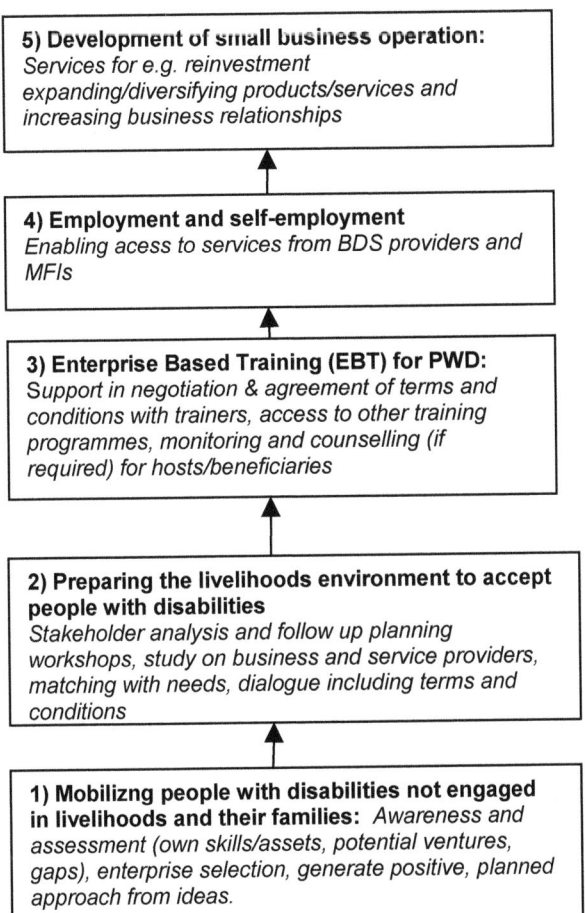

Figure 17.2. Promoting enterprise-based training

regional and district levels), and was designed to facilitate better inclusion of persons with disabilities in the community.

The project struggled, especially in the early stages, with managing expectations of trainees, resulting in part from previous welfare or charitable approaches of intervening organizations, and in part from attitudes present in society. Stimulating this change is a time-consuming area of the project, but successful role models, demonstrating their increased pride and self-esteem, proved to be an effective catalyst.

Follow up and support. Although for some stigmatized groups the key area is overcoming barriers to their initial entry in enterprise activity, some form of support, such as mutual problem-solving groups for people who are breaking new ground, was valued as they developed their enterprises. Additional interventions were also needed to address the challenges of widely varying health more common among PLWHA.

Support groups helped PLWHA to meet openly, compared to earlier days spent in isolation. These, or other groups, were stimulated by a business need to undertake group-based livelihood activities that included resource mobilization, table banking, 'merry-go-rounds' (rotating savings and credit associations), access to market information and bulk sales. It also facilitated access to labour from group members during particular stages of crop production cycles. The formation of support groups changed the social status of PLWHA who were previously living in isolation from the community and family. By the end of the project these support groups were becoming recognized as a regular community structure for both awareness creation among the community and focusing on livelihoods enhancement.

In the DP project, the district disability unions, linked with disabled people's organizations (many of which are impairment specific), also provided support to their members, linking them to services and to each other for enterprise and other types of problem solving.

A form of enterprise legacy planning and insurance against periods of ill health, known as 'shadow workers', was designed to ensure the sustainability of the business and to provide the security that was lost when the wider family network was no longer available. Enterprise beneficiaries were advised to seek assistance, ideally from an elder child of working age, to help to run the business during periods of ill health or treatment. These shadow workers learned the basic skills involved in the business. Their knowledge of local market conditions, sources of credit and local input suppliers helped to retain the lines of communication and the network of associational bonds that are crucial to the survival of a business. However if friends or distant relatives had to be substituted as shadow workers with whom there was inadequate trust, support from this source was limited.

Stimulating attitude change of beneficiaries and their communities. Attitude and behavioural change amongst discriminated groups and their communities is important not only to deliver on sustainable impact of project objectives, but to catalyse and stimulate change to attain levels of outreach in impact. The main stimulant to attitude change was the establishment of successful role models, supported by sustained awareness-raising activities, which included their promotion and publicity.

In the LIFE project, attitude change related to 'positive living', as well as discrimination against women and PLWHA. The volunteer animators acted as role models, together with other key success stories. These were also supported by awareness campaigns, including peer-to-peer strategies using parent, youth and child educators, presentations (choir groups, talks, drama) at schools, churches and social functions (such as markets, funerals, sports tournaments), as well as radio programmes and information materials at events organized by other stakeholders.

The LIFE project had a clear impact on attitude and behavioural change and the reduction of stigma and discrimination. The confidence built among PLWHA was the most notable change in their behaviour brought about by the project, as evident from increased numbers of PLWHA revealing their status in public; positive living and playing an active role in family livelihood development (for example, 98 per cent of women felt they were consulted on family decisions and participated in family events despite their HIV positive status); dealing with markets and the service sector; and standing up for their rights in terms of being remarried or reporting land grabbing. Interviews and focus group meetings indicated that community acceptance of PWLHA can largely be attributed to their success in livelihood and enterprise ventures, supported by awareness-raising within the community (Munasinghe, 2008). Enterprise activities also directly indicated behavioural changes of customers, for example, one of the most popular restaurants in Butula was owned and managed by a PLWHA.

In Uganda, DP have very few role models successfully operating in business to observe. Most have never witnessed a successful disabled business person and find it hard to conceive of themselves as self-reliant. In addition to establishing over 360 DP as positive role models, activities included raising awareness, challenging negative assumptions and promoting examples of successful role models through road shows, radio programmes and TV, as well as positive participation of DP in community clean-up operations and bicycle rides.

Evidence collected from individual interviews and focus group discussions, and an (external) evaluation of the campaigns, reinforced project data that this has had a significant impact on attitudes. Beneficiaries commonly referred to their previous total dependence and not being recognized as people, and to changes in both their own independence and the attitudes around them as others started to see they could support themselves. There were positive changes in public attitudes towards DP. Significantly, observations during the evaluation indicated that the project had gone well beyond its immediate beneficiaries, with evidence of behavioural change in enterprise participation:

- Before the project started, DP in Lira routinely went out onto the streets to beg on a Friday. This was widely acknowledged by the community as 'acceptable'. Since the DP project began, this practice has completely stopped and the community is more used to seeing DP as market vendors than beggars.
- There were a number of examples of DP (non-beneficiaries) establishing microenterprises (for example kiosks) alongside or close to successful role models of the project.
- district disability unions noted individual members opening bank accounts and a 'culture of savings' being generated.

Advocacy for improved (enterprise) services. Advocacy by beneficiaries, and by their representative organizations, for improved and non-discriminatory enterprise service provision is a key area for sustainable change. The establishment of role models and the evidence they provided was a critical stimulating factor, supported by building the capacity of representative organizations to follow up and lobby for demanded services.

The physical demonstration of DP and PLWHA willing and able to learn a wide variety of skills and to run successful businesses was apparent in its effect on local institutions and small businesses. Service providers became aware of how their own negative attitude was, in many instances, the biggest barrier to inclusive participation. Reasons for exclusion included assumptions on their ability to pay; sometimes they were simply disregarded. This fear was mutual – for example DP themselves expressed a reluctance to become involved with micro-credit because of the way they thought they would be treated. DP's limited assets and a lack of credit history were also cited as barriers.

This contributed to a number of changes in service provision among vocational training centres, employers, market linkages and others. Some credit-based examples include:

- PLWHA were able to access credit and purchase shares from Butula Financial Services Association (supported by Kenya Rural Enterprise Programme – KREP), with a range of loan products specifically designed to cater for clients with HIV/AIDS that combine flexible repayment terms with life assurance provision. Without this, PLWHA had been effectively excluded from KREP despite its clientele being poor in terms of incomes and assets and with little business experience.
- The Association of Micro Finance Institutions of Uganda (AMFIU) promoted the inclusion of DP in the MFI sector. They reported a 96 per cent increase in numbers of DP accessing MFI services, with MFIs making decisions based on business plans rather than applicants' impairments.
- There is evidence of banks making their premises accessible to DP.

Working in partnership with relevant specialist organizations. Partnerships between specialist organizations are needed to draw on strengths and knowledge from different sectors. This is needed at different levels – including the overall design and management of the interventions as well as responding to individual needs of beneficiaries.

Both lead partner organizations (NUDIPU and REEP) had specialist knowledge of the client group and their situation and requested assistance to address their clients' expressed need to generate income through enterprise.

Working in partnership with both enterprise and non-enterprise service providers – including in health care, livelihoods and advocacy work – was part of implementing the LIFE project and accessing relevant support to address different facets of beneficiaries' lives. For example, advocacy work on cultural practices such as land and widow inheritance has consequences for both HIV and AIDS, enterprise management and assets. This was also apparent in the DP project, including with respect to the capacity building of communities. district disability unions and disabled people's organizations are to continue advocacy work so that DP are more effectively included in mainstream programmes in the future.

However, in such resource-poor environments, at the grassroots level there is also a need for the beneficiaries' local contacts to have a basic understanding of multiple aspects – someone with the knowledge and understanding of market factors but who also knows about nutrition needs or about the different facets of being discriminated against from birth. Referrals can then be used to access further specialized expertise.

Resourcing the interventions and their sustainability. Clearly there are costs associated with developing a body of volunteers and a sufficient number of role models to stimulate change. There is some justification for subsidizing such programmes that open opportunities for excluded groups to participate – the target beneficiaries are certainly less likely to be able to pay because of the discrimination and associated destitution that they face and the lack of access to assets or the family support normally enjoyed. As they participate they develop the capacity to purchase services.

The projects thus used different strategies for resourcing the interventions:
- attempting to ensure that costs were met by the client as far as possible by assisting with negotiating their contribution;
- embedding costs into the process of establishing the stimulants of change; for example facilitating access to skills or upgrading the facilities of enterprise trainers, including bicycles or other benefits to volunteers that help to promote their area of expertise;
- minimizing on-going running costs to make them appropriate to resource-poor communities and meeting costs in different ways from a variety of local sources. For example EDAs providing training in honey production take a cut from the honey harvest; community health workers became integrated into other health programmes recognized by the Ministry of Health and thus independent from REEP; the choir group that raised awareness was self-sustaining by operating as a social enterprise and charging fees for performances. It is also worth noting that non-financial gains – particularly that of social status – was also a significant contributor to sustaining advice and support.

In the LIFE project, sustainability is achieved by establishing a knowledge base within the community, in the capacity of livelihood animators, community health workers, peer educators, paralegals etc. The use of volunteers was viewed as a good investment in social capital and the establishment of a community resource base, with the ultimate objective of enabling the community members to take on responsibility for running most of the project partners' activities in the future. It relies upon engendering an ethos of positive living, and because the EDAs and community health workers are committed volunteers that in general receive communal approval for their work, the potential for assistance to continue into the future, once LIFE has ended, is greater. Indeed, many REEP EDAs were expected to maintain relationships with their clients when the programme closed.

In Uganda the project established economically successful role models to stimulate attitude change and tackle discrimination in communities in which they live and operate, and among service providers. This established a customer–client relationship between disabled people and local service providers, with employer/trainers more receptive to employing DP in the future; parents more willing to invest in the future of disabled children; and improvement in the livelihoods of DP through their capacity to continue in employment, which will have an impact on their dependants.

In both cases, further long-term monitoring will be required to assess the extent of the outreach and widespread behavioural change obtainable from a relatively small-scale project. Improvements in advocacy capacity will help to apply leverage on a greater scale for more widespread institutional change, bringing national, and potentially international, benefits.

Discussion

What is different about this approach is the deliberate effort to work across sectors – using inclusion in enterprise as a catalyst for change in other aspects that are fundamental to the well-being of the target group, and taking into account the multi-dimensional nature of discrimination. Such an approach and some of the techniques described will be appropriate to other very vulnerable and excluded groups.

The projects described included a range of enterprises and although they are market led, they are not sector defined. By empowering people with the right to choose and stimulating them to tackle discriminatory barriers, this approach was different from analysing a particular sector and making it accessible to one particular group – such as DP. There are sectors that have become accessible to DP (such as blacksmithing in Sierra Leone or certain craft industries in a number of African countries) through tradition or intervention, yet access and acceptance in particular sectors has not led to more mainstreamed inclusion. Catalysing a change of attitude and behaviour across a range of sectors increases the potential of significant scale and outreach, with wide systemic change that mainstreaming can bring. The process is outlined in Figure 17.3.

The complex and multi-dimensional nature of the context facing discriminated groups, including their exclusion from society and services, their low self-esteem and chronic poverty, require a significant change in attitude and behaviour. This is stimulated by change agents/role models demonstrating their capability, supported by appropriate support systems, advocacy and widespread awareness raising. With the successful demonstration of a sufficient cadre, active as employers and employees, attitude and behavioural change is stimulated both among discriminated groups themselves and those providing support – whether in business services, family investment or as customers. Once this is in place there can be better inclusion in other approaches – whether M4P or other wider development processes (for example health and education).

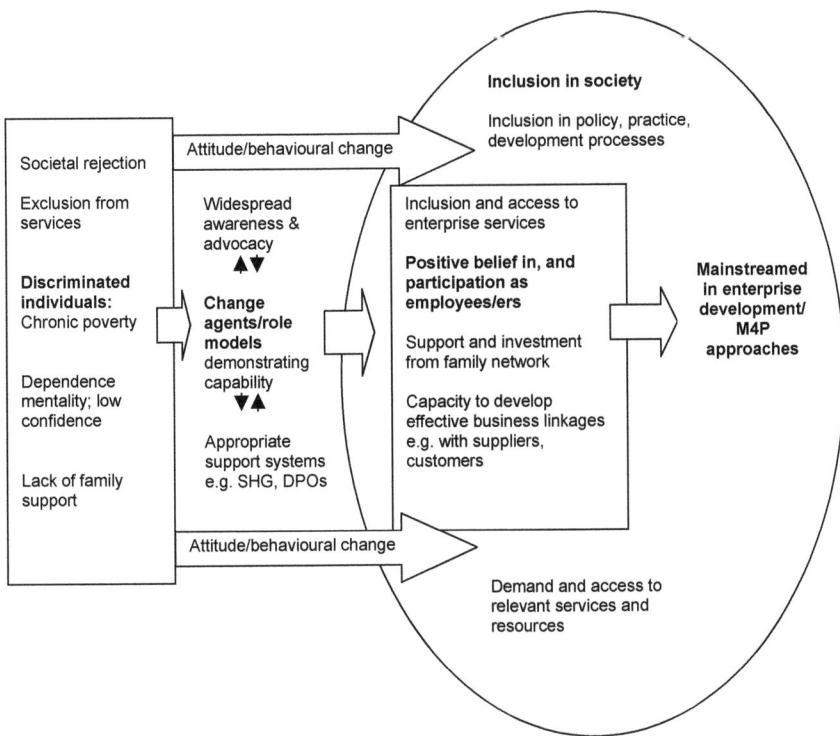

Figure 17.3. Approach to stimulating discriminated groups' participation as employers/employees

Tackling discrimination, stimulating attitude change and establishing a more equitable and inclusive foundation for sector-based programmes, as a preliminary step, is compatible with a number of frameworks. Considerations of these factors should be included in market assessment processes in M4P, used to identify causes of underperformance of all aspects of a market systems, or in other entry analysis that aims to assess what is required to bring about equitable, pro-poor market structure (such as in Oxfam's entry analysis in Carney, 2002). These interventions can be part of an initial response to establish a more level playing field and part of generating a more 'enabling environment' in a market map, as used in the Practical Action Markets and Livelihoods Programme (2007). Initiating activities to precede sector-led microenterprise development programmes is also compatible with SEEP's suggested approach, which proposes a more holistic and coordinated approach to poverty eradication, particularly for people affected by HIV and AIDS, with a staircase of economic strengthening and enterprise development services appropriate for people experiencing different levels of poverty, delivered by institutions or specialists knowledgeable in the use of tools at that level (SEEP, 2008).

Elsewhere, cross-sector approaches are being demonstrated with microfinance as the key entry point for linking economic interventions to concrete health outcomes, for example health-related training at loan centre meetings (Pronyk et al, 2007) or in specific microfinance instruments.

The case studies described help to address the mismatch that arises between client needs and service availability when different development players (such as those working in community-based organization capacity building, health and other sectors, and those promoting sustainable enterprise development and providing business development services) are responding to discriminated and very vulnerable groups. There has often been general reluctance among mainstream project practitioners to get involved in what they see as being specialist advocacy work for minority groups. The disability sector has been especially prone to this because of assumptions made about how much of a role is needed for adaptive support. Also, discriminated groups have often shied away from getting involved in mainstream MED programmes, preferring instead to rely on their own organizations to find ways to provide for them. These are models that enterprise organizations can link with and build on, working in partnership with local organizations (disabled people's organizations etc.) to access and address the needs of very vulnerable groups.

Conclusion

The huge strides in economies of scale and GDP per capita gained through market development approaches can still leave severely marginalized people excluded – or even further marginalized, with inequalities being replicated rather than challenged.

M4P could be more inclusive by drawing on some of the positive elements of these models, by, for example:
- ensuring that service providers are genuinely inclusive and do not multiply and endorse the discrimination present,
- including disability and HIV/AIDS in the analysis in the same way as gender is included,
- providing or linking to additional services that relate to health or other development needs alongside business development interventions.

However, without additional interventions to stimulate attitude and behavioural change, this will not be sufficient for a credible challenge to systemic marginalization and consequent chronic poverty. These case studies have shown it is possible to support discriminated groups to become successful entrepreneurs and employees and in doing so this has helped transform the negative beliefs that underpin their exclusion from society. In future it will be easier for DP and PLWHA in the project areas to be accepted as trainees, employees and business owners, as well as to participate in wider socio-economic processes.

For enterprise development practitioners who wish to maintain the quality and focus of a particular approach and who are interested to increase the participation (or reduce the level of exclusion) of the most vulnerable in markets, effective partnerships are needed to deliver the package of interventions required to overcome ingrained discrimination and exclusion, and reach the most vulnerable.

References

Albu, M. (2004) 'Evaluation of an action-research project by the National Union of Disabled Persons of Uganda (NUDIPU) and APT Enterprise Development', UK.

Braithwaite, J. and Mont, D. (2008) 'Disability and poverty: A survey of World Bank poverty assessments and implications', HDNSP, World Bank, Washington D.C.

Carney, D. (2002) 'Sustainable livelihoods approaches: Progress and possibilities for change', DFID, London.

Elwan, A. (1999) *Poverty and Disability, a survey of the literature*; Social Protection Discussion Paper No. 9932; The World Bank Group, Washington D.C.

Elliot, D., Gibson, A. and Hitchins, R. (2008) 'Making markets work for the poor: Rationale and practice', *Enterprise Development and Microfinance* 19 (2).

Lwanga-Ntale, C. (2003) 'Chronic poverty and disability in Uganda', Development Research Training, Kampala, Uganda.d2003s

Munasinghe, C. (2008) *Building the Capacity of People with Disability in Northern Uganda to Access their Livelihoods: A Handbook for Disability Advocates and Practitioners*, APT Enterprise Development UK/NUDIPU Uganda, Uganda.

NACC (2007) *HIV and AIDS Situation in Kenya*, National AIDS Control Council, Nairobi.

Parker, R. G., Easton, D. and Klein, C. H. (2000) 'Structural barriers and facilitators in HIV prevention: A review of international research' *AIDS* 14: S22–S32.

Pronyk, P. M., Hargreaves, J. R. and Morduch, J. (2007) 'Microfinance programs and better health: Prospects for sub-Saharan Africa', *JAMA – Journal of the American Medical Association* 298: 1925–1927.

SEEP (2008) *SEEP Network Guidelines for Microenterprise Development in HIV and AIDS-Impacted Communities: Supporting Economic Security and Health, Book 2 For Microenterprise Development Practitioners*, SEEP, Washington D.C.

Sumartojo, E. (2000) 'Structural factors in HIV prevention: Concepts, examples, and implications for research', *AIDS* 14: S3–S10.

UNAIDS/WHO (2007) *AIDS Epidemic Update Paper 07*, UNAIDS/WHO.

UNAIDS/WHO (2008) *Kenya Epidemiological Country Profile on HIV and AIDS, Fact Sheet Update*.

About the authors

Alex Daniels is the Programme Development Manager and Andy Jeans is the Chief Executive of APT Enterprise Development, a UK-based NGO that promotes economic empowerment and social change by helping the most vulnerable and disadvantaged achieve sustainable livelihoods and by addressing the barriers that limit their participation.

Index

References to text in figures, tables or boxes are **bold**.

Africa 3, 19, 66, 143–4, **144**
agriculture; *see also* farmers
    agrifood systems 6
    cooperation between formal and informal sectors 20
    employment in 19
    and financial services 153
    growth in 36, 151
    and informal sector 24
    and value chain development 141–3
APT Enterprise Development 201
Azerbaijan 175

Bangladesh
    Katalyst programme and 5, 7, 19, 155, 157; *see also* Katalyst programme
    labour surplus economy of 19
    microcredit in 22
barriers
    to employment in formal sector 17
    to entry in microenterprise 4, 25, 98
BASIX 152–3
BDS (business development services)
    definition 5, 84
    commercialization of 87
    efficacy of 6
    evolution of 130–1
    guiding principles for 5, 84–5
    in Kenya **126**
    and M4P **2**
    and market linkage projects 97, 106, 109–110
    organizational systems in 85
    services provided by projects **100**
best practice
    in Bangladesh fishery 162
    in market development 3
    in market linkage projects 103
    in value chain approach 6
Brazil 26, **88**, 148
bureaucratic failure 15
business associations 45–50, 52–8, 87, 92, 104
business enabling environment **2**, 3, 6, 30, 121, **127**, 129, 141, **142**, 187,
business skills, training in 12, 205–206
businesses 2, 42, 45, 61, 93–4, 121; *see also* firms

competition
    in agricultural sector 149, 174, 181, 183
    between BDS providers 89
    in finance sector 146
    global nature of 139–41
    governments promoting 15
    and PROFIT Zambia programme 172

218 VALUE CHAINS IN DEVELOPMENT

response to in franchising 61
and scale of industry 78, 184
in sub-sector analysis 3, 30
competitiveness
   in agricultural sector 141, 151, 182
   and horizontal linkages 114
   identifying potential for 115
   increasing 114, 117, **123**, 125, 157
   link with sustainable growth 115
   and market structure **123**
   in PROFIT Zambia programme **172**, 173
   of small enterprises 29
   USAID review of 122
   of value chains 6, 113, 119–120, 123
constraints
   analysis of 6
   based on gender 135
   to competitiveness 124
   on finance 55
   on industrial development 33, 114, **116**, 121
   in Pakistan handicrafts sector 133, 135
   reduced attention to 131
   on small business 29, 55
   and value chain analysis 119–120
   of village situation 43
   in Zambian agriculture 180, 183
credit
   in agricultural sector 3, 144
   in BDS programmes 89
   in enterprise development programmes 29, 34–5
   and informal sector 22, 24–5, 98
   letters of 150
   in market linkage projects 102, **104**
   in outgrower schemes 21
   and sub-contracting 23
   and TTO programme 12–13
   and value chain finance **147**
crowding in 15, 167, **183**

design
   for agricultural equipment 74–5
   of BDS programmes 83, 87, 94, 113–14
   in handicrafts value chain 107, 134–6
   of interventions 83–4, 169
   for market development in Pakistan 133
   of regulatory framework 52
   small producers of **99**
disabilities, people with 200, 202, 204, 206, 208, 209, 210, 212
disadvantaged groups 93, 131, 200
Doing Business Report 188, 194
Dominican Republic **122**
donors
   and BDS 83–6, 88–9, 92
   and distributional questions 93
   interventions in Bangladesh 159
   objectives of interventions 115–16
   and project management 185
   requirements for programme evaluation 155–6, 164, 169
   and rural sector 142
   and value chain programmes 113, 120–121

EDOs (enterprise development organizations) 34–8, 43–4
embedded services **2**
enterprise development
   approaches to 1, 33, 35–6
   content of programmes 29
   evolution of 129–130
   and franchising 59–60, 62–3, 66
   and M4P **2**

and poverty reduction 4
responsibility of government
 for 54
rural 36–7
small and microenterprises
 34–5
enterprise development
 organizations, see EDOs
enterprise development programmes
 29
entrepreneurship
and sub-sectoral approach 37
and tasar cultivation 40
equity, challenge of 8, 212
evaluation
of BDS programmes 88, 90
difficulty of 156
in FIT programme 74–5, 77–8
in Katalyst programme 7, 166
of value chain programmes
 125
exit strategies 1, 4, 124–5

facilitation
in BDS programmes 131
distinct from provision 4
and FIT programme 73
of market linkage 101
principles of 121
in PROFIT Zambia programme
 7, 171, 178, 184–5
in value chain analysis 121,
 125
farmers
associations of 157
in Bangladesh 157–64, **161**,
 166–7
in BASIX approach **152**
and finance 143–4, 148–150
and FIT programme 73, 78–9
in Kenya **149**
organizations of 3, **145**, 152;
 see also business associations
and poultry rearing **142**
and value chains 118, 143, **147**

in Zambia 172, 176–180, **176**,
 179, 182–183
finance
access to 146
and agricultural sector 142–143,
 151–2
in agricultural sector 142–4,
 149, 151–2
and BDS 131
for business associations 47,
 50, 56–7
facilitating **149**, 210
in post-communist countries
 54–5
programme 211
restructuring of 153
for tribal peoples 39
and TTO programme 1, 11–14
in value chain **142**
firms
complementarity between large
 and small 20
family ownership of 16–17
links between 18, 22
FIT (Farm Implements and Tools)
 programme 5, 71–81
formalization 190, 192,
frameworks 117,
in PROFIT Zambia programme
 171–72
franchise associations 63, 66–7
franchising **60–2**

GEMINI (Growth and Equity
 through Microenterprise
 Investments and Institutions) 3,
 30–1
good practice 5, 83–6, 92, 94–5; see
 also best practice
in BDS 83–6, 92, 94–5
government policy
and economic signals 88
and informal sector 19–24
towards informal sector 3
and value chain finance 150

governments
   and BDS programmes 87, 91, 93, 131
   communist 45–6
   demand for evaluation 155
   objectives of interventions 115
   and outgrower schemes 21
   reform of 130
   relationship with business associations 47–9, 51–3, 56
   role of in economic environment 15–16
   role of in value chains 151
   and rural sector 142
   services provided by 53–4
   support for franchising 59, 63–6, 68
   and Zambian agriculture 175, 181–2, **183**
Grameen Bank 22, 24
Guiding principles for donor interventions 109–110

handicrafts 23, 98–9, **99**, 101, 106–7, 133
HIV/AIDS, people living with 200, 201, 205, 209, 210, 213

impact assessment
   in BDS 5, 90
   in FIT programme 5
   in Katalyst programme 7, 155–7, 159, 164, **165**, 167, 169
   systems for 164
   in value chain programmes 113, 125, **127**
impact logics 164–9
incentives
   for adding value 114
   to collaborate **123**
   for enterprise development 36, 54, 115
   to improve competitiveness 119–20, 122–4, 127
   in industry upgrading strategy 171
   in informal sector 3, 25
   and PROFIT Zambia programme 172–3, **175**, 181, 183–4, **183**
   in SOC programmes **86**
   in tasar cultivation 40
incomes
   and gender in Pakistan 132
   in informal sector 19, 22–3
   and Katalyst programme 156, 158, 162–3, 166
   of participants in TTO programme 14
   and PROFIT Zambia programme 172
   and rural development 33, 136–7
   and targeting development policy 37
   and value chains 113, 115
India
   informal sector in 25
   poultry rearing in 40
   small farmers in 149, 152
   tribal development programmes 38–9
industry
   growth patterns in 35–6, 115–17
   selection 6, **117**
industry competitiveness
   holistic approach and 131
   Kula's emphasis on 6
   strategies for 6, 120–22, **122**, 124
   and value chains 114–16, **116**, 127, 129
   in Zambian agriculture 184
informal sector 3, 15–27, 33, 63; *see also* microenterprise
   advantages of firms in 17
   characteristics of 17
   and franchising 63
   groupings within 16

growth of 33
resistance of customers to 100
as safety net 15–16
unrealistic depictions of 17–18
women in 3, 17
information, exchange of 46, 66, 68, 160
innovation
    and BDS 83, 92, 95
    and development programmes 79
    franchising as 60
    historical process of 78
    in informal sector 3, 25–6, 98
    market demand for 114
    in PROFIT Zambia programme 171–73, 184
    in services for small business 81
    in tasar cultivation 40
    in value chains 121, 124, 142, 152–3
    in Zambian agriculture **183**
interest rates 13
interventions
    in BDS 83, 85, 87
    cost-effectiveness of 30
    for entire industries 131
    evaluating 90, 113, 115, 137–8, 159, 165–6, 169
    in Katalyst programme 157, 159, 165–7
    minimal 156
    and poverty reduction 107
    to prevent market failure 15–16
    sequencing of 172
    short-term 93
    targeting of 6, 87, 89
    time lag in evaluating 168
    in value chains 2

Katalyst programme 2, 5, 7, 155–9
    case study from **162**
    impact logic example **158**
Kenya
    BDS in **126**
    and FIT programme 71, 73, 77, 80
    and LIFE project 191
    informal sector in 17, 20
    market linkage projects in 97, 101
    value chain finance in **149**
    value chain programmes in 125, **127**
knowledge management 7, 171–73, **173**, 184
Korea 20

Latin America 3, 24, **144**
lead firm 3
linkages
    between formal and informal sector 22
    between government and programmes 181
    between private and public sector 122
    between service providers **100**
    between small and large firms **123**
    brokerage of 101
    market, *see* market linkage
    in sub-sector analysis 30
    in value chains 114, 143, **150**

M4P (making markets work for the poor) **2**, 9, 129, 155–6, 171, 185, 199, 214
market assessments 3, 133, 151
market demand 1, 94, 114, 138
market development programmes 2–6, 130, 156
market linkage projects **99–100**, 103–6, **108**
market linkages 76, 99, 101–102, **104**, 106
    in Pakistan 134
    sustainable 100, 102–3
market research 73–4, 135
market systems 2, 4, 7, 138, 184–5

marketing strategies 76, 105
marketing support 1, 9, 13–14, 59, 103
  and franchising 59, **60**
MEs, *see* microentrepreneurs
Mexico 26
microenterprises 2–3, 29, 34, 94, 97, 107, 113, 129–31, 135, 137
  and enterprise development 129–31
  integration into market systems 3
  and market linkage projects 97, 107
  and poverty reduction 34
  and sub-sector analysis 29
  upgrading of 135
  in value chains 113
microentrepreneurs 1–2, 5, 133
microfinance 83–4, 89–90, 130
models
  agricultural 3
  BASIX livelihood services **152**
  BDS and subsidies 130
  of cooperation between formal and informal sector 20–21
  core-satellite 20
  embedded service 3
  franchising as means for propagating 61
  of industrial development 33
  LAFISE group integrated service **145**
  of linkages between smallholders **127**
  overreliance on theoretical 88, 94
  of poultry rearing 41
  transferability to private sector of 109
  for women microentrepeneurs 135
  for Zambian vet services 182
monitoring
  in FIT programme 74–7

  in franchising **61–62**, 64
  by government of franchising 68
  in Katalyst programme 155–6, 164, 166, 168–9
  in value chain programmes 113, 125
monopolies 15, 135

networks
  among women microentrepeneurs 133–4
  and BDS 89, 104
  in enterprise development 44
  and FIT programme 80–81
  indigenous 92
  and limited resources 94
  of small businesses 73
  in Zambian agriculture **175**, 182
non-financial services
  and BDS 5, 83
  and FIT programme 71, 74, 79–80
  in India 152
  and microenterprises 130
  and sub-sector analysis 3
  in value chain 145

outgrower scheme 3, 21

Pakistan 4, 6, 129–34, 137–8
participatory technology development (PTD) 73
Philippines 4, 65
policy; *see also* government policies
  and lobbying 51–52
  and value chains 141, 153
poultry rearing 4, 40–44, **148**, 167, 181
poverty
  in developing countries 35
  in Pakistan 131
  and sub-sectoral approach 37
  and women in Pakistan 136

poverty reduction
    and informal sector 19
    and Katalyst programme 156, 162, 164–6, 168–9
    and market linkage projects 97, 106, 108, 156
    monitoring impacts on 155
    and private-sector development projects 7
    and PROFIT programme 175
    and small business development 34
    and sub-sectoral approach 41
    and value chain programmes 113–15, 125, **127**
practitioners, and BDS 83–4
PRADAN 33–4, 38–41
PRIDE (Promotion of Rural Initiatives and Development Enterprises) 72–4, 79
private sector
    and BDS 89, 94, 97
    build-up of 51
    and FIT programme 79
    in former communist countries 46, 52
    increase in subcontracting 98
    and Katalyst programme 157, 168
    leading role in value chains 118
    organizations in 45, 54–6
    provision of services for small business 5, 105–6
    relationship with government 53
    representation of 50–1
    role in improving competitiveness 122–3
    role of in market linkage 103
    support for franchising 65
    and value chain programmes 127
    and veterinary services in Zambia **175**, 177, **179**

private sector development (PSD) 155, 188,
pro-poor market development 2
PROFIT Zambia programme 7, 115, 117, 124, 171–8, 180–84, **179**, **183**
public sector 17, 49, 122

quality control
    and BDS programmes 130, 134
    in core-satellite model 21
    in market linkage projects 102, **104**, 105
    in TTO programme 1, 13

regulation 189–91,

safety nets 15–16, 24
scale
    and BDS 89, 94
    challenge of 7
    economies of in TTO programme 13
    and franchising 60
    and horizontal likages 114
    inability to achieve **117**
    and informal sector 17
    in market linkage projects 102
    and poultry rearing 41
    and PROFIT Zambia programme **172**, 176, 179–81, **180**, 184
    scale-up initiatives 4
    and sub-sectoral approach 30, 38, 42–3
    and value chains 151
sectors
    appropriate for franchising 62
    symbiosis between formal and informal 20, 24, 26
SEEP Network 2, 4
service development 5
service markets 2
    in FIT programme 5
    in Katalyst programme 156, 164, 167

and value chain analysis 122–3
weak 5
services
   demand-led 80
   in market linkage projects 103
   subsidized 2
   in value chain programmes 125
Sierra Leone 25–6
silk 4, 38–40, 42–3
Singapore 20
Slovakia 45, 47, 52–3
small business
   associations for 48–9, 51
   co-operation among 105
   comparative advantage of 124
   exhibitions and trade fairs 101
   finance for 1, 55
   and franchising 64
   and globalization 110
   in Hungary 56
   polarity within sector 99
   political support for 48
   and poverty reduction 33
   promotion of 33
   services needed by 53, 55
   and vertical supply chains 29
smallholders
   in FIT programme 79
   and innovation 152
   in Kenya **126, 127**
   symbiosis with agricultural estates 20–21
   and value chain finance 151
   in Zambia 174–5, **175**, 177, 181–3
South Africa 1, 9, 13–14, 66
South-East Asia 4
specialization, flexible 15, 26
Sri Lanka 5–6, 97, 101
star producers 104–6, **104**, 110
strategies
   for competitiveness 113, 120
   of market linkage projects 101, 103
   minimalist 34

for new markets 135
for promoting small business 64
scaling up 184
for sub-sectoral growth 35
sub-contracting 15, 17–18, 22–3, 26
sub-sector analysis
   and BDS 6, 87, 94
   key concepts of 29–30
   practical application of 4
sub-sector maps 3, 30
sub-sectoral approach 3–4, 33–8, 41–43, 72, 87–8, 97
sub-sectors
   definition of 34–5
   growth in 36, 42
   in Pakistan 133
   policy framework pertaining to 43
   targeting of 131
   traditional and new 42–3
   in value chain analysis 125
subsidarity 91
subsidies
   and BDS programmes 91, 93, 130
   in enterprise development 37
   and FIT 73
   for franchising 67
   in traditional enterprise development strategies 36
   and value chain analysis 119, 124
suppliers
   in FIT programme 76, 79–80
   horizontal linkages between 114
   linkages to 107
   to manufacturing sector 21
   and sub-contracting 101
support services
   in BDS programmes 5, 129
   and FIT programme 79
   for franchises 67
   in Pakistan 133–4

INDEX   **225**

for small business   55–6
in value chain analysis   120,
142, 143
sustainability
of BDS interventions   85–6
challenge of   7
of enterprise development   37,
211
of Katalyst programme   163
of market linkage projects   108
and market models   4
of services for small businesses
80
in sub-sector analysis   4
of value chain programmes
124, **126**
Swiss Agency for Development
Co-operation (SOC)   **86**
system failure   156
systems perspective   3

Tanzania   4, 62, 79
tasar, *see* silk
technology
in BASIX approach   **152**
and competitiveness   113–14
development   84, 93
difference between sizes of firms
30
and FIT programme   76
and informal sector   17, 25–6
and ME involvement   4
in poultry rearing   41
shifts in   16
stimulating private interest in
94
and sub-sectoral approach   38,
43
in tasar cultivation   39
and value chains   **126**, 150
titling, property 189, 192–3
tools
cheap imports of   97
for competitiveness analysis
116

for enterprise promotion   131
FIT programme and purchase of
76, 78–9
for improved management   90
in PROFIT Zambia programme
171, 174
for value chain finance   **150**
trade agreements   6
trade associations   4, 123
training
in BASIX approach   **152**
and BDS   84, 130
in enterprise development
programmes   29, 34
in FIT programme   76
and franchising   **60**
government responsibility for
54
and informal sector   24, 27
in Katalyst programme   **158**,
159, 162, 164, 166
in market linkage projects   102,
104, 105
in market linkage projects
and private sector   47, 55–7, 105
programmes in Brazil   **88**
for small enterprise
development   36, 101, 206
for staff of franchisee   **61**, 62
and traditional sub-sectors   42
in TTO programmes   1, 11–12,
14
in value chain programmes   **126**
and Zambian agriculture   **175**
transition economies   4, 46, 50–53
TTO (Triple Trust Organization)
1–2, 11–14

Uganda
disabled people project 202
USAID   6, 66, **117**, **122**, **127**, 171

value chain actors   6, 135
value chain analysis   2–4, **2**, 6,
113–19, **116**, **118**, 131

value chain development 4, 6–7, 129, 141–42
   definition and scope of 2
value chain financing 6, 141–53, **147**, **150**
value chain mapping 119
value chains
   definition of 143
   in agriculture 6, 141–44, 146, 151
   and financial institutions 145, 153
   flows within **144**
   increasing competitiveness of 113–15, 123, 125
   innovation in 152
   integration of small producers 151
   in Katalyst programme 167
   in Pakistan handicrafts sector 129–31, 133, 135–6, 138
   participants in **118**
   place of small firms in 122, 127
   in poultry rearing **148**
   vertical linkages in 114
value chains 2, 142
value chain programmes in **117**, 124
viability 12, 38, 176

women
   and FIT programme 79
   in informal sector 3, 17
   and Katalyst programme 166
   in Pakistan 129–37
   production of milk in India 20
   rural 6
World Bank 19, 33

Zambia; *see also* PROFIT Zambia programme
   beef industry in **174**
   industry selection in 115

www.ingramcontent.com/pod-product-compliance
Ingram Content Group UK Ltd.
Pitfield, Milton Keynes, MK11 3LW, UK
UKHW021835140426
5217IPUK00021B/1462